(En)gendering the Political

What is the relationship between being political and citizenship? What might it mean to be marginalised through both the practices and knowledge of citizenship? What might citizenship look like from a position of social, political and cultural exclusion? This book responds to these questions by treating marginalisation as a political process and position. It explores how different lives, experiences and forms of political action might be engendered when subjects are excluded, made vulnerable and invisible from contemporary forms of citizenship. It aims to contribute to the growing body of literature on the politics of resistance by investigating how complex forms of marginality are not only produced by dominant forms of citizenship but also actively challenge them.

Modernist approaches to politics tend to see the citizen as the ideal type of political agent and citizenship as the zenith of struggles over rights, representation and belonging. This edited volume challenges this approach to political subjectivity by showing how political acts work for but also against/beyond citizenship claims, towards different orientations and as 'acts' of (non) citizen. By bringing together diverse theoretical and empirical contributions, and exploring the emergent politics of marginalised subjects, this collection challenges how we think about citizenship and opens up space for alternative imaginaries of political action and belonging.

This book was originally published as a special issue of *Citizenship Studies*.

Joe B. Turner is a Research Fellow in International Migration at the Department of Politics, University of Sheffield, UK. He is interested in the politics of citizenship and how internal/external borders emerge and are governed in (post)colonial states such as the UK. His work lies at the cross-section of IR, political sociology and historiography. He has previously published work in journals such as *British Journal of Politics* and *International Relations and Citizenship Studies*.

(En)gendering the Political

Citizenship from Marginal Spaces

Edited by
Joe B. Turner

Routledge
Taylor & Francis Group

LONDON AND NEW YORK

First published 2017
by Routledge

2 Park Square, Milton Park, Abingdon, Oxfordshire OX14 4RN
52 Vanderbilt Avenue, New York, NY 10017

Routledge is an imprint of the Taylor & Francis Group, an informa business

First issued in paperback 2018

Chapter 4 © Lucy Mayblin, originally published as Open Access
Chapters 1–3 & Chapters 5–8 © 2017 Taylor & Francis

Notice:
Product or corporate names may be trademarks or registered trademarks,
and are used only for identification and explanation without intent to
infringe.

British Library Cataloguing in Publication Data
A catalogue record for this book is available from the British Library

ISBN 13: 978-1-138-63701-6 (hbk)
ISBN 13: 978-0-367-14299-5 (pbk)

Typeset in Minion Pro
by RefineCatch Limited, Bungay, Suffolk

Publisher's Note
The publisher accepts responsibility for any inconsistencies that may have
arisen during the conversion of this book from journal articles to book chapters,
namely the possible inclusion of journal terminology.

Disclaimer
Every effort has been made to contact copyright holders for their permission to
reprint material in this book. The publishers would be grateful to hear from any
copyright holder who is not here acknowledged and will undertake to rectify
any errors or omissions in future editions of this book.

Contents

Citation Information

The chapters in this book were originally published in *Citizenship Studies*, volume 20, issue 2 (April 2016). When citing this material, please use the original page numbering for each article, as follows:

Chapter 1
Editorial Introduction: (En)gendering the political: Citizenship from marginal spaces
Joe Turner
Citizenship Studies, volume 20, issue 2 (April 2016), pp. 141–155

Chapter 2
Unfamiliar acts of citizenship: enacting citizenship in vernacular music and language from the space of marginalised intergenerational migration
Aoileann Ní Mhurchú
Citizenship Studies, volume 20, issue 2 (April 2016), pp. 156–172

Chapter 3
Contestations in death – the role of grief in migration struggles
Maurice Stierl
Citizenship Studies, volume 20, issue 2 (April 2016), pp. 173–191

Chapter 4
Troubling the exclusive privileges of citizenship: mobile solidarities, asylum seekers, and the right to work
Lucy Mayblin
Citizenship Studies, volume 20, issue 2 (April 2016), pp. 192–207

Chapter 5
Governing the domestic space of the traveller in the UK: 'family', 'home' and the struggle over Dale Farm
Joe Turner
Citizenship Studies, volume 20, issue 2 (April 2016), pp. 208–227

Chapter 6
Between safety and vulnerability: the exiled other of international relations
Amanda Russell Beattie
Citizenship Studies, volume 20, issue 2 (April 2016), pp. 228–242

Chapter 7

Ethiopianism, Englishness, Britishness: struggles over imperial belonging
Robbie Shilliam
Citizenship Studies, volume 20, issue 2 (April 2016), pp. 243–259

Chapter 8

Beyond the nation state: the role of local and pan-national identities in defining post-colonial African citizenship
Gemma Bird
Citizenship Studies, volume 20, issue 2 (April 2016), pp. 260–275

For any permission-related enquiries please visit:
http://www.tandfonline.com/page/help/permissions

Notes on Contributors

Amanda Russell Beattie is a Lecturer in International Relations at Aston University, Birmingham, UK.

Gemma Bird is a Teaching Associate in Politics and International Relations at Aston University, Birmingham, UK.

Lucy Mayblin is an Assistant Professor in Sociology at the University of Warwick, UK.

Aoileann Ní Mhurchú is a Lecturer in International Politics at the School of Social Sciences, University of Manchester, UK.

Robbie Shilliam is a Professor in International Relations at the School of Politics and International Relations, Queen Mary University of London, UK.

Maurice Stierl is a Visiting Assistant Professor at the Graduate Group in Cultural Studies, University of California, USA.

Joe B. Turner is a Research Fellow in International Migration at the Department of Politics, University of Sheffield, UK.

(En)gendering the political: Citizenship from marginal spaces

Joe Turner

Department of Politics, University of Sheffield, Sheffield, UK

ABSTRACT

This introduction sets out the central concerns of this special issue, the relationship between marginality and the political. In doing so, it makes the argument that the process of marginalisation, the sites and experiences of 'marginality' provide a different lens through which to understand citizenship. Viewing the political as the struggle over belonging it considers how recent studies of citizenship have understood political agency. It argues that marginality can help us understand multiple scales, struggles and solidarities both within and beyond citizenship. Whilst there is a radical potential in much of the existing literature in citizenship studies, it is also important to consider political subjectivities and acts which are not subsumed by right claims. Exploring marginality in this way means understanding how subjects are disenfranchised by regimes of citizenship and at the same time how this also (en)genders new political possibilities which are not always orientated towards 'inclusion'. The introduction then sets out how each article contributes to this project.

This special issue concerns the relationship between marginality and the political. It contends that an understanding of this relationship is of central importance for an exploration of contemporary citizenship. In focusing on the production of marginality, the emphasis here is on how marginality or marginal spaces are fashioned but equally how they provide conditions for forms of political becoming and the emergence of 'alternatives'. These articles thus explore how practices, experiences, legacies of marginality *(en)gender* different sites of political struggle, which in turn shape, contest and disrupt citizenship as it is both practised and conceptualised. The collection offers a series of interventions into both how we understand the production of marginality across modern societies but also the way we understand how subjects become constituted as political subjects through the process of marginalisation. They provide theoretically informed but empirically rich explorations by both activists and scholars into how different struggles, acts, events, practices and conduct disrupt the hierarchisation and ordering of social life. The relationship between marginality, citizenship and the political represented here is underpinned by the persistent struggle over belonging. If marginality is the process through which certain subjects and groups' belonging is problematised, then this is often materialised through dominant norms and practices of citizenship. Following McNevin, we can thus read the political as a radical questioning of what it is to belong (2007). *This special issue aims to highlight how the process of marginalisation itself, and the new co-ordinates it makes possible, have (en)gendered this radical form of questioning.*

Broadly conceived, citizenship studies have been at the forefront of exploring the tension between inclusion/exclusion at the heart of modern citizenship, with many studies revealing an emphasis on either inclusion or exclusion. Those scholars focusing on inclusion have tended to rely on a normative commitment to citizenship as an empirically flawed but ultimately inclusive project. Whilst granting citizenship necessitates a privileging and demarcation of rights (citizen/non-citizen), this is often treated as a problem that can be overcome with more pluralistic definitions of (active) citizenship (Çakmaklı 2015; Grugel and Singh 2015; Lister 2007), more progressive border regimes (Sandelind 2015), the detaching of national identity to right claims through multiculturalism (Joppke 2007; Kofman 2002; Kymlicka 2001), etc. The literature on exclusion works against elements of this commitment. Through interlocutors with security and border studies (Muller 2004; Nyers 2009; also see Guillaume and Huysmans 2013), critical approaches to migration (Mezzadra and Neilson 2013; Papadopoulos, Stephenson, and Tsianos 2008) as well as (post)colonial (Rigo 2005), gender and queer theory (Roseneil et al. 2013), there is now a relatively large body of work exploring citizenship as an inherently exclusive mode of political subjectivity (Hindess 2004). Through both legalistic and normative definitions, the case is presented that the *citizen* has been scripted as a liberal, white, bourgeois, heterosexual, man and this inherently leads to the powerful hierachisation and securitisation of others (Basham and Vaughan-Williams 2013). In those accounts treating citizenship as a component of sovereign politics, exclusion from citizenship is linked to process of de-humanisation, exemplified in the abject figure of the 'deportable' asylum seeker or irregular migrant reduced to a form of 'bare life' (Doty 2011; Edkins, Pin-Fat, and Shapiro 2004; Rajaram and Grundy-Warr 2007; Rygiel 2008; Vaughan-Williams 2010). Citizenship maintains its (post)colonial co-ordinates in Western states, where neoliberal ideologies persist to contain racialised and dangerous 'others' outside of the state's 'juridical and spatial confines' (De Genova 2007, 440; Schinkel 2010). Whilst analyses of exclusion(s) are far from monolithic they tend to lean towards an account of state violence; exclusion from citizenship is imagined through a prism of inside/outside.

This focus has produced fascinating accounts of inclusion/exclusion; we now have a far more complex understanding of the assemblages of control and regulation through which certain forms of life are both made possible and denied. However, this focus tends to obscure a view of the active contestation of both practices of inclusion and exclusion. There has been a general absence of analysis of the emergence of political events, moments or 'acts' of resistance in the literature on exclusion (see Guillaume and Huysmans 2013, 9; Isin 2008; Nyers and Rygiel 2012). Equally, the focus on inclusion tends to read the political through the existing narrative of citizenship, as a territorialised regime of rights. Citizenship becomes the key site of political struggles and claims (see Papadopoulos and Tsianos 2013). Arguably, in this context the divergence and heterogeneity of the political is obscured, either through a focus on the extent of the social reach of governmentalities, or because politics is reduced to those events which mobilise around formal rights claims. This special issue thus contributes to a movement in critical citizenship studies which seeks to push beyond the focus on inclusion/exclusion (Bagelman 2015; Guillaume and Huysmans

2013; McNevin 2011; Nyers and Rygiel 2012; Papadopoulos, Stephenson, and Tsianos 2008; Squire 2011; Tyler and Marciniak 2013). This body of work has attempted to subvert the analytical focus on the institutional practices of citizenship in favour of the contestation and refashioning of citizenship through protest and activism. Many of these studies have explored the role of migrants, those classically conceived as non-citizens, in contesting, claiming and effectively 'practising' citizenship (Nyers and Rygiel 2012, 2). In particular these studies seek to understand how global migration, the experiences and practices of mobility and forms of control provide new spaces for (re)shaping and (re)conceptualising citizenship. Exemplifying this move, Nyers and Rygiel (2012, 2) argue that we need to ask 'how, through various strategies of claims-making, non-citizen migrant groups are involved in practices and ways of engaging in citizenship even when lacking formal status'. Drawing upon Engin Isin's now seminal work on 'acts of citizenship', and a wider turn in politics, political and economic geography (Darling 2014; Harvey 2008; Ong 2006; Scott 2009) and International Relations (IR) (Death 2010) towards a focus on resistance, I read these studies as seeking to (re)politicise the analysis of citizenship by bringing into focus those acts which 'protest' exclusory regimes but, in doing, also help delineate the contingency of citizenship itself. This focus is subversive in that it addresses both the (im)possible agency of non-citizen (migrants), against a focus on passivity, victimhood and 'bare life', and equally accounts for changing nature of citizenship 'from below' through active 'transgressions'.

This special issue's examination of how marginality (en)genders the political, aims to extend this emerging literature. It does this in three ways. (1) By unsettling the binary of inclusion/exclusion by exploring how marginality is *productive* of political subjectivity. The role of (en)gendering is important here as it refers to a process of 'emergence' – emergent activism, solidarities, political being. (2) The emphasis on marginality brings into focus a more divergent set of subjects, sites, scales of struggles over citizenship, alongside and beyond the justified yet restrictive focus on the 'migrant'. To use the verb (en)gender thus alludes to feminist scholarship on gender and intersectionality (Hunt and Rygiel 2007) which provides us with unique insights into the production of marginal subjects. (3) It further examines the political as more than a claim to rights. Whilst agreeing that an analysis of rights claims is helpful in understanding contestation, this special issue also recognises the different orientation of acts, events and movements which may not always be subsumed by the existing co-ordinates of citizenship that they contest (also see Tyler and Marciniak 2013, 2; Walters 2008). This means exploring what Aoileann Ní Mhurchú refers to as 'Unfamiliar acts of Citizenship' (Ní Mhurchú 2016), 'Acts against Citizenship' (Tyler and Marciniak 2013, 8), as well as acts that are orientated towards different relations and cosmologies (see Bird 2016; Shilliam 2016).

By exploring marginality, we in this special issue follow the observation that the experience of marginalisation, restriction, social control also constitutes political subjectivities (Nyers and Rygiel 2012). However, marginality is embodied and experienced by a multiplicity of subjects and groups. This means recognising that citizenship has historically related to many different forms of marginalisation and hierarchicalisation, not all of which coalesce around the figure of the migrant, alien or asylum seeker (see Anderson 2013). The racialised, classed, sexualised, gendered dimensions of citizenship produce a complex assemblage of marginality; even when achieved, formal status is differentiated and does not always equate to legitimacy or belonging (see Harrington 2012). The history of the poor, women, homosexuals, the mad and 'feebleminded', colonial subjects, naturalised citizens attests to this. Whilst previous studies have arguably reconstituted the dichotomy between citizen/ non-citizen, this special issue seeks to understand the treatment of subjects along a broad continuum of marginality (intergenerational migrant youth, black minorities, 'Problem Families', Traveller groups, the 'workless') and to explore the (un)familiar processes which constitute the spatiality of the marginal. Marginality is divergent and historical and by exploring marginality as a continuum this means recognising the 'many relay points in the weave of modern politics, which are neither exceptional nor comparable, but simply relational' (Weheliye 2014, 37). Whilst different experiences of marginality are relational, this equally leads to different explorations of the politics of contestation which dispute and interrupt dominant modes of belonging. This special issue brings into focus different (yet related) strategies, practices and solidarities that intertwine between those with formal status and those without. For instance, border practices that (en)gender (temporary) solidarities between activists and irregularised migrants (Stierl 2016), or right to work protests between asylum seekers and trade unions (Mayblin 2016), Irish Travellers and 'No Border' protesters rejecting acts of 'domicide' (Turner 2016), white and black 'Ethiopianist' in the contestation of Imperial sensibilities (Shilliam 2016).

What this emphasis on a stratified continuum helps us engage with are the different sites, scales and character of political acts. Whilst marginality encompasses a spatial dimension so does the political. Investigating the constitution of political subjectivity in liminal spaces means that we need to explore the multiplicity of such sites and the practices relating to them. The articles collected here thus work alongside and beyond the focus on mobility, borders and the bodies of non-citizens to a multitude of sites of marginality and political possibility: street art and music, unmarked graves/yards, the Traveller caravan, the African village, the Rastafari movement. As the individual articles argue, these sites provide the (partial) raw materials for the constitution of subjects and groups into political subjects who can contest the apparently settled boundaries of social life in new ways (Balibar 2012). To think of marginality in terms of different political spaces is also to contest the linear and liberal notion that inclusion 'back in to' normalised modes of belonging and equitable rights is the objective of all struggles. Such a perspective risks leading to a fixed imagination of inside/outside and replays the commonsensical boundaries of citizenship against the cultivation of an 'imaginary and a practical sensibility to what lies after citizenship' (Papadopoulos and Tsianos 2013, 179).

Acts of citizenship/acts after citizenship

Isin's work on 'acts' of citizenship has been influential in reconceptualising the political character of citizenship (Isin 2008). 'Acts' refer to the performances and events through which subjects constitute themselves (or are constituted) as 'those whom the right to have rights is due'. As Tyler and Marciniak (2013, 7) argue

> This redefinition has proved fruitful for thinking about ways in which populations who are disenfranchised by the states in which they reside, and are 'outside of politics' in any normative sense, are able to act in ways that allow them to (temporary) constitute themselves as political subjects under sometimes extreme conditions of subjugation.

However, it is our sense that the radical potential of Isin's formulation is often overlooked in subsequent analysis (with significant exceptions – see Marciniak, and Tyler 2014; McNevin 2011; Tyler and Marciniak 2013), this is because the 'constitution of political subjectivity' is often analysed precisely through the existing co-ordinates of (liberal) citizenship. This is in part to do with a focus on 'right claims'. Exemplary examples of 'acts of citizenship' provided in the literature are those incidents where non-citizens – irregularised migrants, asylum seekers, or the undocumented – protest or involve in activism and thus appear to mirror the expectations and actions of 'good' 'civic' citizens. This seemingly reveals the contingency of boundaries demarcating citizen/non-citizen (see Andrijasevic and Anderson 2008). To Andrijasevic (2013, 54) this 'accounts for those instances that citizens claim rights that they do not have and non-citizens act as if they were citizens'. This is described in relationship to terrorist policy (Jarvis and Lister 2013), sex worker protests (Andrijasevic 2013), the organisation of residents and activists in camps and detention centres. What defines the political in these circumstances (analytically) is how non-citizens *claim* equitable rights, through acting like citizens (also see Benhabib 2004).

Right claims are important but they do not and should not provide the horizon of the political. As contributions to this special issue examine, rights claims provide useful mechanisms to destabilise existing regimes of citizenship and open up new spaces of political possibility (see Mayblin 2016). Equally, those suffering extreme subjugation may claim the right to access state provisions such as health care, education, welfare benefits, the right to work and rely on the materialisation of these rights for survival (Papadopoulos and Tsianos 2013). However, there remains a tension here between claiming legal rights and the reconstitution of citizenship through 'integrationist' strategies, which provide rights on the conditions of behaviour, meritocracy, 'acting' like a good citizen (see Brown 1995, 121; Turner 2014). Does the inclusion of non-citizens as (temporary) citizens not also reproduce the very distinction of legitimate membership that they equally call into question (Honig 2003)? Hoover's (2015) recent work on human rights may provide a way of negotiating the citizen/integrationist bind. He suggests that rather than reproducing a liberal hegemonic project of universalism, claims over human rights have the potential to be radical in that they provide space 'by invoke the universal but ambiguous notion of humanity' (Hoover 2015, 1093) Eschewing a reading of human rights as either a Western-centric or an entirely progressive tradition, this means recognising the possibility of rights through 'an optics of rightlessness' (Odysseos and Selmeczi 2015, 1038). Mayblin (2016) reflects on right claims in similar ways in her article, where the demand for recognition is made not to inclusive membership of citizens but to the appeal of an ambiguous 'humanity' linked together with internationalist traditions of 'worker' solidarity (also see Anderson, Sharma, and Wright 2012). The emphasis here is less on 'acting as a citizen' and instead on the insurrectionist moment that a right claim generates when articulated by marginalised subjects. As Critchely (2007, 91) argues: 'This reveals a novel political function for rights: they can be levers of political articulation whereby hitherto marginalised constituency enters into public visibility by raising a universal claim in relation to a situation of injustice or a wrong'.

Importantly, this special issue situates rights claims as *one* site for (en)gendering the political. In relating the political to a radical questioning of belonging (McNevin 2007), this also means exploring how acts, events and struggles work to rupture, break and reveal the contingencies of what Isin refers to as the 'habitus, practice, conduct, discipline and routine' (Isin 2009, 379) of ordering social life. In doing so, this destabilises the commonsensical mapping of 'belonging'. For instance, in exploring the politics of 'escape', Papadopoulos, Stephenson, and Tsianos (2008) suggest that struggles over everyday life are political but specifically in the refusal to address such struggles to the redistributive power of the nation state. The autonomy of migration literature has thus broadly sought to understand dis-id-enitification, de-subjectification and escape in the potential for reimagining life: 'Escape is a creative, constructive move, one which radically alters the very conditions within which struggles over existence are conducted' (60). I also suggest that escape can be read as a distinctly political 'act', in that is far from passive, it is a refusal to align with the existing co-ordinates of contemporary order and representation. We can see this in line with a tradition of ethical anarchist practice where politics is the constant disturbance of the state (of order), 'prompting isolated moments of negation *without any* affirmation' (Levinas cited in Critchley 2007, 122). This rejects the scripting of the political as the joining together of the disruptive and the affirmative (Darling 2014). If escape is a mode of *being political* that goes beyond and actually contests the very basis of the redistributive function of rights regimes, then we have a far wider lens through which to view the emergence of the political in marginal, everyday spaces.

Marginality and the political

To speak of marginality as (en)gendering, the political is to note a certain relationship to 'conditions of possibility' (Allen 2002). The use of '(en)gender(ing)' is to recognise a process of emergence which blurs our understanding of the 'doing subject or agent'. The political 'acts' which emerge from marginal spaces and experiences are never determined but always work through the historical and social conditions which they equally contest. Nor do they rely upon the exertion of a subject's autonomy which renders them outside of history. To use the concept of (en)gender is to pay homage to emergent social and political formations and the fractured, hybrid nature of subjectivity (Kristeva 1994) but equally to recognise the role that studies of gender and feminism have played in explorations of marginality and exclusion (Hunt and Rygiel 2007). It is to recognise that the process of marginality and the political 'acts' they make possible are always (en)gendered, but that gender is always intersectional:

> Race, ethnicity, gender or class (and we should add sexuality) are the avenues of power that define the social, economic and political map. These are the routes which 'disempowering dynamics' travel. These avenues, or axes of power are sometimes considered distinct from each other. But in reality they overlap and cross each other, and operate in relation to each other, resulting in complex intersections at which two or more of these axes meet. (George cited in Hunt and Rygiel 2007, 3)

It is these 'disempowering dynamics', wrapped around different axes of race, class, sexuality, gender, that are explored in this special issue, specifically through the contestation and politics which they also *evoke*. This is to say that these spaces in themselves offer up different modes of life and belonging – not only as victims which need 'inclusion' but as subjectivities which provide different accounts of what it is to be political. This is not to lapse into the fetishisation or romanticism of marginality. This is avoided by keeping a focused eye on the governmental mechanism which foster and shape (often violently) marginality and by also understanding alternative claims as (im)possible reimaginings which will also, in part, fail.

What is important to emphasise here is the collective experience of *refusal* and *disturbance*, that is the emergent solidarities that disturbance makes possible. Perhaps, the political is always, in part, a failed project of collective experience and struggle. Speaking to this theme, Stierl's (2016) article in this issue draws upon Ranciere's notion of 'impossible identification' to reveal the complex and precarious encounters that subjects experience at the margins (in this case in the contestation of violent EU border practices). He argues that the examples of 'grief activism' practiced by activist, migrants, grieving families constitute acts 'that can foster relationalities and communities in opposition to a politics of division, aban-donment and necropolitics'. What is radical and political transformative about these acts is that they refuse the affirmation of existing rights regimes, the political identities assigned to them by the 'dominant consensual order' and are always failed projects of community making. We can reflect upon the broader implications of this. Marginal solidarities emerge and are always in a process of constant failure brought on by the heterogeneity of their composition, which is often (temporary) aligned in opposition to injustice or wrongs. This works against the traditional logic of community which relies on modalities of homogeny or cohesion (what Nancy (1991) calls 'immanentism'). Stierl (2016) argues for the radical nature of these 'coalitions waiting to be formed':

> While political acts that entail a horizon of failure seem discomforting as they leave the realm of easily assumed (political/ideological) commonness and readability of one another, it is the process of identification despite impossibilities that engenders political potentiality and can point us to modalities of community that surpass traditional ideas of settled and bounded political communities.

If political is the radical questioning of belonging, then *the political is also the possibility of difference that can never be subsumed within a totalising social formation* (see Levinas 1999).

Whilst the contributions in this special issue conceive of the political in slightly different ways, what they share is an ethic to open up the understanding of the political both through and beyond the existing parameters of the politics of citizenship. Right claims can be read as interruptions of the social order (although this is an empirical rather than philosophical question) but equally so can everyday acts of refusal. We need to be open to the orientation, direction and contingency of political acts. This can involve struggles which challenge the boundaries of 'equitable national settlement' (Bird 2016; Shilliam 2016), or that deny integration into the existing rights regimes of 'sedentary' citizenship (Turner 2016), or the precarious encounters found in 'grief activism' (Stierl 2016). Equally, the focus on the everyday, and refusal, means that we can also read collective experiences of music appreci-ation (Ní Mhurchú 2016), narrative and exile (Beattie 2016) as creating forms of political subjectivity. This means attuning ourselves to claims to alternatives forms of politics by exploring the hybridity and ambiguity of political identities and belonging (Ní Mhurchú 2016), global–colonial relations (Shilliam 2016) and decolonial struggles (Bird 2016), the possibility of worker internationalism (Mayblin 2016), keeping alive forms of nomadism (Turner 2016), impossible forms of solidarity and community (Stierl 2016). As individual contributions outline, this is less of a critique of Isin's work on acts but a reassertion of its radical potential to reveal the heterogeneity and (im)possibility of alternative claims to political life.

Marginality

As has already been suggested thus far, marginality can be analysed along a continuum of related experiences. Marginalisation refers to a social, legal, economic, normative and polit-ical process through which subjects and groups are both disempowered and constituted as not belonging. Marginality is the recognition of an injustice through which certain subjects are denied access to the 'common resources' of a political order (Tyler and Marciniak 2013,

7–8). To speak of the marginal is to invoke a spatial imaginary of the social where certain subjects are understood to inhabit the periphery – marginal spaces. It is both a geography and moral economy of hinterlands, colonies, silenced minorities, homelessness, detention centres, prison cells, (un)free labour. In this way, marginality/marginalisation invokes a relation to notions of 'exclusion' and 'abjection' (Wacquant 2007).

However, this is not a retelling of the story of insiders and outsiders (Walker 1992) because that imagines a linear distinction of inclusion/exclusion, it is a recognition of the stratified and contingent way in which subjects are interpolated into stratified and hierarchical social formations. Following such a process, the contributions selected for this special issue focus on the different ways that subjects and groups are marginalised – mono-linguistic nationalism, the racist modalities of Empire, violent EU border practices, the policing of family life. And the political sites and acts this equally (en)genders. This contributes to the work on marginality by treating these experiences of injustice as productive of political subjectivity, but they equally relate to processes of marginalisation in academic knowledge production. They speak of the marginal not just by giving these experiences a 'voice' (see Spivak 1988; Squire 2015) but by articulating an exploration of marginality through drawing upon subjects and methodologies which are often sidelined (especially in mainstream political science and IR). For example, Ethnography and narration (Stierl 2016), autoreflexivism and storytelling (Beattie 2016), cultural studies (Shilliam 2016), music (Ní Mhurchú 2016), Travellers and Gypsies (Turner 2016), 'Let them Work' (LTW) campaigns (Mayblin 2016), African philosophy (Bird 2016). They reveal innovations in the theorisation and representation of marginality just as they provide *interventions* into practices of marginalisation.

The politics of resistance and escape

There is always a risk and tension in exploring the mechanism which produce marginality. By focusing this special issue on the (en)gendering of political acts through the process of marginalisation, there is a danger of prioritising an analyse of marginality *over* the political (Guillaume and Huysmans 2013, 7). By suggesting that marginality is productive of political subjectivity, this might appear to argue that disempowering processes emerge first, only to be resisted and contested by those who are subjugated or marginalised (as is the case with many accounts of resistance). We would like to contest this reading.

It is worth turning again to Papadopoulos, Stephenson, and Tsianos' (2008) conception of escape here and its relationship to control. In their reading, escape and social control are co-constitutive, each defining the parameters of the other. However, whilst social control must map escape, it is *escape* that is prioritised within processes of control. This of course further elaborated on in their commitment to a radical, fleeing and subversive form of 'experience' (which they contrast to political subjectivity):

> Sovereignty manifests in response to escape. People do not escape their control. People escape. Control is a cultural–political device which comes afterwards to tame and eventually to appropriate people's escape. Social struggles come first. (Papadopoulos, Stephenson, and Tsianos 2008, 43)

Whilst escape leads from forms of social control, there is a 'human' or social impulse to escape which in fact defines the need for control – *without escape there would be no need for control*. This offers a way around the conceptual prioritisation of control over the political. And yet inverting the logic of 'resistance' so that escape is prior to control seems to: (1) miss out on the continual constitutive effect of mechanisms of social order and the historical conditions they shape; (2) re-appropriate the autonomous a priori (ahistorical) subject which is beyond social relations (in the 'human' impulse to escape). In this sense, we find Robbie Shilliam's (2015) account of the global–colonial nexus of decolonial struggles a more satisfying formulation (or perhaps 'cultivation'). At the risk of simplify a complex argument, what Shilliam argues (in part) in both his contribution to this issue and in his latest book *Black Pacific* (2015) is that through struggles over decolonisation new solidarities and identities where formed which were 'global-colonial' in their character. Seemingly diverse and fragmented communities subverted national co-ordinates in appropriating experiences and practices from other anti-colonial and anti-racist struggles, forging connections that both subverted and paralleled colonial relations (the 'Black Pacific' relates specifically to the resonance between Maori groups in New Zealand and Black Power movements in the US). Whilst these communities where subjugated through colonial and racist rule, the global reach of colonialism also provided the conditions for new/old dynamics and solidarities to (re)form. The important lesson to be drawn from Shilliam's analysis for an analysis of marginal/political acts is that colonialism (the process of marginalisation and injustice, if we are being crude) provides some of the co-ordinates for new political, social, emotional and spiritual collectivities/connectivities to emerge. It is productive. However, decolonial struggles are never merely the resistance of colonialism in its mirror image; they draw upon knowledge, cosmologies, 'deeper relations' which both *proceed* and *follow* colonial rule (also see Bhambra 2014; de Sousa Santos 2014). Colonialism, as a form of marginalisation, never works in totality, it is always in part a violent yet incomplete project which fails to produce entirely new experiences nor robs people of other ways of living, thinking or belonging. 'Decolonial science', as Shilliam presents it, is the cultivation of knowledge of alternatives and sensibilities that no longer take these co-ordinates as the horizon of truth.

So whilst Shilliam's argument relies upon a particular historical legacy, we would like to suggest that a conceptualisation of marginality and the political can work in familiar ways. Whilst disempowering practices provide the conditions for struggles, oppositional coalitions and refusal, this is mapped out through the diagram of the dominant order. However, in treating practices of ordering as always, in part, over determined and failed projects, there is always an excess to this process. There are always tools, practices and knowledge which are not subsumed by the historical order and provide methods and alternatives that open up (and can be taken up) to maintain other ways of living. This promises both affirmative transformations of citizenship as a desirable project and active refusals of citizenship as a sovereign form of politics. This is a questioning and ambiguous potential that we need to struggle to keep open.

Mapping unfamiliar and impossible acts of citizenship

The first section of the special issue focuses on events, moments and acts which disturb the co-ordinates of existing regimes of citizenship. Ní Mhurchú's (2016) article extends and develops the questions raised in this editorial introduction concerning the existing work on 'acts of citizenship' and the conceptualisation of the political. Arguing that 'acts' are often analysed through a central focus on the 'unfamiliarity of familiar (political) acts', such as irregularised migrants and non-citizens involvement in demonstrations, marches, occupations, she proposes the need to develop our understanding of 'unfamiliar acts'. This means a reimagining of what resistance and the political looks like. Drawing upon studies of 'indirect resistance' (Scott 2014) and the politics of language and musical performance (Maira 2008), Ní Mhurchú argues that forms of word play, vernacular language and musical styles engaged with by intergenerational migrants can be fruitfully understood 'unfamiliar acts of citizenship'. Examples of youth engagement with Verlan and Hip-Hop in France are read as highly political because it disturbs the status quo of mono-linguistic and ethnic categories of national citizenship. This engagement with vernacular music and language is constituted by the precarity and marginality that many intergenerational migrants experience and this becomes a site of hybrid identification which subverts (rather than actively contests) the narrow dualistic definitions of the nation state. To Ní Mhurchú, what designates these engagements as 'unfamiliar acts citizenship' is that whilst they are orientated away from the politics of the nation state, this nonetheless provides for alternative forms of belonging to emerge. Recognising a tension in movements such as French Rap between both their subversive potential and its patriarchal and commercial character, Ní Mhurchú calls us to appreciate the ambivalence at the heart of citizenship. That is 'the need to think about hybridity across inclusion and exclusion within citizenship and precisely to refuse this citizenship beyond citizenship binary'.

Stierl and Mayblin's articles separately examine the potentiality of struggles over the recognition of migrants and asylum seekers; in death (Stierl 2016) and through the politics of work/labour (Mayblin (2016)). Stierl's ethnographic study of three separate protests reveals how the violent marginality induced by EU border regimes is contested within a politics of grief. Through an innovative theorisation of 'grief activism', realised through a reading of both Judith Butler and Jacque Rancière, this explores the fragile encounters and (im)possible solidarities formed around the mourning of border deaths. Responding to fatalities which are produced by the complex vacillating and deterritorialised tendencies of contemporary borders, grief activism works to protest the deaths of those detained, drowned or abused through acts of mourning and by subverting the official state-led process of memorialisation. The article pursues a rich narrative account of different sites of protest peopled by citizen activists, irregularised migrants, grieving families. This again expands our conception of the political in its attention to a 'failed' event of grief activism in Monastir, Tunisia and through an analysis of artistic activism by the Centre for Political Beauty in Berlin. Such events, Stierl argues, (en)gender solidarity at the margins (blurring the distinctions of citizen/non-citizen). However, encounters in grief are equally temporal, precarious and fraught with tensions, 'they are always replete with the possibility of failure'. As well as collective acts that humanise the dead and contest the violent economy of EU borders, these struggles reveal unrecognisable and 'impossible' forms of identification that disturb our existing sovereign understanding of community and citizenship.

Mayblin's (2016) article likewise offers us an analysis of struggles over humanisation against the subjugating and exclusory logics of the UK's policy towards asylum seekers. She argues that the 'LTW' campaign, a movement to allow asylum seekers the right to work in Britain, provided an 'insurrectional moment' in resisting the highly restrictive forms of social control used to govern asylum seekers. The LTW campaign is significant because it legally contests the hegemonic consensus on Asylum, through a divergent assemblage of Trade Unions, Refugee activists and religious groups. The important claim here is that whilst the campaign was unsuccessful in enacting institutional change it provided an opening up and a reimagining of British citizenship which is dominated by (post)colonial narratives of 'otherness'. The contestation of marginalisation through LTW strategies relied on invocations of both the asylum seeker as a potentially equal citizen, included within the social body of 'workers', but also a more radical reimagining of the asylum seeker's right to work hinging on Marxist traditions of internationalism and 'human solidarity'. Whilst there remains a tension in the campaign between idealising the asylum seeker through the distinction of 'good'/'failed' citizen (those who contribute and work and those who don't), Mayblin argues that the significance of this movement is the 'mobile solidarities' which it (en)gendered and the potential this reveals for future disruption.

Turner's work follows on this theme of the tension between marginality and the type of oppositional politics this (en)genders. Drawing on William Walters' reading of domopolitics and Anne McClintock's work on domesticity, he argues that domestication is central to the production and regulation of marginal groups in the UK (relying on a certain raced, gendered classed, sexed assemblage). Focusing on the marginalisation of Traveller groups, he argues that familial domesticity provides a site of anxiety regarding the (re)production of social difference but equally remains a site of contestation. Turner reads these dynamics in the exemplary example of the eviction of Irish Traveller's from the Dale Farm site in Essex in 2011. The modern push to regulate Traveller life is in part constituted by their apparent failure of domesticity, leading to state-led 'domicide'. However, this form of marginality always (en)genders forms of resistance, however violent domestication is. He argues that what we see in the protest over the Dale Farm eviction by both residents and activists is a powerful counter-narrative that offers up a different claim to family life and home. Whilst familial domesticity provides both a moral and biological diagram of British citizenship, it also provides the material through which alternative ways of living are kept alive.

Reimagining citizenship from marginal spaces

The acts and encounters which emerge from marginal spaces provide both disturbances of citizenship and equally provide alternative ways of accounting for and understanding the political. Recognising the radical potential of marginalised acts can open up ways of conceptualising existing regime of citizenship and new political constellations which work both *within* and *beyond* citizenship. In Beattie's (2016) contribution, she reflects upon a personal trauma (relating to the violence of securitised border regimes) which opened up her understanding of both Cosmopolitan theory and the contradictory enactment of global regimes of control. Beattie utilises Cynthia Weber's conception of 'Safe Citizenship' and Isin's 'affective' citizenship to theorise a personal experience of deportation and 'exile'. Beattie situates her experience of exile in the ethical potential it has to create previously unthinkable and impossible connections with 'others'. She thus reveals how an account of exile helps us (re)think the boundaries of sovereign politics, security and move towards an affective mode of political subjectivity. Exile is often an extreme form of marginalisation and is often violent, what Beattie suggests is that storytelling opens up a process of politicisation within this experience which can be both personally and socially therapeutic.

Shilliam (2016) works takes up this engagement with (re)imagining citizenship and the political but through a historical and archival re-reading of anti-colonial struggles. Shilliam retells the history of 'Ethiopianist' movements in the 1930s as an opening up of the contradictory logics and racist underpinnings of British Empire (and identification). The outcry over Britian's inaction over the Italian invasion of Ethiopia in 1935 (by both white subjects and members of the Black diaspora in the UK) helped to reveal the racist and exclusive script of Britishness which had previous been offered as a mode of 'Imperial belonging'. Shilliam provides an interlocutor with cultural studies to understand how Afri-centric Ethiopianism was orientated around global–colonial struggles over race, marginalisation and belonging. This provides a re-reading of commonsensical approaches to citizenship and the political. Shilliam argues that cultural studies (and (post)colonial studies of citizenship) have tended to read black political movements in the UK as orientated around claims to 'equitable national settlement' i.e. a demand to be 'included' in the frame of rights and belonging offered by 'multicultural' citizenship. Contesting this both *historically* and *politically,* he reveals that the global–colonial coordinates of anti-colonial politics reach both *within* and *beyond* the narrative of citizenship. The legacies of Afri-centric Ethiopianism continue to resonate in Rastafari movements and campaigns demanding colonial reparations, these are not located within a national-territory struggle over rights or membership per se but rely on relational appeals to the global solidarities (en)gendered by European colonial encounters (enslavement, violence, prospective African liberation). These movements provide and practice different 'cartographies of belonging' which help us reimagine and resist contemporary citizenship.

The last article by Bird (2016) equally focuses on decolonial struggles and the lessons this has for our understanding of citizenship. Her article looks at the work of African philosopher 'statesman' as a means of rethinking 'acts' of citizenship in different historical contexts. Whilst the acts of citizenship literature have tended to focus on localised acts 'from below' (also see Mayblin 2016; Ní Mhurchú 2016) she suggests that the marginalised voices from African philosophy provide us with new ways of creatively conceptualising citizenship. What is significant in the accounts of thinkers such as Julius Nyerere and Léopold Sédar Senghor is the liberating potential they present in the cultivation of political subjectivity linked to both the 'village' and 'Pan-African' solidarities. To Bird the (failed) promise of these interventions is found in both a reimagining of the Europeanist sovereign (white, colonial) citizen and the desire for a re-humanisation of the African self; a self which no longer has to prove anything to colonial masters and can tell its own history (and future). As with many of these explorations of the disturbances and (re)imaginings of citizenship, this remains an unfulfilled and failed project. Whilst decolonisation opened up a potentially emancipatory move in African history, the failure of (post)colonial state-led projects reveals another darker story. Whilst philosopher statesman's work may still hold a radical conceptualisation of decolonial citizenship, the Authoritarian nature of their regimes and the persistence of imperial power through developmentalist capitalism reveals the impossibility of the reimagining that it (en)genders.

References

Allen, Amy. 2002. "Power, Subjectivity, and Agency: Between Arendt and Foucault." *International Journal of Philosophical Studies* 10 (2): 131–149.

Anderson, Bridget. 2013. *Us and Them?* Oxford: Oxford University Press.

Anderson, Bridget, Nandita Sharma, and Cynthia Wright. 2012. "'We Are All Foreigners': No Borders as a Practical Political Project." In *Citizenship, Migrant Activism, and the Politics of Movement,* edited by Peter Nyers and Kim Rygiel, 73–92. Abingdon: Routledge.

Andrijasevic, Rutvica. 2013. "Acts of Citizenship as Methodology." In Engin Isin and M. Saward, eds. *Enacting European Citizenship*, 47–65. Cambridge: Cambridge University Press.

Andrijasevic, Rutvica, and Anderson, Bridget. 2008. "Sex, Slaves and Citizens: The Politics of Anti-trafficking." *Soundings: A Journal of Politics and Culture* 40: 135–145.

Bagelman, Jennifer. 2015. *Sanctuary City: A Suspended State*. Basingstoke: Palgrave-Macmillan.

Balibar, Etienne. 2012. "The 'Impossible' Community of the Citizens: Past and Present Problems." *Environment and Planning D: Society and Space* 30 (3): 437–449.

Basham, Victoria M., and Nick Vaughan-Williams. 2013. "Gender, Race and Border Security Practices: A Profane Reading of 'Muscular Liberalism.'" *British Journal of Politics and International Relations* 15 (4): 509–527.

Beattie, Amanda. 2016. "Between Safety & Vulnerability: The Exiled Other of International Relations." *Citizenship Studies* 20 (2): 228–242.

Benhabib, Seyla. 2004. *The Rights of Others*. Cambridge: Cambridge University Press.

Bhambra, Gurminder. 2014. *Connected Sociologies*. London: Bloomsbury.

Bird, Gemma. 2016. "Beyond the Nation State: The Role of Local and Pan-national Identities in Defining Post-colonial African Citizenship." *Citizenship Studies*. 20 (2): 260–275.

Brown, Wendy. 1995. *States of Injury: Power and Freedom in Late Modernity*. Princeton: Princeton University Press.

Çakmaklı, Didem. 2015. "Active Citizenship in Turkey: Learning Citizenship in Civil Society Organizations." *Citizenship Studies* 19 (3–4): 421–435.

Critchley, Simon. 2007. *Infinitely Demanding: Ethics of Commitment, Politics of Resistance*. London: Verso.

Darling, Jonathan. 2014. "Asylum and the Post-political: Domopolitics, Depoliticisation and Acts of Citizenship." *Antipode* 46 (1): 72–91.

De Genova, Nicholas. 2007. "The Production of Culprits: From Deportability to Detainability in the Aftermath of 'Homeland Security.'" *Citizenship Studies* 11 (5): 421–448.

Death, Carl. 2010."Counter-conducts: A Foucauldian Analytics of Protest." *Social Movement Studies* 9 (3): 235–235.

Doty, Roxanne Lynn. 2011. "Bare Life: Border-crossing Deaths and Spaces of Moral Alibi." *Environment and Planning D: Society and Space* 29 (4): 599–612.

Edkins, Jenny, Véronique Pin-Fat, and Michael J. Shapiro. 2004. *Sovereign Lives: Power in Global Politics*. London: Routledge.

Grugel, Jean, and Jewellord Nem Singh. 2015. "Protest, Citizenship and Democratic Renewal: The Student Movement in Chile." *Citizenship Studies* 19 (3–4): 353–366.

Guillaume, Xavier, and Jef Huysmans, eds. 2013. *Citizenship and Security: The Constitution of Political Being*. Abingdon: Routledge.

Harrington, Jack. 2012. "Orientalism, Political Subjectivity and the Birth of Citizenship between 1780 and 1830." *Citizenship Studies* 16 (5–6): 573–586.

Harvey, David. 2008. "The Right to the City." *New Left Review* 53: 23–40.

Hindess, Barry. 2004. "Citizenship for All." *Citizenship Studies* 8 (3): 305–315.

Honig, Bonnie. 2003. *Democracy and the Foreigner*. Princeton: Princeton University Press.

Hoover, Joe. 2015. "The Human Right to Housing and Community Empowerment: Home Occupation, Eviction Defence and Community Land Trusts." *Third World Quarterly* 36 (6): 1092–1109.

Hunt, Krista, and Kim Rygiel. 2007. "(En)Gendering the War on Terror: War Stories and Camouflaged Politics: An Introduction." In *(En)Gendering the War on Terror: War Stories and Camouflaged Politics*, edited by Krista Hunt and Kim Rygiel, 1–27. Aldershot: Ashgate.

Isin, Engin F. 2008. "Theorising Acts of Citizenship." In *Acts of Citizenship*, edited by Engin Isin and Greg Neilsen, 15–44. London: Zed Book.

Isin, Engin F. 2009. "Citizenship in Flux: The Figure of the Activist Citizen." *Subjectivity* 29 (367–388): 379.

Jarvis, Lee, and Michael Lister. 2013. "Disconnected Citizenship? The Impacts of Anti-terrorism Policy on Citizenship in the UK." *Political Studies* 61 (3): 656–675.

Joppke, Christian. 2007. "Beyond National Models: Civic Integration Policies for Immigrants in Western Europe." *West European Politics* 30 (1): 1–22.

Kofman, Eleonore. 2002. "Contemporary European Migrations, Civic Stratification and Citizenship." *Political Geography* 2002, 21 (8), 1035–1054.

Kristeva, Julia. 1994. *Strangers to Ourselves*. New York: Columbia University Press.

Kymlicka, Will. 2001. *Politics in the Vernacular*. Oxford: Oxford University Press.

Levinas, Emmanuel. 1999. *Totality and Infinity: An Essay on Exteriority*. Pittsburgh, PA: Duquesne University Press.

Lister, Ruth. 2007. "Inclusive Citizenship: Realizing the Potential1." *Citizenship Studies* 11 (1): 49–61.

Maira, Sunaina. 2008. "'We Ain't Missing' Palestinian Hip-Hop: A Transnational Youth Movement." *The New Centennial Review* 8 (2): 161–192.

Marciniak, Katarzyna, and Imogen Tyler. 2014. *Immigrant Protest: Politics, Aesthetics, and Everyday Dissent*. New York: SUNY Press.

Mayblin, Lucy. 2016. "Troubling the Exclusive Privileges of Citizenship: Mobile Solidarities, Asylum Seekers, and the Right to Work." *Citizenship Studies*. 20 (2): 192–207.

McNevin, Anne. 2007. "Irregular Migrants, Neoliberal Geographies and Spatial Frontiers of 'The Political'." *Review of International Studies* 33 (4): 655–674.

McNevin, Anne. 2011. *Contesting Citizenship*. New York, NY: Columbia University Press.

Mezzadra, Sandro, and Brett Neilson. 2013. *Border as Method, or, the Multiplication of Labor*. Durham, NC: Duke University Press.

Muller, Benjamin. 2004. "(Dis)Qualified Bodies: Securitization, Citizenship and 'Identity Management'." *Citizenship Studies* 8 (3): 279–294.

Nancy, Jean Luc. 1991. *Inoperative Community*. Minneapolis: Minnesota University Press.

Ní Mhurchú, Aoileann. 2016. "Unfamiliar Acts of Citizenship: Enacting Citizenship from the Space of Marginalised Intergenerational Migration." *Citizenship Studies* 20 (2): 156–172.

Nyers, Peter, ed. 2009. *Securitisations of Citizenship*. Abingdon: Routledge.

Nyers, Peter, and Kim Rygiel, eds. 2012. *Citizenship, Migrant Activism, and the Politics of Movement*. Abingdon: Routledge.

Odysseos, Louiza, and Anna Selmeczi. 2015. "The Power of Human Rights/The Human Rights of Power: An Introduction." *Third World Quarterly* 36 (6): 1033–1040.

Ong, Aihwa. 2006. *Neoliberalism as Exception*. Durham, NC: Duke University Press.

Papadopoulos, Dimitris, Niamh Stephenson, and Vassilis Tsianos. 2008. *Escape Routes: Control and Subversion in the Twenty First Century*. London: Pluto Books.

Papadopoulos, Dimitris, and Vassilis S. Tsianos. 2013. "After Citizenship: Autonomy of Migration, Organisational Ontology and Mobile Commons." *Citizenship Studies* 17 (2): 178–196.

Rajaram, Prem Kumar, and Carl Grundy-Warr, eds. 2007. *Borderscapes: Hidden Geographies and Politics at Territory's Edge*. Minneapolis, MN: University of Minnesota Press.

Rigo, Enrica. 2005. "Citizenship at Europe's Borders: Some Reflections on the Post-colonial Condition of Europe in the Context of EU Enlargement." *Citizenship Studies* 9 (1): 3–22.

Roseneil, Sasha, Isabel Crowhurst, Ana Cristina Santos, and Mariya Stoilova. 2013. "Reproduction and Citizenship/Reproducing Citizens: Editorial Introduction." *Citizenship Studies* 17 (8): 901–911.

Rygiel, Kim. 2008. "The Securitized Citizen." In *Recasting the Social in Citizenship*, edited by Engin F. Isin, 268–300. Toronto, ON: University of Toronto Press.

Sandelind, C. 2015. "Territorial Rights and Open Borders." *Critical Review of International Social and Political Philosophy*. 18 (5): 487–507.

Schinkel, Willem. 2010. "From Zoepolitics to Biopolitics: Citizenship and the Construction of 'Society'." *European Journal of Social Theory* 13 (2): 155–172.

Scott, James C. 2009. *The Art of Not Being Governed: An Anarchist History of Upland Southeast Asia*. New Haven, CT: Yale University Press.

Scott, James C. 2014. "Leaking Away and Other Forms of Resistance." In *Youth Resistance Research and Theories of Change*, edited by E. Tuck and K. W. Yang, 59–71. Abingdon: Routledge.

Shilliam, Robbie. 2015. *The Black Pacific: Anti-colonial Struggles and Oceanic Connections*. London: Bloomsbury.

Shilliam, Robbie. 2016. "Ethiopianism, Englishness, Britishness: Struggles over Imperial Belonging." *Citizenship Studies* 20 (2): 243–259.

Spivak, Gayatri. 1988. "Can the Subaltern Speak?" In *Marxism and the Interpretation of Culture*, edited by Cary Nelson and Larry Grossberg, 271–313. Chicago, IL: University of Illinois Press.

de Sousa Santos, Boaventura. 2014. *Epistemologies of the South: Justice against Epistemicide*. Abingdon: Routledge.

Squire, Vicki. 2011. *The Contested Politics of Mobility: Borderzones and Irregularity*. Abingdon: Routledge.

Squire, V. 2015. "Acts of Desertion: Abandonment and Renouncement at the Sonoran Borderzone." *Antipode* 47 (2): 500–516.

Stierl, Maurice. 2016. "Contestations in Death – The Role of Grief in Migration Struggles." *Citizenship Studies* 20 (2): 173–191.

Turner, Joe. 2014. "Testing the Liberal Subject: (in)Security, Responsibility and 'Self-improvement' in the UK Citizenship Test." *Citizenship Studies* 18 (3–4): 332–348.

Turner, Joe. 2016. "Governing the Domestic Space of the Traveller in the UK: 'Family', 'Home' and the Struggle over Dale Farm." *Citizenship Studies* 20 (2): 208–227.

Tyler, Imogen, and Katarzyna Marciniak. 2013. *Protesting Citizenship: Migrant Activisms*. Abingdon: Routledge.

Vaughan-Williams, Nick. 2010. "The UK Border Security Continuum: Virtual Biopolitics and the Simulation of the Sovereign Ban." *Environment and Planning D: Society and Space* 28: 1071–1083.

Wacquant, Loïc. 2007. *Urban Outcasts: A Comparative Sociology of Advanced Marginality*. Cambridge: Polity Press.

Walker, R. B. J. 1992. *Inside/Outside*. Cambridge: Cambridge University Press.

Walters, William. 2008. "Acts of Demonstration: Mapping the Territory of (Non) Citizenship." In *Acts of Citizenship*, edited by Engin Isin and Greg Neilsen, 182–207. London: Zed Book.

Weheliye, Alexander. 2014. *Habeas Viscus*. Durham: Duke University Press.

Unfamiliar acts of citizenship: enacting citizenship in vernacular music and language from the space of marginalised intergenerational migration

Aoileann Ní Mhurchú

School of Social Sciences, University of Manchester, Manchester, UK

ABSTRACT
Conceptualising citizenship as an act rather than a status enables us to rethink the familiarity of both 'who' can be a citizen and the type of 'practices' that can be understood as citizenship. This paper focuses on unfamiliar practices of citizenship per se by exploring the liminal site from which intergenerational migrant youth resist the taken-for-granted space of citizenship through a turn towards vernacular music and language. It considers how citizenship is resisted here through the unfamiliar act of turning away from either identifying or, failing/refusing to identify with the nation-state. It explores the effect of this move in challenging narrow national linguistic and ethnic ideologies through the development of non-standard language practice and cross-cutting musical styles. It argues that citizenship is enacted in this move by creating a space *in* vernacular music and language for expressions of hybrid political identity and belonging.

An act does not exist as a now within a series of nows. Rather, acts are continually becoming and arriving in various forms. (Morrison 2008, 223)

[T]he struggle at the heart of migrant politics is a battle not only over what kinds of protest and protestors can be seen and heard (as politics) but also more fundamentally what kinds of resistance are imagined as possible. (Tyler 2013, 213)

Introduction

The notion of citizenship as an act (a practice) rather than a status (Isin and Neilson 2008) has brought about a huge challenge to the dominant idea of 'active citizenship' and thereby to how we understand what it is to be political in the social sciences. Whereas the idea of active citizenship emphasises familiar ways of being political, which are tied up in ideas of belonging as a right and associated duties, the notion of citizenship as an act has enabled explorations into *unfamiliar* and *disruptive* possibilities of being political by focusing on how rights-claims are constantly remade in the name of belonging (Isin and Nyers 2014b;

Isin and Saward 2013). This paper contributes to this latter engagement with disruptive and unfamiliar possibilities of being political, looking specifically at migrant youth and the subtlety of political enactment undertaken by them.

Conceptualising citizenship as an act (Isin and Neilson 2008) links citizenship to the process of claiming and performing rights to belong; it thus enables us to rethink 'who' can be a citizen beyond the already-existing rights-bearing liberal subject. It also enables us to rethink what type of 'practices' can be understood as citizenship, beyond the repetition of practices that merely affirm socio-historical patterns, but as actions which also disrupt, and rupture these. In the context of migration studies, particular attention has been paid thus far to the former – namely to how unfamiliar actors such as undocumented adult migrants undertake familiar practices of resistance – such as marching, withdrawing labour, voicing descent, strikes, protests, raising/waving of flags and sit-ins – thereby interrupting existing socio-historical patterns. These are actions whose target is the state and its institutions or other existing polities such as the European Union, which have demanded a range of issues, from redistribution to more formal and substantive rights (e.g. Ashutosh 2013; McNevin 2011; Nyers 2008). Such work has challenged the figure of 'who' is understood to be able to claim citizenship.

Increasingly, there is an emphasis on thinking about practices of citizenship linked to less immediately perceptibly political acts in order to further recognise the multiple and contested nature of political subjectivity (cf. Morrison 2008; Neveu 2014). This paper contributes to and extends these inquiries, and thereby our understanding of the unfamiliar disruptive possibilities of being political more generally, by exploring the liminal site from which intergenerational urban migrant youth resist the taken for granted space of citizenship. It looks at how they do so by turning away from identifying or failing/refusing to identify with the nation-state (without grounding belonging at the city or international level either) *towards* vernacular music and language. It explores the effect of this move in challenging standardised national language and ethnicity ideologies through the development by youth of non-standard regional language practices and cross-cutting musical styles which mix together and undermine mono-linguistic and mon-ethnic affiliations. Doing so, this paper contributes to our understanding of 'everyday resistance' as an indirect practice linked to subtle destabilisations (which draw upon rather than oppose) dominant national spaces of political identity and belonging. This complements work thus far which has captured more direct challenges (clearly articulated dissatisfaction) to the national space of political identity in migrant activism.

This paper firstly looks at how conceptualising citizenship as an act foregrounds *social struggle* (what people do rather than who they are). This allows us not only to think about citizenship as a direct challenge to an existing polity, such as the nation-state, the city or an international body – and a re-configuration of this – but also to imagine citizenship beyond (working through but not limited to) these existing polities. It subsequently explores how marginalised intergenerational migrant youth's experiences at the level of the everyday invoke important questions about belonging in terms of vernacular music and language. I consider the political effect of this turn towards vernacular music and language: namely that it indirectly challenges a narrow national linguistic space which has tended to be based around normally one, or only several prioritised languages ('monoglot standardization' [Blackledge 2004, 72]) and ethnicity ideology (the symbolic linking together of ethnicity and culture). I posit that by taking this political effect into account, this turn towards vernacular music and language can be read as an act of citizenship given that it involves creative processes of drawing on and mixing up sanctioned 'national' and 'non-national' resources by young people, which produce different understandings of who they are/can be *beyond* the dominant national space of political identity and belonging. The paper considers in the third part how practices of engagement in vernacular music and language can be understood not only as disruptive acts into hegemonic understandings of citizenship but as enacting a form of hybrid citizenship.

Broadening the concept of citizenship

Traditionally, citizenship studies have explored citizenship as a realm of familiar ordered linear, formal and legal status which the individual negotiates, where the importance of enabling progressive rights and duties to reduce inclusive/exclusive hierarchies across citizenship is stressed (Ní Mhurchú 2014a). In contrast, by focusing on ideas of rupture in existing socio-historical patterns about 'who' can be a citizen and 'what practices' can be associated with citizenship, the acts of citizenship literature has brought to the fore ideas of complex and irregular belonging and identification; and thereby unfamiliar ways of being political (Isin and Neilson 2008; McNevin 2011). It has drawn attention to ambiguous, complex and irregular political agency which exceed the traditional citizen/second-class citizen dualism. It emphasises instead a messy unordered collective of neurotic citizens, irregular citizens, abject citizens, illegal citizens and ambiguous citizens (Isin and Nyers 2014a, 2014b; Ní Mhurchú 2014b). These are citizens who are caught between many different polities – polities of various levels of formal authority including the European Union, the United Nations, the city, as well as various covenants, agreements and charters that constitute these polities. Within migration studies, the emphasis in this area has tended to be on the unfamiliarity of the irregular migrant subject. While unfamiliar 'acts' do emerge at present; therefore, their unfamiliarity is often based on contradictions across familiar acts rather than unfamiliar acts per se. For example, the acts themselves which are pointed to include demands made by irregular migrants for recognition through demonstrations, occupations and marches, which are all familiar acts in discussions about citizenship traditionally. It is the way in which irregular migrants make these demands – for example, both in the national language and in the presence of foreign-language placards, music, dress and performances – that is unfamiliar (cf. Butler and Spivak 2007; McNevin 2011) because of its contradictory nature. It is the unfamiliarity of familiar acts therefore which is disorienting in this existing literature rather than unfamiliar acts themselves.

As Morrison (2008) notes in the opening quote, the notion of citizenship as an act which is both disruptive of the status quo *and* in itself ('continually becoming and arriving in various forms') emphasises the idea of unfamiliar acts of citizenship per se. It is by following this line of inquiry that this paper extends analysis in the field of critical citizenship studies. It stretches our understanding of the nature of citizenship *as* an act in keeping with the multiplicity of political agency within the context of migration (Nyers and Rygiel 2012). For, understanding citizenship as a process of 'negotiating different situations and identities, and articulating ourselves as distinct from, yet similar to, others in our everyday lives' (Isin and Nyers 2014a, 4) as critical citizenship studies does, emphasises (and opens up) the question of social struggle itself through which a sense of rights and duties vis-à-vis a 'polity' can be *established*. It indicates that this can involve foregrounding the process through which people engage with each other on a day-to-day basis to articulate themselves *as part of* a polity, as well as by enacting a challenge to existing polities.

To build on these existing insights in critical citizenship studies, I turn to a group which tends to be the focus of much debate about the intersection of migration and citizenship, but whose possibility as political subjects very rarely *inform* such discussions: marginalised intergenerational migrant youth. This group is normally only implicitly linked to this intersection through the actions, views and experiences of migrant adults, in particular migrant mothers (cf. Lentin 2003; Tyler 2013). Even when focused upon, it is often only as people who have been failed by the existing liberal democratic regime(s) rather than people who challenge this in a substantive way (cf. Bhabha 2009; Cohen 2005).[1] This is in contrast to a growing literature within youth studies which has in recent decades emphasised the specificities of young people's political agency in all its (un)familiarity, and in particular of migrant youth (e.g. Boehm et al. 2011; Hoerder, Herbert, and Schmitt 2005; Kallio and Häkli 2013; Maira and Soep 2005; Nortier and Svendsen 2015). This paper, as such, does not turn away from thinking about (ir)regular migrants as an important group in the context of how we understand 'acts of citizenship'; but it considers how a nuanced understanding of the different generational experiences (as social locations) of migrant groups, helps us think further about the unfamiliar nature of their acts.

Marginalised intergenerational migrant youth: turning away from existing polities

The term intergenerational migrant youth refers to those who migrated at a very young age (below 12) often called the '1.5 generation' and those born in a country which their parent(s) or grandparent(s) migrated to – often called 'second generation migrants'. Portes and Zhou (1993) called this group 'The New Second Generation' and distinguish their experience of adaptation from those of adult migrants. I focus specifically on the lives of marginalised intergenerational migrant youth – that is, intergenerational migrant youth who experience discrimination due to their own precarious status, that of their parents/ immediate family members or that of their family's historical relationship with the state (and often a combination of these). By 'youthful agent', I draw on Kallio and Häkli's definition (2013, 7) of someone 'who occupies a minor position in her/his specific geo-economic and socio-cultural community and society'.

Intergenerational migrant youth are often linked to both citizenship and migration, however normally at different times, for different purposes and without much discussion as to what the implications of linking them to *both* citizenship and migration might be for how we understand 'citizenship' (Ní Mhurchú 2014a). It is as people caught between these categories – rather than falling into one category or the other and/or straddling them equally – that I focus on them here. I argue that the actions of intergenerational migrant youth force us to rethink how we have come to understand the politics of citizenship because their actions are not directed at overtly challenging the boundaries of existing polities such as the nation or state, city or international polity but involve turning away from these towards music and language. Such actions can be understood, I argue, in a way that avoids the blackmail of needing to define them as either political or non-political if we theorise them as 'a mode of political presence' and think about how some modes of political presence first appear as political absence (Kallio 2012, 294).

One of the difficulties with focusing on youth when thinking and talking about citizenship is that young people find themselves residing within a 'generational milieu' (Hoerder, Herbert, and Schmitt 2005, 15) where past, present and future meet processes of change and rupture (Boehm et al. 2011). As inhabitants of this generational milieu, young people are at the epicentre of where identities, power relations and social change engage and interact; however, because most societies naturalise socialisation by adults of youth, and elevate the culture of adults during working life to the position of 'the' culture, youth are rendered invisible often *from* questions about the choices, challenges and changes involved in cultural *negotiation* and transfer (ibid.). In effect, the power relations through which young people resist and navigate their everyday lives – which involve negotiating relations of peer cultural communities, following and engaging in familial and local norms, forging and protecting bonds in their personal relationships – take place at the intersection of *various* temporal and spatial senses of place, locality, globality, culture, symbolic significance, futurity and possibility which render them less visible. Youth have many possible ways of grounding this sense of self that they must negotiate and voice, which can be less visible given their messy nature. Yet, it is precisely often at this intersection and atypical voice that they make present their political subjectivities.

For example, in their study of 1.5 generation migrant youth growing up in Ireland, Ní Laoire et al. (2011) look at how young people articulate their sense of political identity and belonging in ways which indirectly confound categories such as 'Irish' and 'migrant' as useful hierarchies for understanding national processes of othering. Youth did so through practices and relationships linked to *combinations* of music, fashion, school, sport and language across national and international as well as regional and local spaces. In other words, some youth did not simply reject hierarchies of sameness and difference which underpin national processes of othering – thus acknowledging them *in* such a rejection – but by turning away from them. Their actions lacked immediate clarity of message.

Most notably, some young people when faced with discourses of exclusion – which included forms of othering ranging from more benign to overtly racist claims about their lack of 'Irishness' – did not seek to challenge these and demonstrate alternative ways in which they were integrated 'Irish' citizen nationals at the level of the state, the city or the European Union (for example, by emphasising their links to Ireland, such as being born there, coming from countries with colonial links to Ireland or having families who contributed financially to Ireland (see, McNevin [2011] on how the *Sans Papiers* do this)). Rather, they began to associate exclusion *with* the dominant national identity; in this case, 'being Irish' was seen as 'a way of being in the world firmly rooted in the local and indifferent to other ways of doing, being and perceiving' (Ní Laoire et al. 2009, 74). Some migrant youth opted as a result to turn away from this: even from the process of identifying the limitations of the national polity in favour of other types of international or sub-national polity. They turned instead towards, most notably, music and language which are often associated with subversive subculture within a given society (Hebdige 1981).[2]

The groups looked at in this study by Ní Laoire et al. (2011) for whom this was a feature included youth from African backgrounds and Latin American youth living in Ireland, many growing up in the asylum system. What became important for such youth was developing belonging via globalised culture, including through music (such as rap) and languages (in particular code-switching) among like-minded peers in response to experiences of marginalisation and isolation (ibid.). One way of seeing these, I argue, is as manifestations of attempts by some intergenerational migrant youth to develop a hybrid self and a polity based on such hybridity in the face of exclusion from existing national polities which they do not fall into: to create 'the proverbial "room of one's own"' (Mushaben 2008, 508). What we can think about is the possibility of 'artistic phrasing' *in* music and language by youth to 'reshape terms and meanings in the interest of self-distinction' (Fernandez-Kelly and Konczal 2007, 1165) in response to marginalisation in society associated with national culture. I posit such acts as political by understanding 'everyday resistance' (being political) as a practice and thus not reducible to intentions but as that which can be explored through its effects across society (Foucault 1978; Vinthagen and Johansson 2013). This allows us to link 'being political' to even subtle challenges to dominant power relations (with all the messiness this entails) rather than merely dialogue whereby a clear message is conveyed through intentions. Specifically, I argue that the turn to vernacular music and language described above and explored further below should be seen as a political act as it involves a refashioning of the self by youth by destabilising the dominant narrow national space of political identity and belonging.

To explain, the Irish nationalist project has following independence from the British Empire in the early nineteenth century been deeply cultural, with the Celtic language, music and heritage seen as a bridge to past generations of the imagined Celtic nation (Dowling 1997). Put simply, the Irish nationalist political project is deeply anchored in the idea of two official languages (Gaelic and English), official music (Gaelic music) and Celtic heritage. Despite official adherence to interculturalism in Ireland (based upon ideals of diversity and tolerance), 'interculturalism' is institutionalised under 'integration' which is underpinned clearly by a linguistic hierarchy as well as an ethnic understanding of 'Irishness'. Most notably, the Irish citizenship test requires fluency in either English or Gaelic and in recent decades it has become increasingly difficult for those born in Ireland to automatically acquire Irish citizenship without the necessary Gaelic ethnic background (due to major changes introduced under the 2004 Irish Citizenship Referendum) while it has remained very possible for those born abroad to automatically acquire Irish citizenship *through* Gaelic ethnic heritage (Mancini and Finlay 2008). Yet, the turn to vernacular music and language engaged in by people in Ireland challenges this national space of belonging by drawing aspects of existing 'national' language and music together with various other music and linguistic influences – in particular African American hip hop – in ways which are unsettling and disrupting, not least because they are familiar *and* unfamiliar at the same time. It allows for creative processes of drawing on and mixing up sanctioned 'national' and 'non-national' resources through which young people can experiment with different understandings of 'who' they are/can be, as I discuss further below. These however remain *ungrounded*, thus distinguishing them from ideas about 'multiculturalism' which emphasise various groundings of difference.

Language, music and resistance

The relationship between music and resistance has been widely documented, in particular in relation to slave-songs, post-war youth mod and rocker music as well as hip hop (Keyes 2002; Sullivan 2001). Hip hop itself, in particular has become synonymous with youth subculture and resistance, originating as it did in the US among disadvantaged youth of colour as a medium for bringing attention to the social and political realities in which they were forced to live. Nonetheless, in recent decades, a number of studies have demonstrated new developments around engagement in hip hop and language use by immigrant youth in diversely populated urban areas (e.g. Hoerder, Herbert, and Schmitt 2005). Exposure to multiple cultures and linguistic influences in such spaces, and increased global awareness, have been shown to be developing novel (albeit not unique) practices of language mix and hip hop due to the specificities of the local–global influences in each given context (Nortier and Dorleijn 2013; Nortier and Svendsen 2015).

Maira (2008), for example, has explored the resistant practices against exclusion and discrimination (linked to imperialism, racism, inequality) enabled by Palestinian-American hip hop affiliated youth in a post-9/11 security-oriented highly diverse urban context. She focuses in particular on the tangibility of descent in the words used in hip hop here. That said, she elsewhere (Maira 2005, 69) points to aspects of 'reframing the basis of citizenship' within such youth practices; in particular the possibility in them of 'a complex set of political affiliations and social *boundary crossings*' in subtle ways (emphasis added). Others such as Schmitt (2005) and Cutler and Royneland (2015) have drawn a specific link between vernacular music such as hip hop and vernacular language; in particular pointing to increasing *mixtures* of local, indigenous and migrant languages which form the base language for hip hop. This allows us to think about how hip hop not only conveys a message (acts as a medium) to express dissatisfaction with society and point to wrongs but also has become a tool to 'establish solidarity with fellow community members and to strengthen their position in society' (ibid., 140) by infusing a variety of cultural linguistic and musical influences into hip hop itself in a way that cuts across traditional categories of ethnicity or language use. This work points, as such, to the need to think further about the processes and effects of vernacular music and language: that is, about what is gained by those who engage in them (rather than just what can be expressed verbally through them). This paper builds on such literature by foregrounding the importance of the subtlety of engagement with vernacular music and language: both how the process facilitates creative hybrid refashioning of self, and its indirect impact on undermining dominant ideals of national linguistic and ethnic identity and belonging, which involve *drawing on* these dominant ideals and mixing them up with others, rather than opposing them.

Verlan and hip hop in France

One of the places where language and music have been linked in various ways to the experiences and actions of marginalised intergenerational migrant youth is in France (Drissel 2009; Durand 2002; Lefkowitz 1991). Pointed to are young people, in particular those from North African families, who grow up in France yet are relegated to the peripheries of French society: both physically by being housed on the outskirts of cities in France's banlieues, and symbolically through their identification as yet another generation of migrants (a 'second generation'). These are people born in France often without being recognised as 'French', yet are not 'migrants' either given that their only tie with their parent's birthplace is frequently simply an occasional visit or vacation. In an attempt to deal with exclusionary discourses – their experiences of falling short of the image of a 'French citizen' given that they are 'caught between the culture of their parents, which they no longer possess, and the French culture to which they don't have complete access' (Lefkowitz 1991, 137) – many have displayed what can be understood as a turn away from the existing national, city or international polity towards music and language in their use of the slang 'Verlan' and rap music.

Verlan is linked to an ancient form of wordplay (called Argot) which involves inverting syllables. It uses French as a base language but draws on vocabulary from across immigrant languages and involves creative modifications across speech and grammatical structure (Nortier and Dorleijn 2013).[3] Verlan forms a key part of French rap, the second largest rap market in the world. Both rap and Verlan are known for their informal and cross-cultural references. Speaking about Verlan, one woman explains when asked why she uses it (quoted in Doran 2004, 93) that it is part of an attempt to produce oneself as a subject and as part of a polity: 'because we are looking for ourselves', and we can't find ourselves' in either 'French' or the alternatives of 'non-French' culture, but always as a mixture of both and neither.

The turn to rap and Verlan in France can be seen as political because of the huge role language has played in French nation-building. The French language has historically served as 'the major vehicle for the transmission of the national culture and … revolutionary ideology' (Safran 1992, 793) with the Académie Française set up in 1635 to protect it, and French institutionalised as the sole language of instruction in 1891. This continues today with the French language seen as the vehicle for national unity in the face of growing diversity (Villard and Yan-Sayegh 2013). Any attempts to undermine the centrality of the French language are still understood by the Académie Française as threatening 'French identity', and this is a view echoed by the French Senate which vetoed attempts to recognise regional languages in the French Constitution as recent as 2008 (ibid., 244). Any ethnic differences furthermore in the French ideal of the Republic are presumed to be subsumable into a 'French' common nationality forcing people to choose between being French or not. As explained by Drissel (2009, 121), however, "French hip-hoppers are involved in a complex process of reconfiguring and synthesising relevant idioms and vernaculars found not only in global hip-hop and their 'native' culture but also in their 'host' country of France". The use of language mix and hip hop is thus understood to be both reflecting and influencing the *construction* of hybridised identities which undermine the spaces of national linguistic homogeneity and ethnic identification: the latter is the space where a national language is linked to an originary overarching culture (ethnicity) and this is imposed on everyone on the basis of facilitating integration.

Indeed, there has been in recent decades increased emphasis in countries of inward migration in Europe on the need for language homogeneity or a standardised national language (Blackledge 2004). In some countries, there is one prioritised national language such as in France (French) or Germany (German); in other countries there is more than one choice such as in Ireland (English or Gaelic) and in Belgium (French or Flemish). However, hierarchy and a narrow element of choice is a defining feature here across all despite the reality of large linguistic diversity (ibid.; Alexander Edwards, and Temple 2007). What is articulated in vernacular music in its form (as I further tease out below) is a refusal of the idea that national identity and belonging can be fit into one space *rather than* another space. As one hip hop artist Stromae (whose name is a Verlan inversion of 'Maestro') notes in his song 'Bastard': you are told 'either you are one or the other … Are you Flemish or Wallonian? … Are you white or brown, eh?'[4] Having grown up in a French Belgian suburb with a Flemish Belgian mother and a Rwandan father, Stromae's upbringing mirrors the mixed linguistic and ethnic urban environment of immigrant youth pointed to in existing literature (Nortier and Svendsen 2015). His refrain is that he is neither and never has been: 'neither one nor the other I am; I was and I will remain myself'.[5]

Marginalisation, irregularity and hybridity

In many of the examples above, the migrant youth are those who have some form of status in the societies in which they live – this can be by virtue of being born there and acquiring citizenship at birth, by virtue of having a citizen parent and/or by virtue of being a child and having rights linked to education and welfare as a child regardless of status. For example, in many European countries, children regardless of status are entitled to free access to primary and secondary school education as well as health care; as such they possess a form of status – understood as entitlement to rights – which their parents do not enjoy, simply by virtue of being under 18. However, at the same time they are people whose status is precarious given their broader family circumstances which can include having parent(s) who are asylum seekers, on short-term visas, or who cannot be deported for various reasons linked to their connection to a citizen (for example, having a child who becomes a citizen) but who are still not entitled to work or to other rights.

This emphasises the differences between how youth and adults experience precarity (irregularity) in their daily lives (albeit drawing distinctions between generational experiences on the basis of positionality rather than entrenched cultural identity).[6]Whereas, irregular adult migrants may be in danger of immanent deportation and/or find it very difficult to avail of basic services (such as health, employment, education), marginalised intergenerational migrants will often be in school, and able to avail of basic services for free as typical 'citizens' do; as such they experience less explicit forms of exclusion than adults often do, as their exclusion is often defined through their wider family situation rather than linked merely to themselves and their status. Marginality however does not rest only in access to formal status. The example of France similarly demonstrates that intergenerational migrant youth may have formal citizenship and live within families where all members also have formal citizenship, but their family's history of migration may have resulted in disenfranchisement which has persisted across generations.

It often makes sense therefore for irregular adult migrants to challenge their explicit exclusion through overt political gestures of outright resistance which are directed at the political authority which excludes them – the state, city, European Union or convention. For intergenerational migrant youth, however, whose exclusion is implicit as much as explicit, the problem can appear as the authority (polity) itself; as a link *between* Ireland, France, Europe, etc and exclusion. This is expressed by one youth as follows in a study on use of Verlan: 'I don't like the French system. In France, it's each person for himself' (Doran 2004: 114). It is in this context that music and language can be understood to provide a space in which different conceptions of identity and belonging are experimented with, explored and enabled, ultimately challenging a restricted national linguistic space and restricted ethnic cultural affiliation.

Indeed, as intergenerational migrant youth negotiate belonging across a range of spatio-temporal sites – including school, home, peer-groups, music, fashion, etc, – something that unites these claims to belong is how they draw on multiple, often overlapping ideas of belonging which are paradoxical and very rarely straightforward (Ní Laoire et al. 2011, 47). What I want to suggest is that vernacular music and language provides a space to develop such contradictory claims of belonging and being with others who they see as like-minded rather than of a particular nationality or ethnicity, etc, albeit not necessarily in a direct, deliberate way. This does not create a distinctive polity, understood as an organised society, akin to a state or a city or a common humanity. But rather a highly fluid space in which belonging, identity and affiliation so integral to the foundations of citizenship are constantly re-enacted. It is highly fluid because although there are lots of signifiers – of nationality, ethnicity, race, gender, etc – these are not grounded in a particular nation, ethnicity or form of statehood based around one or two languages and ethnicities. This is a space defined *by* hybridity *across* languages and ethnicities.

Creative resources for hybrid self-expression in vernacular street music and language

When looking at intergenerational migrant youth in Ireland and their responses to discourses of marginalisation, Ní Laoire et al.'s (2011) work shows that the problem identified by youth themselves was not just that they didn't fit simply into the categories of 'Irish' and 'non-Irish' or 'African' but that they also didn't fit into the newly hyphenated identities of 'African-Irish' or 'New-Irish' which were opening up. Key issues with fitting into such categories are to do with the number of places intergenerational youth identify as 'home': including their neighbourhood, their city, their parent's country of birth, their own country of birth and their current place of residence, as well as their multiple linguistic affiliations and broader cultural identifications – which are often contradictory given that not all of these are places which they visit or spend much time in, nor languages which they speak very well, nor cultures which they are necessarily very familiar with (cf. Lee 2002; Yau 2007). What ensues is a negotiation of home and belonging in multiple contexts through simultaneous notions of attachment and detachment to particular places in a way that disrupt(s) 'any simple opposition between roots and routes, or movement and attachment' (Ní Laoire et al. 2011, 48).

As discussed above, unlike many adult migrants who can less problematically act and exist as individuals in the present, youth are situated in their collective and intergenerational relations across times (past present and future) and many spaces (here, there, ancestral home, current home, parents home) many of which (unlike their parents) they will have had little direct access to (Kallio and Häkli 2013, 11; Ní Laoire et al. 2011). Speaking different languages is often a key way in which intergenerational migrant youth perform and embody belonging as a result (Darmody, Tyrrell, and Song 2011; Nortier and Svendsen 2015). The point is that intergenerational youth may be exposed to several languages which they may use at different times and in different places depending on who they are talking to (whether it is their parents, teachers or friends) and where they are (at home, in school, on the street) (Doran 2004; Ní Laoire et al. 2011). Rather than identity being reflected through language or visa-versa, these become mutually constitutive.

The turn to vernacular language, such as slang, and music such as rap, in the multiple fashion that it is being engaged today, within highly diverse urban environments, can thus be seen as a way in which intergenerational migrant youth negotiate the multiplicity of their lives. Vernacular music and language provide a milieu which enables hybridity – inconsistency and overlap – rather than requiring coherency and consistency. We might therefore see them as milieus which enable subversive 'noise' (Hebdige 1981; Kallio 2012); as sites of disagreement which convey political contestation in their effect of undermining the idea of a single nationally defined culture or language *without* necessarily positing a coherent alternative or reifying clear cultural difference. Although they don't voice their concerns through existing politically recognisable channels or as forms of direct dissatisfaction, I suggest that youth can be seen to 'noise' (Kallio 2012, 295) their concerns nonetheless *in* their use of vernacular language and music by presenting different variants of political belonging in Ireland and France which indirectly challenge a narrow choice of language (French, or Gaelic and English) and a clearly defined ethnicity (French or Arab; African or merely African-Irish.)

As Ní Laoire et al. discuss (2011, 68): "For some African/Irish young people the appeal of particular fashions, styles or music was that they were globalised – that they weren't [just] 'Irish' or 'Nigerian' or 'Somalian' or 'Kenyan'". This demonstrates how fluidity is prioritised. These categories are not unimportant to intergenerational migrant youth; on the contrary, the point is that *many* of these categories are very important and significant to how they identify themselves rather than just one or two of them. Through globalised vernacular music and language they can mix these together, however, to allow different presentations of the self which result in a more fluid ongoing (re)mapping of political imaginaries (Drissel 2009; Perry 2008).

The way in which such hybrid (mixed) presentations of the self come together in music, for example, can be seen in how French rap is a synthesis of influences from around the world including French, African American, North African and African Caribbean expressive culture, and draws on pre-existing musical genres from French traditional music, rock, jazz and gospel. This is furthermore inseparable from the informal language of Verlan which is seen as key to its expressive wordplay and poetic depiction of life in French banlieues (Durand 2002). What is enabled is a type of 'third space' (Bhabha 1994) in which 'a complex, multicultural, working-class identity … [can] be both performed and recognised in a way that they are not within the larger society' (Doran 2004, 95). One of the things to note therefore is the creative resource in music such as rap and in slang like Verlan. It provides the opportunity to mix the old with the new; to be adapted and changed to fit circumstances. To some extent this can be said about any type of music; however, it also depends on the extent to which music and language is tied to the vernacular (Rosenthal and Flacks 2012). Music such as rap, blues and jazz, for example, and 'contact languages' (Nortier and Dorleijn 2013) whose development is as street vernacular (everyday music and language) due to their lack of grammatical and linguistic rigidity, can be reworked over and over again in ways that enable them to adapt and incorporate multiple cultural influences (ibid.; Rosenthal and Flacks 2012). Here, we get away from the idea of fixed cultures simply coming together towards movement, change and disruption; in particular it emphasises young people's agency in (re)forming ideas of political identity and belongings: reforming what it means to identify in France or Ireland via multiple (rather than only one or several narrow) languages and ethnicity (Ní Laoire et al. 2011; Perry 2008). For example, the lack of grammatical rigidity enables those engaging in Verlan to draw on and draw together many different influences from Arabic, Creole and African languages as well as Romani and Argot. Its meanings constantly adapt and move within and among these influences where youth combine different grammatical elements of various languages in ways that break rules within these individual languages all the while using French as the base language (Doran 2004; Nortier and Dorleijn 2013). Verlan and rap, as such articulate not only the poverty and disaffection of the banlieue(s) but also the hybrid linguistic, ethnic make-up *of* the banlieues. Youth deal with contradictions between competing understandings of 'home' by mixing and matching different influences to undermine a dominant national idea of 'home' linked to a particular ethnicity and language.

The idea of 'indirect resistance' (those acts of resistance which ignore, transcend or move beyond what they are resisting) as a form of everyday resistance here thus presents I argue an alternative to the oppositional understanding of 'everyday resistances' which is stressed elsewhere. For example, Scott (2014, 62) argues that it is 'opposition' which gives everyday resistance meaning; saying '[w]e can't understand British youth culture of mods and rockers without seeing it in contrast to the clerk with the furled umbrella and the bowler hat as the standard bourgeois male Londoner'. However, rather differently from Scott's statement above, the meaning of 'indirect resistance' lies in how it draws *upon* dominant practices (e.g. dominant linguistic and ethnic markers) and *plays with* these (by mixing them up with others) in order to undermine them rather than by opposing dominant practices.

Re-enacting citizenship

Although there is increasingly more written about the multiple and often very diverse forms of adaptation among intergenerational migrant youth, these are often reluctantly linked to citizenship per se. Instead, citizenship in such instances is often contrasted (juxtaposed) with hyphenated identities: for example, Mushaben (2008, 508) talks about how 'Berliners of Turkish descent have decided that rather than waiting for Germany to accept them as full citizens, they would carve out their own hyphenated identities'. This is because 'citizenship' is often associated with a Eurocentric theory of belonging which is state-bound, masculinist, singular and individualistic. The possibility of 'hyphenated' (ibid.) or 'transnational' (Tyler 2013) identifications which are fluid is contrasted in such work *with* the singular, fixed and rigid identifications which sovereign citizenship maintains through 'its deployment as a technology of biopolitical governance in local regimes of mobility control' (ibid., 218). What is emphasised is the failure of the democratic promise of citizenship and, as such, the need to think about acts of citizenship in terms of how they move *beyond* (are "'acts' against") citizenship (Tyler and Marciniak 2013, 146).

I suggest that a danger of seeing belonging and identity invested in music and language as beyond or outside citizenship is that it reifies them and associates them with a problematic political space outside of (certain) struggles about inclusion and exclusion. It furthermore undermines the diversity of 'citizenship' broadly understood as contestations over rights (Isin 2002). Indeed, a Foucauldian understanding of power as relational behoves us to recognise the ongoing relationship between politics and struggle: to understand 'politics' as a struggle *in terms of* meaning and identity across inclusion(s) and exclusion(s). This is not to reduce all experiences of political identity and belonging to citizenship rather than beyond citizenship. It is to emphasise instead the need to think about hybridity across inclusion and exclusion *within* citizenship (Bosniak 2006); and precisely to refuse this citizenship/beyond citizenship binary.

The turn to music and language as explored above, although very much tied to more fluid and hybrid forms of linguistic and ethnic identity and belonging which shift and change given the vernacular nature of their grounding (and thus ungrounding) in street music and language, does not forego inclusionary and exclusionary logics. On the contrary, they produce/enact various lines of inclusion and exclusion through the different ways in which they link together national, subnational and international, as well as linguistic and musical concepts. For example, rap and Verlan are linked to particular historical experiences, cultural characteristics and linguistic abilities as well as ethnic signifiers. It is by virtue of linking these together in particular ways that various forms of community are enabled as 'French rap' or 'Verlan' or 'Popular/global Rap'. As Ní Laoire et al. note (2011, 69), living in Ireland as predominantly young black men and women in a largely white culture, the turn to rap music and artists by intergenerational migrants 'make as well as reflect acceptable ways of being black in Irish society'. Lapassade (1996, 52–65) elsewhere insists that 'noirceur' (blackness) is critical to rap, thus confirming the significant ways in which lines of inclusion and exclusion are drawn through rap despite its vernacular nature (see also Perry 2008).

This emphasis however placed on blackness is articulated to a large extent in ways which are not rigidly deterministic, unlike with sovereign statist citizenship. For example, in the French banlieues, rap is also linked to identifications *across* the colour spectrum uniting many groups in their marginality – where being black is associated with being racialised – rather than the colour of one's skin (Durand 2002). The point is that identification with a community in rap and slang does not transcend or bypass ideas of nationality, statehood and internationality nor of ethnicity and cultural specificity and the question of inclusion and exclusion. It does not provide a universal or a cosmopolitan envisaged space where identifications no longer matter or people have come to ignore these. Instead, it interweaves various political identifications together in different ways at different times by trying not to ground them rigidly but nonetheless constantly re-grounding them in someways rather than others.

Thinking about identification in vernacular music and language as struggles over inclusion and exclusion and thus as forms of citizenship, allows us to address questions, for example, about rap's highly deterritorialised nature which can celebrate the global at the expense of the local, as well as its highly consumerist nature which can result in prioritising neoliberalism at the expense of questions about structural inequalities. Another issue is rap's often problematic misogynistic nature, and the patriarchal hegemony which this perpetuates. These are all key aspects of the musical and linguistic space which marginalised intergenerational youth have carved out for an alternative fluid form of linguistic and ethnic identity and belonging which cannot be dismissed, but nor should it be reduced simply to these factors. This emphasises the complexity of 'resistance' in this context. Engagement in vernacular music and language challenges mainstream national mono-lingualism and clear ethnic identification, and is thus linked to an understanding of the subversive. Yet, there are often many aspects which reinforce parts of the mainstream including its patriarchy and its narrow neoliberal capitalist ideology; a problem pointed to within studies about contemporary 'subcultural' practices (Hebdige 1981; Huq 2001). My argument is thus that thinking about engagement with vernacular music and language as a form of citizenship helps us because it allows us to think about how these are realms of immanent relations and struggles which provide alternative ideals of national community and identity *at the same time* as they remain a site of struggle over inclusions and exclusions which draw on aspects of these very same ideals.

Conclusion

The idea of citizenship as an act – something that is seized (rather than bestowed) and trans-formed (rather than replicated) – emphasises the constantly in-formation, practice-oriented 'incipient' (Isin and Nyers 2014a) nature of citizenship(s). Doing so it reminds us of the need to continually question and reassess what it is that we call citizenship – i.e. what we imagine as possible acts of resistance – as well as questioning who can be a citizen. With this in mind, this paper has turned to an under-theorised group within citizenship studies and also more generally within political studies – that of marginalised intergenerational migrant youth – to try to build on existing insights into the association between unfamiliar-ity and acts of citizenship, and to think about how unfamiliarity of acts challenges what we presume resistance to citizenship looks like. In the spirit of opening up our understandings of the various ways in which migrant communities resist citizenship from the 'margins', it considers the importance of recognising that marginalised intergenerational youths do so in different ways from marginalised migrant adults, although not simply reducing these actions to the question of youth.

This paper looked at the process itself through which some marginalised intergenera-tional migrants turn away from identifying or contesting their belonging and identity at the level of the nation-state towards vernacular music and language and produce cross-lingusitic and ethnic expressions of self. This is what I am identifying as an act of citizenship: under-stood as an interruption by youth into existing socio-historical practices which currently define national language in mono or very narrow dualistic terms and designate ethnicity in a clear fashion. Such an act is interruptive in a way which is unusual (unfamiliar) as it is not a challenge to statehood, nationality or international society directly; it does not demon-strate the limits of these polities by questioning outright ('contesting' McNevin 2011) their boundaries. The latter gestures are the ones which we have come to recognise as ways of 'resisting' citizenship. The point is not that the categories associated with nationality (e.g. Irish, French, American, African), statehood (e.g. France, Ireland, America, Nigeria) or an international polity (such as Europe, or Africa) longer apply or make sense here. Rather, ideas of nationality are interwoven together *without* being grounded in statehood or an international polity – which is then resisted. Their only grounding is in vernacular music and language which at the same time results in their ungrounding, given the colloquial, non-standard nature of this music and language.

Notes

1. An exception is literature on the undocumented youth known as DREAMERS and their various acts of civil disobedience including 'coming out of the shadows' rallies, sit-ins, mock(ing) graduations and hunger strikes. These acts are however focused on acquiring formal citizenship and directed at the federal and state level unlike the indirect acts focused on in this paper.
2. This is not to ignore how music, language and fashion can be used also to reinforce cultural hierarchies in keeping with active citizenship (acts that re-entrench existing socio-historical practices) rather than acts of citizenship (acts that disrupt socio-historical practices). Ní Laoire et al. (2011) also, for example, explore how some youth drew on language, fashion, music and sport in the form of traditional Irish dancing, the Irish Celtic language and Irish Gaelic football or hurling to try to reaffirm their 'Irish' identity.
3. The official term of this 'slang-like linguistic style' is a multi-ethnolect (ibid.).

4. *Sois t'es l'un ou soit t'es l'autre…Flamand ou Wallon?… Mais t'es blanc ou bien t'es marron, hein?*
5. *Ni l'un ni l'autre, je suis; j'etais et resterai moi*
6. This leaves open the possibility of recognising shared intragenerational experiences in other respect which puts into practice what some people like Anthias (2009) stress is very important when thinking about migration across generations.

Acknowledgements

I would like to thank Reiko Shindo and the two anonymous reviewers for detailed and constructive engagement with earlier drafts of this paper. A draft of this paper was presented at the European Consortium for Political Research (ECPR) in Glasgow in September 2014 and at the University of Manchester Critical Global Politics Research Seminar series in December 2014 where it benefited from questions and comments from audience members and fellow panellists.

Disclosure statement

No potential conflict of interest was reported by the author.

References

Alexander, C., R. Edwards, and B. Temple. 2007. "Contesting Culture Communities: Language Ethinicity and Citizenship in Britan." *Journal of Ethnic and Migration Studies* 35 (5): 783–800.

Anthias, F. 2009. "Translocational Belonging, Identity and Generation." *Finnish Journal of Ethnicity and Migration* 4 (1): 6–15.

Ashutosh, I. 2013. "Immigrant Protests in Toronto: Diaspora and Sri Lanka's Civil War." *Citizenship Studies* 17 (2): 197–210.

Bhabha, H. 1994. *The Location of Culture*. Abingdon: Routledge.

Bhabha, J. 2009. "The 'Mere Fortuity of Birth'? Children, Mothers, Borders, and the Meaning of Citizenship." In *Migrations and Mobilities*, edited by S. Benhabib and J. Resnik, 187–227. New York: New York University Press.

Blackledge, A. 2004. "Constructions of Identity in Political Discourse in Multilingual Britain." In *Negotiation of Identities in Multilingual Contexts*, edited by A. Pavlenko and A. Blackledge, 68–92. Clevedon: Cromwell Press.

Boehm, D. A., H. Meredith, C. Coes, H. Rae-Epinoza, and R. R. Reynolds, eds. 2011. *Everyday Ruptures: Children, Youth and Migration in Global Perspectives*. Nashville, TN: Vanderbilt University Press.

Bosniak, L. 2006. *The Citizen and the Alien*. Princeton, NJ: Princeton University Press.

Butler, J., and G. C. Spivak. 2007. *Who Sings the Nation State?* London: Seagull.

Cohen, E. 2005. "Neither Seen Nor Heard: Children's Citizenship in Contemporary Democracies." *Citizenship Studies* 9 (2): 221–240.

Cutler, C., and U. Royneland. 2015. "Where the Fuck Am I from? Hip-Hop Youth and the (Re) Negotiation of Language and Identity in Norway and the US." In *Language, Youth and Identity in the 21st Century*, edited by J. Nortier and B. A. Svendsen, 139–164. Cambridge: CUP.

Darmody, M., N. Tyrrell, and S. Song, eds. 2011. *The Changing Faces of Ireland*. Rotterdam: Sense Publishers.

Doran, M. 2004. "Negotiating between Bourg and Racaille: Verlan as Youth Identity Practice in Suburban Paris." In *Negotiation of Identities in Multilingual Contexts*, edited by A. Pavlenko and A. Llackledge, 93–124. Clevedon: Cromwell Press.

Dowling, M. 1997. "'The Ireland That I Would Have' De Valera and the Creation of an Irish National Image." *Contemporary History* 2 (5).

Durand, A. P. 2002. *Black, Blanc, Beur: Rap Music and Hip-Hop Culture in the Francophone World*. Oxford: Scarecrow Press.

Drissel, D. 2009. "Hip-Hop Hybridity for a Glocalized World." *The Global Studies Journal* 2 (3): 121–142.

Fernandez-Kelly, P., and L. Konczal. 2007. "Murdering the Alphabet: Identity and Entrepreneurship among Second-Generation Cubans, West Indians, and Central Americans." *Ethnic and Racial Studies* 28 (6): 1153–1181.

Foucault, M. 1978. *The History of Sexuality*. Vol. 1: An Introduction. New York: Random House.

Hebdige, D. 1981. *Subculture: The Meaning of Style*. London: Routledge.

Hoerder, D., Y. Herbert, and I. Schmitt, eds. 2005. *Negotiating Transcultural Lives*. Toronto: University of Toronto Press.

Huq, R. 2001. "Rap à la Française [Rap French Style]." In *Transitions of Youth Citizenship in Europe*, edited by A. Furlong and I. Guidikova, 41–60. Strasbourg: Council of Europe Publishing.

Isin, E. 2002. *Being Political: Genealogies of Citizenship*. Minneapolis, MN: University of Minnesota Press.

Isin, E., and G. M. Neilson, eds. 2008. *Acts of Citizenship*. London: Zed.

Isin, E., and P. Nyers. 2014a. "Globalizing Citizenship Studies." In *Routledge Handbook of Global Citizenship Studies*, E. Isin and P. Nyers. Abingdon: Routledge.

Isin, E., and P. Nyers, eds. 2014b. *Routledge Handbook of Global Citizenship Studies*. Abingdon: Routledge.

Isin, E., and M. Saward, eds. 2013. *Enacting European Citizenship*. Cambridge: Cambridge University Press.

Kallio, K. P. 2012. "Political Presence and the Politics of Noise." *Space and Polity* 16 (3): 287–302.

Kallio, K. P., and J. Häkli. 2013. "Children and Young People's Politics in Everyday Life." *Space and Polity* 17 (1): 1–16.

Keyes, C. L. 2002. *Rap Music and Street Consciousness*. Chicago, IL: University of Illinois Press.

Lapassade, G. 1996. *Le Rap ou La Fureur de Dire* [Rap or the wrath to speak]. Paris: Loris Talmart.

Lee, W. A. 2002. "Passing as Korean-American." In *Relocating Postcolonialism*, edited by D. T. Goldberg and A. Quayson, 282–293. Oxford: Blackwell.

Lentin, R. 2003. "Pregnant Silence: (En)Gendering Ireland's Asylum Space." *Patterns of Prejudice* 37 (3): 301–322.

Lefkowitz, N. 1991. *Talking Backwards Looking Forwards: The French Language Game Verlan*. Tübingen: Gunter Narr.

Maira, S. 2005. "The Intimate and the Imperial: South Asian Muslim Immigrant Youth after 9/11." In *Youthscapes*, edited by S. Maira and E. Soep, 63–81. Philadelphia, PA: University of Pennsylvania Press.

Maira, S. 2008. "'We Ain't Missing' Palestinian Hip-Hop: A Transnational Youth Movement." *The New Centennial Review* 8 (2): 161–192.

Maira, S., and E. Soep, eds. 2005. *Youthscapes: The Popular, the National, the Global*. Philadelphia, PA: University of Pennsylvania Press.

Mancini, J. M., and G. Finlay. 2008. "'Citizenship Matters': Lessons From the Irish Citizenship Referendum." *American Quarterly* 60 (3): 575–599.

McNevin, A. 2011. *Contesting Citizenship: Irregular Migrants and New Frontiers of the Political*. New York: Columbia University Press.

Morrison, I. 2008. "Unintentional Acts of Citizenship (the Joke)." In *Acts of Citizenship*, edited by E. Isin and B. Turner, 221–223. London: Zed Books.

Mushaben, J. M. 2008. "Gender, Hip-Hop and Pop-Islam: The Urban Identities of Muslim Youth in Germany." *Citizenship Studies* 12 (5): 507–526.

Neveu, C. 2014. "Practicing Citizenship from the Ordinary to the Activist." In *Routledge Handbook of Global Citizenship Studies*, edited by E. Isin and P. Nyers, 86–95. Abingdon: Routledge.

Ní Laoire, C., N. Bushin, F. Carpena-Mendez, and A. White. 2009. *Tell Me about Yourself*. Cork: UCC.

Ní Laoire, C., F. Carpena-Mendez, N. Tyrrell, and A. White. 2011. *Childhood and Migration in Europe*. Farnham: Ashgate.

Ní Mhurchú, A. 2014a. *Ambiguous Citizenship in an Age of Global Migration*. Edinburgh: Edinburgh University Press.

Ní Mhurchú, A. 2014b. "Citizenship beyond State Sovereignty." In *Routledge Handbook of Global Citizenship Studies*, edited by E. Isin and P. Nyers, 119–127. Abingdon: Routledge.

Nortier, J., and M. Dorleijn. 2013. "Multi-Ethnolects." In *Contact Languages*, edited by P. Bakker and Y. Matras, 229–272. Boston, MA: De Gruyter Mouton.

Nortier, J., and B. A. Svendsen, eds. 2015. *Language, Youth and Identity in the 21st Century: Linguistic Practices across Urban Spaces*. Cambridge: Cambridge University Press.

Nyers, P. 2008. "No One is Illegal between City and Nation." In *Acts of Citizenship*, edited by E. Isin and B. Turner, 160–181. London: Zed Books.

Nyers, P., and K. Rygiel, eds. 2012. *Citizenship, Migrant Activism and the Politics of Movement*. Abingdon: Routledge.

Perry, M. D. 2008. "Global Black Self-fashionings: Hip Hop as Diasporic Space." *Identities: Global Studies in Culture and Power* 15: 635–664.

Portes, A., and M. Zhou. 1993. "The New Second Generation: Segmented Assimilation and its Variants." *The Annals of the American Academy of Political and Social Science* 530: 74–96.

Rosenthal, R., and R. Flacks. 2012. *Playing for Change*. London: Paradigm Publishers.

Safran, W. 1992. "Language Ideology and the State in French Nation-Building." *History of European Ideas* 15: 793–800.

Schmitt, I. 2005. "Germany Speaking? Rap and Kanak Attak and Dominant Discourses on Language." In *Negotiating Transcultural Lives*, edited by D. Hoerder, Y. Herbert, and I. Schmitt, 213–234. Toronto: University of Toronto Press.

Scott, J. C. 2014. "Leaking Away and Other Forms of Resistance." In *Youth Resistance Research and Theories of Change*, edited by E. Tuck and K. W. Yang, 59–70. Abingdon: Routledge

Sullivan, M. 2001. *African-American Music as Rebellion: From Slavesong to Hip-Hop*. Ithaca, NY: Cornell University.

Tyler, I. 2013. "Naked Protest: The Maternal Politics of Citizenship and Revolt." *Citizenship Studies* 17 (2): 211–226.

Tyler, I., and K. Marciniak. 2013. "Immigrant Protest: An Introduction." *Citizenship Studies* 17 (2): 143–156.

Villard, F., and P. Yan-Sayegh. 2013. "Redefining a (Mono)Cultural Nation: Political Discourse against Multiculturalism in Contemporary France." In *Challenging Multiculturalism*, edited by R. Taras, 236–256. Edinburgh: Edinburgh University Press.

Vinthagen, S., and A. Johansson. 2013. "'Everyday Resistance': Exploration of a Concept and its Theories." *Resistance Studies Magazine* 1: 1–46.

Yau, N. 2007. "Celtic Tiger, Hidden Dragon: Exploring Identity among Second Generation Chinese in Ireland." *Translocations: Migration and Social Change* 2 (1): 48–69.

Contestations in death – the role of grief in migration struggles

Maurice Stierl

Cultural Studies, African American and African Studies, University of California, Davis, USA

ABSTRACT

This article explores forms of 'grief-activism' commemorating those who have perished on the move, in the waters surrounding EUrope, at physical border barriers or on EUrope's streets and in its detention centres. Contestations in death protest the differential distribution of vulnerability and a politics of division, abandonment and necropolitical violence on which EUrope's border regime thrives. Mobilising both Judith Butler's notion of grievability and Jacques Rancière's proposition of an 'impossible identification' as a heterological form of politics, this article examines what occurs in attempts to form solidarities in precarious moments of collective mourning. While a politics that seeks to include lost others must always be replete with impossibilities, it is argued that grief-activist practices that counter-perform exclusions in transformative political encounters engender imaginaries of what it might mean to create community 'beyond borders'.

Introduction

Death is of the EUropean border regime.[1] On the very day of beginning to write this article, the 10th of February 2015, news broke of yet another shipwreck in the Central Mediterranean Sea. Twenty-nine travellers died of hypothermia when leaving Libya on an overcrowded rubber vessel, trying to reach Italy. It emerged only gradually that there were more, in fact, four vessels that had embarked on this dangerous journey with several hundred passengers on board, the majority of which froze to death or disappeared and presumably drowned (WatchTheMed 2015). These are amongst the first of several hundreds, probably thousands, of EUrope's border deaths to come in 2015.

Border fatalities, as the ultimate, lifeless evidence of unwantedness, point to the diffuse but connected registers of death-inducing violence that underpin the contemporary EUropean border regime. These bodies, found or unfound, identified or unidentified, speak of police and borderguard brutality, of mental and physical abuse experienced in detention, of push-backs at sea and forcible deportations, of abandonment and the failure to render assistance when in need, even of policies that redirect human movement or that foreclose the very ability to move and escape in the first place, rendering millions bound to local conditions of hardship (Weber and Pickering 2011).

Border deaths occur not merely along the external borders of EUrope but deep inside and far beyond of what is commonly considered EUropean sovereign territory, revealing the increasingly vacillating, deterritorialising and externalising tendencies of border governance. Even if these deaths morbidly speak of the circumstances that led to the loss of life, dominant reactions in EUrope tend to embed them in humanitarian narratives or silence them altogether. What becomes wilfully sidelined, in either reaction, are the circumstances that suggest a necropolitical condition of EUrope's border regime and its 'subjugation of [migrant] life to the power of death' (Mbembe 2003, 39).

This article enquires into a politics of grief that responds to these continuous subjugations. Turning to the external borders of EUrope, three activist contestations in death illustrate attempts to find traces of those who, swallowed by the sea or discarded into nameless mass graves, all too often remain unidentified and unmourned. Grief-activism constitutes a transformative political practice that can foster relationalities and communities in opposition to a politics of division, abandonment and necropolitical violence on which EUrope's border regime thrives. By enacting different communal possibilities, such activism questions, interrupts and displaces sovereign citizenship as a foundational and identitarian arrangement of community and engenders alternative imaginaries of ways of being-with one another. Formulating a politics around death in migration struggles poses a series of important questions relating to solidarity, identification and, ultimately, ethics. While grief-activism must necessarily entail a horizon of failure and moments in which solidarity does not materialise and identification breaks down, it is the risking of oneself in complex encounters that, rather than pre-emptively formulating what community constitutes, pose community as a question continuously anew.

The article is organised in three main sections. Section one provides 'snap-shots' of three migration struggles that made use of collective commemorations, in two of which I participated: the *Boats4People* solidarity campaign of 2012, the 2013 *Traces Back* project and the artistic interventions by the *Centre for Political Beauty* in 2014. Section two explores, with help of Judith Butler's notion of grievability (2009), what occurs when grieving border fatalities, often taking place in the most precarious of spaces. I propose that, while fostering a 'political community of a complex order' as suggested by Butler, these forms of grief-activism form 'impossible' acts of identification. The third section draws from Jacques Rancière's proposition of an 'impossible identification' to argue that these contestations in grief, despite remaining incomplete and fallible, form a heterological politics that seeks alternative ways of being-with one another at the margins. It is this dimension, the concluding section suggests, that distinguishes mourning mobilised as a radical political engagement with loss at borders from official practices of commemoration employed by state and EU leaders that stage selective humanitarian border spectacles.

Grief-activism

Grief and commemoration have found widespread expression in contemporary migration and border struggles that are surging throughout a world in which fatalities give evidence to its bordered state. Border deaths are mourned by family and community members, friends and colleagues but also by those who may have never encountered the particular life before it was lost and who, nonetheless, seek to mourn an absence. Protest campaigns responding to lethal border violence and the disappearance of un/known others have taken on a variety of forms and foster complex solidarities. They certainly are part of what Imogen Tyler and Katarzyna Marciniak referred to as 'an explosion of "immigrant protests", political mobilizations by irregular migrants and pro-migrant activists', in the past decade (2013, 143).

Located in London, I participated in public vigils and protests surrounding border fatalities 'at my doorstep' (2013, 2014). Jimmy Mubenga died when he was placed in the 'carpet karaoke' position that cut off his air supply during his deportation. Despite audible 'I can't breathe' outcries, the restraining continued until Mubenga died of positional asphyxia. Public commemorations celebrated the life of LGBT rights activist Jackie Nanyonjo who was brutally beaten and injured during her deportation flight to Uganda and who died weeks later in the place she had once successfully escaped (2013). A demonstration was organised also at the French embassy in London for Noureddin Mohamed who died under unknown circumstances in Calais/France, with campaigners assuming police involvement (2012). These border deaths constitute a mere fraction of those who, already within the sovereign spaces of EUrope, died when the 'border crossed them'. They were known, and relatives, friends and allies made sure that their fates did not remain unnoticed, even if their deaths went largely unpunished.

As an activist-researcher engaged in political campaigns, I was fortunate to witness and become involved in 'contestations in grief' along EUrope's external borders, at the Southern end of Italy and the Eastern shores of Greece. It is there that thousands go missing in the attempt to overcome dangerous border zones. Rather than providing an exhaustive account of the three campaigns, the focus is placed on a significant element in these border struggles: the many practices of commemoration that allowed for encounters in collective grief. What, as Butler queries, can be gained through these commemorations, 'from remaining exposed to [grief's] unbearability?' (Butler 2003, 19) She argues:

> Many people think that grief is privatizing, that it returns us to a solitary situation and is, in that sense, depoliticizing. But I think it furnishes a sense of political community of a complex order. (Butler 2004, 22)

Inspired by Butler's conceptualisation of grief as a transformative practice, this article asks: How can we imagine the creation of a political community in scenes of collective grief, formulated around the loss of (other) life, life that may remain unknown to many of those mourning, and whose existence may have only emerged due to its absence?

Boats4People, 2012

The Boats4People solidarity campaign of summer 2012 saw freedom of movement activists located in various settings travel to a particularly lethal space, the border zone between Italy and Northern Africa. Considered one of the best monitored seas in the world, it is in the Central Mediterranean Sea that thousands disappear and die year after year. While mainly from EUrope and the 'global north', Boats4People formed as an international coalition and included groups from Mali, Niger and Tunisia with the aim 'to end the dying along the maritime borders and to defend the rights of migrants at sea'. The campaign accused EU border practitioners of violating their obligation to rescue at sea and the principle of non-refoulement and, more profoundly, of having created the very conditions for so many deaths to occur in the first place, including the border regime's 'repressive policies which

Figure 1. Waterfront in Palermo/Italy; Credit: Leona Goldstein/zapanka.net.

seek to criminalize migration towards Europe more and more each day' (Boats4People 2012a, 2012b).

The idea for the campaign first emerged in summer 2011 as a response to the growing number of border deaths at a time when the turmoil of the 'Arab Uprisings' prompted many to leave Northern African countries. With the authoritarian regimes of Libya and Tunisia crumbling in the wake of revolutionary upheaval, their ability to continue cooperation with EUrope in matters of migration defence waned. The civil war in Libya, NATO's military intervention and 'the active role of Gaddafi's regime in forcing migrants onto boats' prompted an estimated 26,000 people to cross the Mediterranean Sea towards Italy (Pezzani and Heller 2013, 290). Also, in the same year, about 28,000 people who had left Tunisia reached Italian shores. Those who did not arrive were most certainly more than the 1500 migrants who *are known* to have died in the Mediterranean Sea in 2011 (Council of Europe 2012).

When first conceived, the Boats4People campaign was envisioned as an intervention at sea with a fleet of vessels that would possibly enforce encounters with EUropean coastguards or Frontex in order to monitor their activities (Boats4People 2014a). When the campaign was launched in 2012, it was only the Oloferne, a small sailing boat, that embarked on the journey. While the desired intervention in maritime space remained largely symbolic, the Oloferne became, as activist Lorenzo (2014) suggested, a 'good catalyst to bring together people from all the different places'. On the 7th of July, a group of activists boarded the Oloferne and went on a journey to Palermo and Pantelleria in Italy, Monastir and Ksibet El Mediouni in Tunisia and finally to the island of Lampedusa, carrying survival rations in case of encounters with migrant vessels. Activists followed by other means of transport and organised events along the route. During the campaign, the actuality of migrant plight was cruelly confirmed when 54 people died of dehydration or drowned on their way to Italy with only one man surviving. Boats4People activists learned about this incident in the media and some visited the survivor in hospital. In his testimony, he recounted the odyssey in which he lost two brothers and his sister. Waving to vessels that passed by without coming to help, he survived by tying himself to the remains of the boat (Boats4People 2014b; UNHCR 2012).

The death and disappearance of so many along EUrope's maritime borders were reason for and intimately woven into the campaign and found expression in moments of collective grief. Rather than mere fateful tragedies, Boats4People considered these deaths direct consequences of EUrope's expanding border security practices, policies and infrastructures that curtail secure migration routes ever-more, leaving for particular individuals and groups only the most precarious and dangerous paths and corridors. In Palermo, Monastir and Lampedusa, as well as in Berlin in December 2012, public commemorations were held, constituting both solemn vigils and angry protests (Figure 1). During these commemorations, candles were lit, banners held, speeches given and the long list of documented deaths, collected by UNITED, was unrolled, showing times, places and causes of death, countries of origin and names, if known. (Migrant) Activists read out the few fragments of lives that were revealed through their death:

> On the 2nd of May 2012, name unknown, 16 year old boy from Afghanistan, stowaway, suffocated in a truck into which he had hidden to avoid the border police checks. […] On the 1st of May 2012, name unknown, from Somalia, died in a boat during a week-long voyage from Libya to Malta, boat came ashore at Rivera Bay. […] Names unknown, 9 year old girl, 55 year old man, Afghanistan, missing after they tried to cross the river Evros between Greece and Turkey, part of a group of 15. (UNITED 2012)[2]

The reading out of the little that is known of the deceased was understood as an attempt to reveal traces of those who risked and lost their lives for an anticipated but violently denied future. Those missing, as Edkins holds, 'reveal the status of the rest of us' (Edkins 2011, 14). The banner notes the deaths that EUrope does not count, that remain un-noteworthy. Increasingly sophisticated and centralised security infrastructures gather more and more data and create nuanced identities of traveller histories but fail to acknowledge the thousands who pass away while travelling.

These emotionally charged commemorative practices had performative effects on those participating but also on those passing by. In Palermo, along the waterfront that signifies one of EUrope's outposts at the maritime frontier, many passers-by listened for a moment, sought conversation and scrutinised some of the listed fates while others turned away, ostensibly discomforted by, and unwilling to engage with, the deads' written presence. Survivors of border crossings gave speeches, condemning the violence that a deterrence-based politics must entail and commemorated those who were not fortunate or physically strong enough to survive. In Lampedusa, floral wreaths were thrown into the sea from the deck of the Oloferne with many gathered on the edge of Lampedusa's coast, beside the 'Gate to Europe' memorial erected for border deaths. The Boats4People commemoration in the busy main train station of Berlin, months later, intruded into the festive pre-Christmas atmosphere and sought to connect the supposedly distant suffering of many with the role of geographically non-peripheral EU countries in the making of external border obstacles. The banner was laid out in a central space so that many travellers had to awkwardly step over it, an act often pursued with such caution as to demonstrate, to everyone else, awareness and respect for the dead.

Travelling to the Tunisian side of the border, activists also organised encounters in Monastir. Grieving publicly together with the parents of the disappeared, Boats4People sought to foster a sense of togetherness while acknowledging the difficulty of finding 'common ground' between those directly affected and activists, many from the global North. In complex encounters, activists supported the families in protests against their children's disappearance, but the abyss of suffering often remained unfathomable to those who did not experience its violence. At the harbour of Monastir, accompanied by relatives of the dead or disappeared, the event was planned as a way to engage with the local community. However, overburdened by the many tasks at hand, the activists had only hastily prepared the commemoration. The idea of having the Oloferne arrive in the harbour for the ceremony did not materialise as water levels were too low and the paper lanterns that activists had provided as a symbolic gesture of grief were lit by Tunisian youths and carried by strong winds into the crowd of people. Activist Nina (Boats4People 2014c) recalled:

> The memorial in the harbour was a particularly difficult moment, when some of the weeping women collapsed on the rocks and I had the feeling that necessary structures to support them were not there. We could not talk to them and hardly knew them and thus might not have been the right contact persons anyways, and at the same time, this emotionally charged moment was a common experience.

The commemoration in Tunisia went astray and the attempt to encounter one another and grief collectively failed since, as Christoph stated, 'the local population did not really understand what we were there for'. In this instance, the absence of sufficient time and preparation to foster mutual understanding meant that the intent behind the grief-act could not be communicated. For Christoph, grief-activism 'needs to be handled with caution and in Monastir it became grotesque. It was not a commemoration' (Boats4People 2014d).

The Boats4People campaign intervened in and thereby animated one of the deadliest border zones in the world in order to strive 'for a Mediterranean that will become a place of solidarity and cease to be a mass grave for migrants' (Boats4People 2012c). Such solidarity was enacted in public memorials that sought to promote dialogue and forms of communal being-with one another. However, seeking togetherness at the margin, and often despite the margins, is necessarily riven, precarious and problematic from the very beginning. Spatial, cultural, linguistic, racial, political, historical, economic, or gender differences often underlie and impact solidarity attempts, turning questions of power-relationalities, hierarchies and privilege into central concerns. The scene in Monastir illustrates the fragility and sensitivity of such politics of grief that seems always replete with the possibility of failure. Nonetheless, attempts to collectively mourn set into motion discomforting but necessary encounters that embodied a different politics, one that sought complex forms of togetherness in opposition to a EUropean politics of division. This other politics, formulated around loss and '"missingness" that makes the person irreplaceable', is a politics 'in which the person-as-such is acknowledged' (Edkins 2011, viii–ix), and whose forceful disappearance demands a collective response.

Traces Back to the Border, 2013

> Those commemorated are not the victims of a natural catastrophe; they are the dead of a border regime for which some are politically responsible. Simply said: if it had been possible for them to just buy a ferry ticket and to move wherever they wanted and needed to, they would

Figure 2. Harbour of Thermi, Lesvos/Greece; Credit: w2eu.

certainly be still alive. All those for whom we grieve [...] lost their lives due to a senseless border regime (w2eu and YWB 2014, 52).

The island of Lesvos, the largest of the Greek islands in the North-Eastern Aegean Sea, is for many the first point of entry into EUropean space and separated from mainland Turkey only by the narrow Mytilene Strait. Standing at the shores of Lesvos, Turkish buildings and infrastructure on the other side, roughly six miles away, are easily visible. Ferries with tourists on board travel frequently back and forth, return trips can be purchased for as little as ten Euro, at least by those whose documents are 'in order'. It is here, in the strait, that in December 2012, 21 Afghan travellers drowned and at least 6 went missing. Bodies were recovered in the sea or washed up in Thermi, near the island's capital Mytilene (WatchTheMed 2014). In March 2013, 6 Syrian nationals died in their attempt to reach the Greek island and another tragedy occurred in January 2014, with 12 people drowning, after what seems to have been yet another illegal 'push-back' operation by Greek coastguards (Amnesty International 2013; BBC 2014). They are amongst hundreds of counted persons who have lost their lives in the Aegean Sea (Pro Asyl 2013). For most of those who survive the perilous journey that can cost several hundred Euros for those travelling 'irregularly', Lesvos is a point of transit, not of settlement, and it is here that many experience EUrope and its detention cages for the first time. As one of EUrope's outposts, Lesvos is becoming, more and more, another symbol of EUrope's violent border practices and struggles over migration, just as Lampedusa, Ceuta and Melilla already are.

In October 2013, the activist networks *Youth without Borders* and *Welcome to Europe* organised 'Traces Back 2013', a political project allowing those who had once passed through Lesvos as minors to trace their first steps in EUrope, to meet friends still 'stuck in Greece', and to come together in protest against continuous violence against migrants. Those who came back to Lesvos now reside in several EUropean countries, work or go to school and are granted the freedom to move within the EU, even if only temporarily. They come back as migrants and refugees, but inasmuch so as EUropean residents and activists, as carpenters, pupils, fathers, friends, cricket-players, world-travellers, as those who found ways out of Greece, who resisted and survived the EUropean border regime (Birds of Immigrants 2013). Most arrived on the island between 2005 and 2010 and many were imprisoned in the notorious detention centre Pagani, described (even) by the Deputy Civil Protection Minister Vougias as 'Dante's Inferno' (UNHCR 2009). The centre was shut down in 2009, after protests inside and NoBorder activist solidarity outside. For many participants of the project, Lesvos and Greece as such remain places of traumatising experience, abuse, fear and violence, but also ones of encounter, support, hope and friendship.

A significant aspect of 'Traces Back 2013' was the attempt to foster a 'culture of commemoration' on Lesvos. Besides various political campaigns, including demonstrations in the city centre of Mytilene and at the new detention centre near the village of Moria, the mourning of lost life was central to the journey 'back to the border'. Already in 2010 and 2011, activists had organised commemorations in Greece, at both land and sea borders after discovering a mass grave in the Evros region that contained the remains of up to 200 people (Rygiel 2014).

> Only a sign, riddled by many gun-shots, tells that this is the cemetery of the illegal immigrants where the corpses are buried. It is not immediately obvious that it is a mass grave. Upon closer inspection, one can however see holes that were excavated and again filled up by bulldozers and that can contain up to ten corpses. (w2eu 2010)

The activists drew public attention to the mass grave and the undignified burial that disregarded traditional customs and thereby prompted widespread condemnation leading to the transformation of the site into an actual cemetery, including individual graves. Commemorative plaques and a fountain 'along a road frequently travelled on by refugees' form reminders of those who did not make it and a place of rest for future travellers (w2eu and YWB 2014, 54).

In October 2013, in the heat of the afternoon sun, a large crowd gathered at the small harbour of Thermi. It was here that local fishermen had found a lifeless body and went out to sea to recover more. Some participants of 'Traces Back 2013' stayed behind in our tent camp; for them, the idea of gathering in grief seemed too painful and unsettling. Syrian relatives of the drowned took part and carried 'in their pockets the pictures and also the passports of their losses':

> [The relatives] were speaking about the tragedy of this whole incident: they had not been able to save their relatives through family reunion because even after many years in Greece they had not received papers. We made photos of the passports and we put them on the memorial. They went to look for plants and they prepared the place of the memorial. (w2eu and YWB 2013, 51)

The Syrian relatives encountered fishermen, local residents and supporters, activists and 'border-survivors' to collectively mourn. While forming a collectivity in the act of grief, the reasons for their presence were manifold:

> Some came to mourn their lost relatives. […] Some live here on the island and experience regularly dead people being found on the beach. Some of us here have had the experience of recovering bodies. Some are here on a journey back to the place of their first arrival in Europe. […] Some came already several times […] [to] protest against this deadly border regime. (45–46)

A commemorative plaque was attached to two wooden paddles and images of the deceased were placed beside it, depicting many children and young adolescents (Figure 2).

Besides the remembering of these particular losses, the speech read out by activists and border-survivors was fuelled not only by anger but also by a feeling of shame that 'we failed in our attempt to stop this murderous regime and to create a welcoming Europe':

> Here and today, at this place of failure and loss, we want to stop for a moment and create a space for all those who lost their lives. Remembering here means to save the stories of the uncounted who died at the borders of Europe. They had been on the way to change their lives on their own. Their death is the death in search for freedom. And that concerns all of us. [...] This Europe is not safe, human rights and refugee rights have lost all relevance! The victims ask the ones alive to take action against this Europe of Frontex – borders and walls. They demand us to struggle and to invent a Europe of solidarity, overcoming the deathly migration regime. [...] For the ones who will pass by in the future, the fountain that will be built later on should be a place to rest on their further way, providing them with water and the feeling that they are welcome. We invite you to have a rest – and then to move on: to tear down the borders and to build another, a welcoming Europe. (47–50)

Many listened closely to the speeches given, but some needed more distance and looked upon the site of memorial from afar, often comforted by others. The commemoration brought those together who had been differentially exposed to border violence: those whose relatives succumbed to it, those who found their lifeless remains, who survived such violence and returned, and those who responded to it in activist protest. Often folding into one another, these subjectivities and mobile identities, formed, indeed, a 'political community of a complex order', one that may only temporarily establish itself in grief and in opposition to a general economy of violence that disappears people and creates asymmetrical experiences of violence for differentiated, categorised and racialised individuals, groups and populations. The commemoration came to a close and one border-survivor recalled:

> After the memorial ends, we walk along the harbour. Many of us have cried a lot, in grief about various losses. In memory of lost friends from school in other places and other boats, and other times. In memory of their own fear to die on the trip once with a small rubber-boat in a rough sea without being able to swim ... We walk along the harbour and back into life. (52)

Centre for Political Beauty, 2014

In November 2014, the Germany-based artist collective 'Centre for Political Beauty' (Zentrum für Politische Schönheit) declared the first European 'Mauerfall', the fall of external EU borders. Coinciding with the 25th anniversary of the crumbling of the inner German border and official commemorations of border deaths, a 'battle group against inhumanity' removed 14 white crosses with inscribed names of German border-victims from their usual location beside the German Parliament in Berlin and brought them to EUrope's external borders. Some of the crosses migrated to those living in the Moroccan forests near Melilla, who seek to, one day, overcome the high border fences to the Spanish enclave or to embark on boats leaving towards Southern Spain. Referring to these and other external borders as death strips, reminiscent of the 'Todesstreifen' of Berlin's wall, the performers emphasised not only similarities of historic and contemporary border obstacles but pointed to the dramatic scale of border fatalities at EUrope's borders where nearly every year more people die than in the entire period of existence of the Berlin wall between 1961 and 1989 (Figure 3).

> The dead of the wall fled in an act of solidarity to their brothers and sisters beyond the external borders of the European Union. To be precise: to the future dead of the wall. 30.000 deaths were claimed by the external EU borders since the fall of the iron curtain. The memorial crosses fled from the 'Oktoberfest-like' memorial to those whose lives are acutely endangered by the

Figure 3. Forests of Gourougou/Morocco; Credit: Centre for Political Beauty.

external EU borders and thereby expanded the self-involved German commemoration by a crucial dimension: the present. (Centre for Political Beauty 2014, my own translation)

The names of Germany's border-victims remained at the site in Berlin, scribbled on post-it notes to which a sentence was added: 'hier wird nicht gedacht'. The phrase's savvy double meaning refers both to the absence of commemoration as well as to a lack of thought or general reflection. Besides the emigration of the white crosses, about 100 'peaceful revolutionaries' went on a journey to Bulgaria, hoping to tear down border fences. At departure in front of the Gorki theatre in Berlin, they were met by a hundred-person-strong police unit that surrounded the theatre and searched for bolt cutters, claiming that the Centre for Political Beauty had called for 'serious criminal offence'. The artist-activists embarked nonetheless but remained under surveillance, regularly controlled when crossing European borders and persistently escorted by police forces in Serbia, Bulgaria and Greece. Facing large police units blocking pathways towards the border fence in Bulgaria, the activists, after a minute of silence for all of EUrope's border fatalities, announced the end of their artistic intervention.

While the activists were unable to physically tear down EUrope's walls and 'bring home a piece of fence as a souvenir' as planned, their performance caused widespread condemnation throughout Germany's political landscape, especially amongst the conservatives. Proudly presented on their own website, the Centre for Political Beauty (2014) quotes the President of the German Parliament Lammert (CDU) who stated: 'the white crosses were stolen with a heroic attitude and a pseudo-humanitarian reason that can only be described as sheer cynicism'. Berlin's Minister for the Interior Henkel (CDU) denounced the act as 'despicable', CSU General Secretary Scheuer described the linking of the current border regime to a past totalitarian system as an 'awful act' and for Graf (CDU), the 'theft of the wall crosses debases the memory of those who died for freedom and transcends any moral form of discussion of the matter at hand'. The artists reacted by suggesting that the victims of the German wall were not 'disturbed in their rest' by the movement of their crosses, but that their stories were 'betrayed' by contemporary border deaths that were the result of a militarised border regime:

> Since we sent out the press release on the campaign on Monday, the whole of Germany is getting worked up over the disappearance of 14 – albeit large and important – symbols. In the meantime, the death of 24 refugees on a boat near Istanbul was only worth a tiny notice. Our campaign is on Germany's front pages. This reveals the true face of German society. Every society only mourns its own victims. […] We can only fully pay tribute to those who died at the Berlin wall if we also think about the new victims. (Centre for Political Beauty 2014)

Despite confusion over who actually 'owned' the white crosses, the police started an investigation due to 'aggravated theft' and, in December, criminal investigators began proceedings against Phillip Ruch, the director of the Centre, accusing him of 'theft of antiquities and art' (Centre for Political Beauty 2015).

The staging of a counter-memorial on Germany's official day of mourning provoked a scandal over grievability, over the question of what counts for whom as life worth grieving. The outrage over the absent crosses illustrated not merely unwillingness to draw parallels between past and present border regimes and their deadly natures but, in essence, expressed disbelief that German life was dared to be equated with other, non-German, even non-EUropean life. For many, it seemed, the memories of fallen Germans were not desecrated simply by an act of pure 'vandalism', the removal of the crosses from their 'rightful' place, but indeed by their mis-placing into wrong hands, into black hands of future border crossers or deaths. The reactions to the artistic appropriation of an official commemoration supposedly demonstrating national unity and identity exposed the differential distribution of grievability, where the suffering and death of some simply do not count as much. In January 2015, the Centre for Political Beauty announced that all those who participated in the art project in the forests of Gourougou, had successfully overcome EUrope's external walls. In June, the artists intensified their grief-provocations by launching the novel campaign 'the dead are coming'. With the permission of relatives, bodies of deceased border crossers that were either buried in an undignified way or left to rot in a hospital container in Italy were identified, disinterred and brought in coffins to Berlin, one of the centres of EUrope's 'deterrence regime' as the activists stated (Centre for Political Beauty 2015). At different cemeteries the bodies were buried, following cultural customs. As the last act of the campaign, thousands of protestors moved towards the German Parliament, some carrying shovels with which they dug holes into the parliament's lawn, leaving about 100 symbolic graves behind.

The potentiality of counter-memorialisation

> What might be done to produce a more egalitarian set of conditions for recognizability? What might be done, in other words, to shift the very terms of recognizability in order to produce more radically democratic results? (Butler 2009, 6)

Grief-activism has become a significant facet of contemporary migration struggles – wholly unsurprising when death is so intimately woven into practices of border governance. The acts of grief and commemoration practiced by Boats4People, Traces Back and the Centre for Political Beauty as central aspects of their campaigns sought to identify (with) those who suffered EUropean border violence, even if those others were, and often remained, unknown. Grief was not hidden but openly displayed, countering the dominant, but as Katherine Hite (2012, 3) notes, 'implicit insistence that others' grief take place behind closed doors [which] borders uneasily on complicity, on enlarging the void rather than on imagining how we might begin to fill the void, through collective mourning'. While the commemorations organised by the campaigners of Boats4People and Traces Back were meant to create and reinforce lasting processes and material sites of mourning, encounter and togetherness 'beyond borders', the artistic intervention performed a momentary dis-placement of Germany's official commemoration of historic border deaths and connected them to those of the present. What all three campaigns had in common was their merging of grief for particular and general losses with a radical critique of the EUropean border regime.

When we engage the question previously posed, as to what occurs in moments of collec-tive grief and what kinds of political community can emerge in these scenes, Butler's notion of grievability is particularly helpful. For her, lives are subjected to conditions that make some apprehendable as livable lives and others as losable lives that continuously fall out of frames of recognisability. Ungrievable lives are those that, 'not conceivable as lives within certain epistemological frames, […] are never lived nor lost in the full sense (Butler 2009, 1)'.

> In fact, a living figure outside the norms of life not only becomes the problem to be managed by normativity, but seems to be that which normativity is bound to reproduce: it is living, but not a life. It falls outside the frame furnished by the norm, but only as a relentless double whose ontology cannot be secured, but whose living status is open to apprehension. (8)

Alive or not, these absences suggest that '"there is a life that will never have been lived," sustained by no regard, no testimony, and ungrieved when lost (15)'. Having fallen out of dominant epistemological frames of recognition, most of those who die along EUrope's borders constitute such unrecognisable lives whose actual loss need neither be counted nor accounted for. Certain individuals, groups and populations simply are 'differentially exposed to injury, violence, and death' (25), and those who travel precariously seeking to 'irregularly' overcome EUrope's borders can certainly be regarded as subjects exposed to such heightened risk. The commemorative practices of the three campaigns can be under-stood with Butler as attempts to contest and shift these frames by affirming life that has been lived and violently lost. Responding to an other's disappearance, grief-activism seeks to foster some lives' recognisability, thereby rupturing the frames that consistently subdue these lives and reinforce the unequal distribution of harm. In this sense, as Edkins holds, the 'disappeared return to haunt the authoritarian systems that disappeared them in the first place' (2013, ix).

Turning against the normalisation of discrepant global conditions of vulnerability, the different acts of grief discussed connected moments of silent mourning with angry denun-ciations of those deemed responsible for border fatalities. As Butler suggests:

Open grieving is bound up with outrage, and outrage in the face of injustice or indeed of unbearable loss has enormous political potential. It is, after all, one of the reasons Plato wanted to ban the poets from the Republic. He thought that if the citizens went too often to watch tragedy, they would weep over the losses they saw, and that such open and public mourning, in disrupting the order and hierarchy of the soul, would disrupt the order and hierarchy of political authority as well. (39)

The potentiality of grief as a significant political practice has been noted also by Leanne Weber and Sharon Pickering who suggest that memorialisation can help develop '[a] richer picture of death at the border [that] is needed if we are to overcome the processes that collectively normalize the deaths that are occurring (2011, 6)'. By tracing the fates of border deaths, the authors provide a disconcerting account of suffering at global barriers that speak of a complex economy of violence that leads to human losses. In the increasingly diffuse thicket of migration governance, border deaths mark out the 'complex performances of state power staged at multiple locations through technologies of detection, selection, deterrence, expulsion and pre-emption, directed towards specifically targeted groups (13)'. Inspired by Laleh Khalili's notion of 'counterhegemonic commemorative practices', Weber and Pickering argue that acts of memorialising and accounting can formulate 'powerful counter-narratives of border deaths' that form 'a necessary precondition for identifying the complex chains of accountability and responsibility for the bodies that are found, never found, recorded and unrecorded in relation to border control (70, 6)'.

Counter-memorialisation, then, seeks to 'democratise' absence by protesting the radical inequalities that continue to exist and continue to make some more apprehendable, intelligible and mournable than others, both in life and in death. Public grieving and commemorating as radical political acts have become widespread practices, also, as Hite notes, 'in part because memory is constitutive of who we are and how we interpret the here and now, and for many, many people, the here and now is deplorable (2012, 1)'. Counter-memorial movements, for her, 'raise questions crucial to debates on the politics of memory regarding grief, empathy, and collective action (2)'. As Hite illustrates in her analysis of sites commemorating violent struggles, memorials 'are vessels for the multiplicity of representations, where individual and collective subjectivity can enter into dialogue with Otherness to help process and represent meaning (118)'.

In the next section, I seek to add to these accounts of counter-memorialisation by drawing out how this process of attempting to engage in 'a dialogue with Otherness' entails both immense possibilities as well as the 'impossibility of identification'. This dialogue, and its attempt to maintain 'grief as part of the framework within which we think our international ties', seems bound up with complex processes and feelings of dislocation that emerge in the confrontation with 'the radically inequitable ways that corporeal vulnerability is distributed globally' (Butler 2003, 19). Inspired by the work of Jacque Rancière, grief-activism is discussed as transformative politics that seeks to create complex communities in precarious encounters, unable, however, to ever shake the horizon of failure that accompanies such political practice.

Acts of impossible identification

The activist campaigns of Boats4People, Traces Back and the Centre for Political Beauty formed enactments of solidarity at the margins that must always-already be riven from the beginning. The different realities, 'Lebenswelten' (life-worlds), and affected positionalities of those encountering one another meant that despite attempts to create cross-identities, an impasse necessarily remained. Rather than regarding this 'impossibility of identifica-tion' as giving evidence to a 'weakness' of such political practices, this section portrays the rejection of easy solidarities as a necessary component of grief-activism in which subjects risk themselves in often painful and discomforting encounters without knowing whether such practices have been 'successful' or not.

The idea of impossible identification is embedded in Rancière's notion of heterology that he relates to a form of political subjectivisation in which the subject refuses the 'right names' assigned to her by the dominant consensual order, involving 'a process of disidentification or declassification' (Rancière 1992, 61). Rather than reiterating the widely used Rancièrean conceptualisations of 'politics', 'equality' or 'emancipation' that have become prominent in recent critical scholarship (Edkins 2011; Nyers 2003; Rajaram and Grundy-Warr 2007), the focus is placed on this rather under-acknowledged aspect. Nearing a definition of heterology, Rancière (1992, 62) holds:

> First, it is never the simple assertion of an identity; it is always, at the same time, the denial of an identity given by an other, given by the ruling order of policy. Policy is about 'right' names, names that pin people down to their place and work. Politics is about 'wrong' names – mis-nomers that articulate a gap and connect with a wrong. Second, it is a demonstration, and a demonstration always supposes an other, even if that other refuses evidence or argument […]. Third, *the logic of subjectivization always entails an impossible identification.* (emphasis added)

Political subjectivisation, for Rancière, is the merging of two worlds in one, and is based on 'a logic of the other'. This process, it seems, must always remain incomplete, leaving the subject in in-between spaces without identitarian stability, always exposed to difference and conflict where the sense of the self is always-already ruptured. Providing an example of an always failing but nonetheless significant attempt to identify, Rancière states:

> [T]o take a personal example, for my generation politics in France relied on an impossible identification – an identification with the bodies of the Algerians beaten to death and thrown into the Seine by the French police, in the name of the French people, in October 1961. We could not identify with those Algerians, but we could question our identification with the 'French people' in whose name they had been murdered. That is to say, we could act as political sub-jects in the interval or the gap between two identities, neither of which we could assume. (61)

Seeking solidarity with these bodies beaten to death meant neither the process of becoming or embodying another nor the process of turning inward to oneself in the attempt to secure some form of identitarian stability. Rather, the process of identification entailed continuous uncomfortable movement in a precarious struggle towards political subjectivities forged by a new name, a 'cross name'. Following Rancière, this struggle seemed saturated by an impossibility: the distance towards the 'dead bodies' could never be fully bridged, and the privileges attached to being a 'French citizen' were not, and could not be, abandoned in attempts to identify with those murdered 'non-citizens'.

Rancière's notion of impossible identification helps explore what occurs in moments of collective grief in which participants enter these in-between states, 'between several names, statuses, and identities; between humanity and inhumanity, citizenship and its denial' (61), and even between life and death. Embracing grief as significant and central political moments, the three campaigns relied on several in-between identifications as transform-ative processes, complicating subjectivities and (their) assumed positionalities. Seeking cross-identification and the simultaneous disidentification with overarching narratives of the EUropean project, shielded by a managerial–humanitarian border regime, the campaigners sought to foster a community of solidarity beyond margins that are so rigid for some and permeable for others. Through their grief-practices, they challenged 'the framing of migrant deaths in terms of simple arithmetic or biopolitics that objectify individuals in the management of life and death of populations' (Rygiel 2014, 66). Encounters with the parents of the deceased and disappeared in Tunisia, with relatives of border deaths in the Aegean Sea or somewhat macabrely with 'future border deaths' in Morocco brought together those who bore the principal violence of the border regime with those who were its supposedly 'protected' subjects. In these moments of encounter, exclusions were counter-performed in complex processes of communal becoming-with others at the margins.

However, a politics that centres on or entails moments of grief must necessarily be formulated around a multitude of impossibilities, not merely the irreversibility of death itself which forms a primary impossibility. While commemorations for unknown others may facilitate a post-mortem apprehension of a 'life that has been lived', they come, in a sense, always-already too late, the life has been violently taken and the manifest absence of another signifies an enduring failure. This sentiment was expressed repeatedly during the memorial on Lesvos when activists voiced their feeling of shame of having 'failed' to prevent deaths and create a welcoming Europe, promising to understand such failure as mandate to counteract ongoing and future border-violence. Besides this foregrounding impossibility, the encounters between activists and the families of the deceased did not always result in processes of reciprocal identification but, at times, in incomprehension, confusion and manifest difference. The commemoration in Monastir points to this horizon of failure where the coming-together of different struggles in solidarity did not materialise due to a lack of preparation and mutual understanding. Moreover, seeking solidarity between those who had lost a known someone and those who mourned for an unknown other always entailed the impossibility of sharing the pain felt. The relatives' despair and the unbearability of loss could never be 're-felt' despite emphatic togetherness. In these encounters, the activists also had to be cautiously aware of the possibility of slipping 'between empathy and pity in white Western consideration of "global others"', as Clara Hemmings has pointed out. For her, empathy that fails 'may lead to sentimental attachment to the other, rather than a genuine engagement with her concerns' or may even 'signal a cannibalisation of the other masquerading as care (2012, 152)'.

However, the possibility of 'failing empathy' seems to be unavoidably woven into grief-activism 'beyond borders', necessitating continuous engagement and critical reflection. When protesting the unequal distribution of vulnerability, for many partaking in the activist campaigns, experiences of violence and precariousness could merely be acknowledged and challenged but never fully comprehended. The unequal distribution of global suffering and privilege meant that the process of disidentifying with the prerogatives of European citizenship would ultimately always be incomplete. Similar to the 'Algerian bodies thrown into the Seine', border deaths were subjected to a violence largely unfathomable to activists who, as predominantly 'European citizens', could emphatically be with the relatives without fully comprehending a violence that asymmetrically subjects only some to extreme hardship.

The incompleteness saturating a politics of collective grief meant that commonness or unity as the groundwork for a political community could not be assumed. Nonetheless, as 'potential coalitions waiting to be formed', the need for being-with one another seemed imperative to all (Crenshaw 1991, 1299). While political acts that entail a horizon of failure seem discomforting as they leave the realm of easily assumed (political/ideological) commonness and readability of one another, it is the process of identification despite impossibilities that engender political potentiality and can point us to modalities of community that surpass traditional ideas of settled and bounded political communities. For Rancière, a heterological politics entails 'no consensus, no undamaged communication, no settlement of the wrong' but, instead, 'being together to the extent that we are in between – between names, identities, cultures (1992, 62)'. Impossible identification does not preclude the possibility of finding commonness, but questions simplistic assumptions and easy solidarities and entails the risking of oneself in unsettling embodied encounters. As Butler holds:

> It is not easy to understand how a political community is wrought from such ties. One speaks, and one speaks for another, to another, and yet there is no way to collapse the distinction between the Other and oneself. When we say 'we' we do nothing more than designate this very problematic. We do not solve it. And perhaps it is, and ought to be, insoluble. (2003, 14)

Solidarity conceived as 'impossible' does not assume sameness or expects common objectives from the start but recognises the entwined nature of different struggles. Its impossibility may, in some ways, even allow for its inventive capacity as it counters the idea of 'full identification', 'unity' or even 'becoming-the-other' as a precondition for collective political action. The idea of impossible solidarity resonates in several ways with Butler's (2005) understanding of 'ethics':

> [T]he question of ethics emerges precisely at the limits of our schemes of intelligibility, the site where we ask ourselves what it might mean to continue in a dialogue where no common ground can be assumed, where one is, [as] it were, at the limits of what one knows yet still under the demand to offer and receive acknowledgement: to someone else who is there to be addressed and whose address is there to be received (21-22). [...] [W]e must recognize that ethics requires us to risk ourselves precisely at the moments of unknowingness. [...] To be undone by another is a primary necessity, an anguish, to be sure, but also a chance – to be addressed, claimed, bound to what is not me, but also to be moved, to be prompted to act, to address myself elsewhere, and so to vacate the self-sufficient 'I' as a kind of possession. (136)

If we comprehend ethics as Butler does, then the encounters in grief discussed in this article were certainly both political and ethical practices. Meeting at the limits of intelligibility without an assumed common ground, the collective commemorations entailed the risking of those involved in moments of incomprehension, surprise and unknowingness, and the possibility of becoming hurt and misunderstood. In these encounters, ties were formulated in practices that unbundled and exceeded sedentary and identitarian frames of community, cautiously enacting a 'we' in moments of collective grief.

Conclusion

EUrope's political leaders have mastered the art of public displays of grief. After a particularly gruesome 'tragedy' in the Mediterranean Sea in October 2013, various state and EU leaders voiced sadness about the lives lost, evincing sympathy for families and communities, promising humanitarian measures to ensure that this dying would be 'not in vain', even considering granting the dead citizenship. These leaders have learned to display their dismay over border deaths in what could be referred to as acts of selective humanitarian grief. After his visit to Lampedusa, then EU Commission President Barroso (2013) publicly stated:

That image of hundreds of coffins will never get out of my mind. […] Coffins of babies, coffins with the mother and the child that was born just at that moment. This is something that profoundly shocked me and deeply saddened me. I also saw the desperate eyes in many survivors, […] [in] the reception centre. […] I saw in some of them […] also some hope, and I believe now we have to give reason for that hope. To show that that hope in the middle of this suffering can be justified.

The hope, besides the desperation, that Barroso so adeptly detected in the 'eyes of survivors', when walking through the 'reception' centre was justified by the president's promise to enhance Frontex operations and maritime surveillance through Eurosur. In Barroso's understanding, intensified border-militarisation, shamelessly sold as a humanitarian rescue mission, would adequately respond to those killed by 'fate' and 'nature' or at the hands of 'ruthless traffickers'. When Italy held an official commemoration in Sicily, survivors of the shipwreck were prevented from attending the ceremony while representatives of the Eritrean government as well as Barroso and Italy's Prime Minister Letta were present. In outrage, Eritrean protestors held a banner reading: 'The presence of the Eritrean regime offends the dead and puts in danger the living' and Barroso and Letta were heckled on their way to the service (Miller 2013). What the protestors exposed was a memorial service that did not grieve the dead but instrumentalised them instead, taunting survivors, relatives and supporters. The cruel exclusion of the survivors who faced fines and deportation, silenced outrage and despair so that the stage was set for a humanitarian event. In these public commemorations, EUropean leaders perform a schizophrenic 'border spectacle' (De Genova 2013), reproducing a humanitarian imaginary of EUrope in the very moment of burying its border fatalities. The losses from a particular shipwreck were not connected to a general economy of violence underlying the EUropean border regime. These official humanitarian grief-events do not prompt a consideration of the shared, though unequally distributed exposure to harm. They do not allow one to be transformed in the moment of mourning, 'when one accepts that by the loss one undergoes one will be changed, possibly forever'. (Butler 2003, 11) Rather, the other's vulnerability becomes a sign of (racial) weakness, victimhood and degeneration that can be responded to only with humanitarian generosity.

In contrast to such 'a politics that misses the person, a politics of the *what*, not the *who*' (Edkins 2011, 9), the collective commemorations enacted by Boats4People, Traces Back and the Centre for Political Beauty counter-performed exclusions that divided the living and even the dead. In difficult encounters, the suffering of another was not hidden or turned into a moment for false hope. The abyss of suffering of the relatives of the disappeared or deceased remained often unsettling and inapproachable, but their pain was encountered, not instrumentalised, their outrage not appeased by emphatic avowals of good will, but shared in moments of togetherness and pain, understood as part of interwoven political struggles. Turning collective grief into a 'resource for politics', in these practices in which identification remains in question, those involved risked themselves at the limits of intelligibility where solidarity is rife with impossibility but where, and maybe *therefore*, an emergent community is cautiously formed.

Notes

1. This paper speaks of 'EUrope' throughout. This way, it seeks to problematise frequently employed usages that equate the EU with Europe and Europe with the EU and suggests, at the same time, that EUrope is not reducible to the institutions of the EU.
2. This is not a direct quote but reflects the way the names and fates were read out during the commemorations.

Acknowledgements

I would like to thank Kim Rygiel as well as two anonymous reviewers for providing inspirational feedback on earlier drafts.

Disclosure statement

No potential conflict of interest was reported by the author.

References

Amnesty International. 2013. "Refugees Dying on Dangerous Routes to Asylum in Europe." Accessed October 6, 2013. http://www.amnesty.org/en/news/refugees-dying-dangerous-routes-asylum-europe-2013-03-20

BBC. 2014. "Inquiry Calls after Migrants Die under Tow in Greece." Accessed January 23, 2014. http://www.bbc.co.uk/news/world-europe-25843559

Birds of Immigrants. 2013. Accessed February 10, 2014. http://birdsofimmigrants.jogspace.net/

Boats4People. 2012a. "Flyer May 2012." Accessed October 12, 2012. http://www.boats4people.org/index.php/en/news/press-releases/49-welcome

Boats4People. 2012b. "Final Press Release." Accessed October 12, 2012. http://www.boats4people.org/index.php/en/news/press-releases/587-boats4peoples-first-campaign-is-a-success-the-maritime-borders-of-the-eu-remain-are-as-deadly-as-ever

Boats4People. 2012c. "Transnational Newsletter No. 1." Accessed May 7, 2013. http://www.boats4people.org/index.php/en/news/modulenewseng/385-transnational-newsletter-no-1-april-2012

Boats4People. 2014a. "Interview with Activist Hagen." March 12, 2014.

Boats4People. 2014b. "Interview with Activist Lorenzo." March 19, 2014.

Boats4People. 2014c. "Email Exchange with Activist Nina." March 19, 2014.

Boats4People. 2014d. "Interview with Activist Christoph." March 07, 2014.

Butler, Judith. 2003. "Violence, Mourning, Politics." *Studies in Gender and Sexuality* 4 (1): 9–37.

Butler, Judith. 2004. *Precarious Life, the Powers of Mourning and Violence.* New York: Verso.

Butler, Judith. 2005. *Giving an Account of Oneself.* New York: Fordham University Press.

Butler, Judith. 2009. *Frames of War, When is Life Grievable?* New York: Verso.

Centre for Political Beauty. 2014. "Mauerfall." Accessed December 12, 2014. http://www.politicalbeauty.de/mauerfall.html

Centre for Political Beauty. 2015. "Facebook." Accessed February 5, 2015.

Council of Europe. 2012. "Lives Lost in the Mediterranean Sea: Who is Responsible?" Accessed November 3, 2012. http://assembly.coe.int/CommitteeDocs/2012/20120329_mig_RPT.EN.pdf

Crenshaw, Kimberle. 1990–91. " Mapping the Margins: Intersectionality, Identity Politics, and Violence against Women of Color." *Stanford Law Review* 43: 1241–1299.

De Genova, Nicholas. 2013. "Spectacles of Migrant 'Illegality': The Scene of Exclusion, the Obscene of Inclusion." *Ethnic and Racial Studies* 36 (7): 1180–1198.

Edkins, Jenny. 2011. *Missing, Persons and Politics.* London: Cornell University Press.

European Commission. 2013. "Statement by President Barroso following His Visit to Lampedusa." Accessed March 16, 2014. http://europa.eu/rapid/press-release_SPEECH-13-792_en.htm

Hemmings, Clare. 2012. "Affective Solidarity: Feminist Reflexivity and Political Transformation." *Feminist Theory* 13 (2): 147–161.

Hite, Katherine. 2012. *Politics and the Art of Commemoration*. London: Routledge.

Mbembe, Achille. 2003. "Necropolitics." *Public Culture* 15 (1): 11–40.

Miller, Barbara. 2013. "Lampedusa Migrant Shipwreck Survivors Blocked from Memorial Service in Sicily." *ABC News*. Accessed March 15, 2014. http://www.abc.net.au/news/2013-10-22/lampedusa-migrant-boat-italy-refugees-memorial/5036848

Nyers, Peter. 2003. "Abject Cosmopolitanism: The Politics of Protection in the Anti-Deportation Movement." *Third World Quarterly* 24 (6): 1069–1093.

Pezzani, Lorenzo, and Charles Heller. 2013. "A Disobedient Gaze: Strategic Interventions in the Knowledge(S) of Maritime Borders." *Postcolonial Studies* 16 (3): 289–298.

Pro Asyl. 2013. "Pushed Back, Systematic Human Rights Violations against Refugees in the Aegean Sea and at the Greek-Turkish Land Border." Accessed June 6, 2014. http://www.proasyl.de/fileadmin/fm-dam/l_EU_Fluechtlingspolitik/proasyl_pushed_back_24.01.14_a4.pdf

Rajaram, Prem Kumar, and Carl Grundy-Warr, eds. 2007. *Borderscapes*. Minneapolis, MN: University of Minnesota Press.

Rancière, Jacques. 1992. "Politics, Identification, and Subjectivization." *The Identity in Question* 61: 58–64.

Rygiel, Kim. 2014. "In Life through Death: Transgressive Citizenship at the Border." In *Routledge Handbook of Global Citizenship Studies*, edited by Engin F. Isin and Peter Nyers, 62–72. New York: Routledge.

Tyler, Imogen, and Katarzyna Marciniak. 2013. "Immigrant Protest: An Introduction." *Citizenship Studies* 17 (2): 143–156.

UNHCR. 2009. "Greece Shuts down Migrant Detention Centre on Island." Accessed January 10, 2014. http://www.unhcr.org/cgi-bin/texis/vtx/refdaily?pass=463ef21123&id=4aefd83b5

UNHCR. 2012. "One Survivor, 54 Die at Sea Attempting the Voyage to Italy from Libya." Accessed March 15, 2014. http://www.unhcr.org/4ffc59e89.html

United For Intercultural Action. 2012. Accessed March 23, 2012. http://www.unitedagainstracism.org/

WatchTheMed. 2014. "Thermi Wreck." Accessed January 8, 2014. http://watchthemed.net/reports/view/14

WatchTheMed. 2015. "More than 300 People on Four Rubber Vessels Die in the Central Mediterranean Sea." Accessed February 14, 2015. http://watchthemed.net/reports/view/95

Weber, Leanne, and Sharon Pickering. 2011. *Globalization and Borders, Death at the Global Frontier*. Basingstoke: Palgrave Macmillan.

w2eu. 2010. "Mass Grave of Refugees in Evros Uncovered." Accessed March 10, 2015. http://infomobile.w2eu.net/stories/accidents-and-death-at-the-border/

w2eu and Youth Without Borders. 2013. "Journey Back to Lesvos." Accessed February 15, 2015. http://lesvos.w2eu.net/files/2014/02/Lesvos2013-Screen-DS.pdf

w2eu and Youth Without Borders. 2014. Accessed February 20, 2015. http://lesvos.w2eu.net/files/2015/02/Doku-Lesvos-2014_web.pdf

Troubling the exclusive privileges of citizenship: mobile solidarities, asylum seekers, and the right to work

Lucy Mayblin

Department of Politics, University of Sheffield, Sheffield, UK

ABSTRACT

This article discusses asylum seekers and the right to work in the UK. Differential access to the labour market is one of the ways in which the state maintains a distinction between British citizens, who 'belong', and non-citizens who do not. While such a policy approach garners widespread support amongst the general public of citizens, it does not go uncontested. This article discusses a UK-based campaign, 'Let Them Work', which has sought to influence the government in extending the right to work to asylum seekers. In doing so, it demonstrates the ways in which the stratified regime of citizenship rights is contested politically, and explores how such contestation troubles the exclusive privileges of citizenship by enacting mobile solidarities from marginalised spaces.

Introduction

The right to work is a restricted privilege to which migrants are granted unequal access in relation to citizens. On a sliding scale of privilege some migrants are able to obtain visas to work in the UK relatively easily, while for others (notably asylum seekers and irregular migrants) working is prohibited. This differential access to the labour market is one of the ways in which the state maintains a distinction between British citizens, who 'belong', and non-citizens who do not. This situation might be understood as a stratified regime of rights (Morris 2012). While such a policy approach garners widespread support amongst the general public of citizens, it does not go uncontested. In this article, I discuss a UK-based campaign, 'Let Them Work' (LTW), which has sought to influence the British government in extending the right to work to asylum seekers. I do this in order to demonstrate the ways in which the stratified regime of citizenship rights is contested politically, and to explore how such contestation troubles the exclusive privileges of citizenship by enacting mobile solidarities from marginalised spaces.

The analysis focuses on two key issues: First, how citizenship was represented in the campaign and to what extent this moved beyond dominant scripts. Two main representations of citizenship are identified: citizenship as something which must be struggled for, which contrasts with the government's conception of earned citizenship; and citizenship as a liberal social project but one which involves all who are present, not just those granted citizenship rights by the state; second, the ways in which 'mobile solidarities' (Squire 2011) were invoked and by what means. The campaign invoked two different mobile solidarities: worker solidarity and human solidarity. Both involved the eliding of citizen/non-citizen distinctions in the creation of collective political subjects – workers and human beings – in order to mobilise around the right to work in a manner which sees migration as legitimate, and the multiple diversities which it brings about positively.

The paper draws on textual evidence from the LTW campaign, which ran 2008–2010. This includes speeches, leaflets, press releases, media reports, campaign briefings and archived web materials. Grey literature was gathered via correspondence with LTW activists and the timeline of events verified with these individuals. Texts were gathered and coded using Nvivo data analysis software. The article is structured as follows: the next section outlines the situation of asylum seekers in Britain, unable to work and forced into welfare dependency, and introduces some of the ways in which this policy approach has been resisted. The following section outlines more fully the uneasy relationship between citizenship rights and the category 'asylum seeker' within a stratified regime of rights. Here, I make the case for using the concepts 'acts of citizenship' (Isin and Turner 2007; Isin 2008) and 'mobile solidarities' (Squire 2011) in analysing examples of resistance to this stratified regime of rights, and particularly in the case of the LTW campaign. Following this, LTW is introduced more fully and the unfolding of the campaign described in order that the breadth, depth and transformative potential might be demonstrated. The remaining sections address the case study in an analysis of the representations of citizenship and the invocation of mobile solidarities, before finally bringing together the key themes in the conclusion.

This is a campaign which was ultimately unsuccessful, despite broad cross-party support and a mounting weight of evidence that denying asylum seekers the right to work was an ill-advised policy. The question of why it was unsuccessful is a topic for another paper, but it is worth stating here that the fact of its ultimate failure to change the law does not take away from the transformative power of the campaign in terms of potentially building solidarities between citizens and asylum seekers, and in facilitating a rethinking of citizenship amongst those involved beyond the parameters of the exclusionary state regime. Of interest here, then, is not the ultimate success or failure of the campaign, but the reframing of the parameters of citizenship and the blurring of artificially created boundaries between citizens and non-citizens within it.

Asylum and work in Britain

As Morris (2002, 411) has pointed out 'access to employment readily illustrates a stratified system of inclusion and exclusion'. In Britain, the effective exclusion of asylum seekers from employment is used by the government as a policy tool to socially exclude and marginalise asylum seekers (Mayblin 2014a). Successive governments have argued that this deters potential asylum seekers from coming to the country, though there is no evidence to support this assertion. Until 2002, asylum seekers could apply for the right to work if they had been residing in the UK and awaiting a decision on their claim for six months or more. The 2002 Immigration and Asylum Act took away the right to work, but in 2005 the UK opted in to a European Union Directive on asylum reception conditions (European Commission 2003) and as such the government was forced to re-extend the right to work. Unwilling to fully acquiesce to the aims and scope of the Directive, the UK government allowed asylum seekers to apply for the right to work only 12 months following their initial application for asylum, and only if the delay was not seen to be their fault. From 2010, if granted the right to work, asylum seekers were restricted to jobs on a government's shortage occupations list. This list is so selective that it in effect presents a total barrier to legal employment for the vast majority of asylum seekers (UKBA 2013; Mayblin 2014a).

The governments of most liberal nation states have sought, in recent decades, to exclude asylum seekers as far as possible territorially, socially and economically. Within the context of the stratified regime of rights they stand above only those designated 'illegal immigrants', who have almost no rights at all (Dembour and Kelly 2011). Asylum seeking is linked to welfare support and is therefore seen as an unfair economic burden (Sales 2002). Meanwhile, the response of politicians to suggestions that asylum seekers be allowed to work is that such a policy would act as a pull factor for economic migrants posing as asylum seekers (e.g. see HC 12.10.11. cc44-5WS). There is a large body of work which discredits this claim (e.g. Middleton 2005; Crawley 2010). Equally, if welfare support is too generous, 'bogus' applicants will be attracted, providing a justification for limiting assistance as much as possible (Sales 2002; Dwyer 2005). Within the context of debates around 'deserving' and 'undeserving' welfare recipients more broadly, 'asylum seekers have been cast as the "undeserving", while denied the means (employment) by which to join the "deserving"' (Sales 2002, 459). Anderson (2013) describes this tension in terms of a discourse of 'failed citizens' and 'non-citizens' (such as asylum seekers) who threaten what she terms the 'community of value' made up of 'good citizens'. Measures of control targeting 'failed citizens' and non-citizens seek to marginalise these perceived threats to the community of value from within and without.

This policy targeting both failed citizens and non-citizens for punitive measures of control is nevertheless challenged from within the community of value. In relation to the exclusion of asylum seekers from work, activists have focused their work in two key areas. First, legal channels have been used to challenge particular aspects of the law. These challenges have largely related to access to welfare support for particular groups of asylum seekers who are identified for exclusion (see Morris 2009, 2012 for a detailed discussion on legal challenges to government policy in this area). The second, and the focus of this article, was the launching of a large-scale national campaign in 2008 – 'Let Them Work' (LTW) – which sought to expand the right to work to include asylum seekers awaiting a decision on their claim. Before moving on to a discussion of LTW, the next section addresses the topic of asylum seekers and citizenship with reference to Isin's (2008) work on 'acts of citizenship' and Squire's (2011) on 'mobile solidarities'.

Asylum seekers and citizenship

Asylum seekers inhabit an ambivalent space vis-a-vis citizenship. In a legal sense, they are of course external to citizenship, they are non-citizens. Indeed, if we take the view that citizenship is a territorially based set of rights and privileges to which a relatively sedentary and homogenous community has access, we are left with a clear delineation of 'insiders', who have the full suite of rights associated with citizenship, and 'outsiders' who do not. Asylum seekers thus have formal access to none of the three spheres of rights (civil, political, social) described in Marshall's (1950) developmental account of citizenship. And yet, in reality the human rights conventions and other international agreements (such as free movement of workers within the EU) necessitate a response to international migration which is not wholly exclusionary. The result is a differentiated and hierarchical regime of partial membership in response to the presence of migrants (who have recourse to internationally recognised rights) in territories of settlement (Morris 2002; Sales 2002). What we have, then, is a system of stratified rights.

Asylum seekers, within this context, are neither fully included nor fully excluded from the community of citizens and the rights to which they have access. For example, by their very presence they make demands for privileges which are, partially or wholly, usually reserved for citizens: work and welfare. In the UK, where the vast majority of asylum seekers do not have the right to work, recourse to welfare is necessary for survival, and is granted in order that their human rights are not violated (Morris 2012). In this sense, asylum seekers as mobile subjects are the embodiment of an international web of rights and obligations. They carry 'these webs of rights and obligations with them and further [entangle] them with other webs of rights and obligations' (Isin 2008, 15). This situation makes asylum seekers never fully excludable, though of course many states seek to exclude them as far as is legally possible (Marfleet 2006; Squire 2009).

Yet, listing formal rights – as full, partial or absent – does not get at the full range of activities which make up the experience of citizenship. Nor does it account for the ways in which legal definitions of citizenship might be contested through political struggle for recognition, or through enacting solidarities which breach the insider/outsider divide. There is a growing body of work exploring the political mobilisations of irregular migrants and others of insecure status, as well as activists who campaign on their behalf (e.g. McNevin 2006; Nyers 2010; Darling 2014). This work exposes 'the contradictions and inclusionary/ exclusionary dynamics of contemporary modalities of citizenship' (Tyler and Marciniak 2013, 144) at the same time as offering examples of how activists are disarticulating citizen/ non-citizen borders in ways which open up spaces for collective resistance (e.g. Rigby and Schlembach 2013). This article contributes to this literature by focusing on asylum seekers, and on an under-researched topic in relation to asylum seekers: the right to work.

The campaign which I focus on was not led from the grass roots as many of those previously studied have, but by two large non-governmental organisations. Asylum seekers were involved, but it was not *their* movement. Nevertheless, what I want to focus on in this article is how we might understand this campaign as entailing 'acts of citizenship' which built solidarity across the citizen/non-citizen divide. Acts of citizenship (Isin 2008) are distinct from, but related to, the status of citizenship and are based on fluid subject positions 'which sit on a spectrum of intensity ranging from hospitality to hostility: citizens, strangers, outsiders and aliens' (ibid., 19). For Isin, 'becoming a subject involves being implicated in this spectrum' (ibid.) and as such the dialogical principle of citizenship always involves otherness. Isin is therefore interested in how beings decide between solidaristic, agonistic and alienating acts towards others and what actualizes those acts.

If citizenship studies often focus on extent (rules/norms of inclusion and exclusion), content (rights and responsibilities) and depth (thickness or thinness of belonging), to look at *acts* of citizenship is to investigate what comes prior to these three spheres, to those acts that produce citizens and their others (Isin 2008). Since citizenship is something that is periodically (more or less frequently) remade and reimagined, this is an ongoing process rather than a look back to an imagined beginning. As Balibar (2012, 438) points out 'the history of citizenship … is a permanent dialectical tension between moments of insurrection and moments of constitution, in the sense of more or less stable, more or less hegemonic relation of social forces'. The focus on acts, then, is interesting because it asks 'what accounts for subjects refusing, resisting or subverting the orientations, strategies and technologies in which they find themselves implicated, and the solidaristic, agonistic and alienating relationships in which they are caught'? (Isin 2008, 38) While we are all caught up in formal, historically embedded, modes of inclusion and exclusion, they can guide but do not *determine* our enactments. In contesting, the formal citizenship regime actors engage in modes of being political, and sometimes transform the boundaries of citizenship in law.

Isin (2008) argues that in researching acts of citizenship one needs to investigate how subjects become activist citizens. He contrasts 'activist citizens' with 'active citizens'. While activist citizens 'engage in writing scripts and creating the scene, active citizens follow scripts and participate in scenes that are already created. While activist citizens are creative, active citizens are not …' (Isin 2008, 38). The concept of scripts is helpful in that it draws attention to the discursive – how ideas of citizenship are communicated, and how this may result in social action. Isin further observes that 'acts produce actors that become answerable to justice against injustice' (ibid., 39). In the case of LTW, which I describe more fully below, this is certainly the case. In creating actors who come to realise that they are in a relationship with each other and that this relationship is underpinned by injustice, activists are those who choose to become answerable against that injustice. What I want to look at here, then, is a case in which the scope of citizenship rights was/is reimagined and formal rules for inclusion and exclusion were/are challenged from below – an 'insurrectional moment' (where hegemonic social forces are challenged) in Balibar's terms (Balibar 2012). Though the challenge has thus far been unsuccessful, the acts of citizenship involved have reconceived what it means to be citizen and to be 'other', or in other words have recreated political subjectivities and social formations, if only in select contexts.

Squire's (2011) work on 'mobile solidarities' is helpful here. She points out that legalistic and culturalist conceptions of citizenship and belonging overlook 'enactments of solidarity in which cultural categories and legal distinctions disappear or are relatively unimportant' (292). Mobile solidarities are 'the creation of collective political subjects through mobilisations that promote the physical movements of people as well as the multiple diversities that such movements bring about' (ibid.). Squire explores mobile solidarities within the UK-based City of Sanctuary movement and the Strangers into Citizens campaign, and she identifies these as collective engagements 'through which social hierarchies are disrupted or overturned' (ibid.). Importantly, the solidarities built around these two campaigns fit neither with the legalistic idea of a political community nor the essentialistic frame of a cultural community. These solidarities, rather, are built on heterogeneity and difference. They are solidaristic in that they entail 'minor' acts of citizenship – on the scale of the everyday – which necessitate the blurring, or even disavowal of legally inscribed status labels.

Mobile solidarities, then, are implicated in acts of citizenship. What I want to argue here is that in the example discussed below, mobile solidarities are created and actuated, and acts of citizenship made possible. This concept thus offers analytical purchase for researching acts of citizenship in the case of non-citizens. What is particularly interesting about the LTW example is that citizens, who have often been told by politicians, the media, and other citizens that they are (or will be) disadvantaged by the expanding of employment rights to migrants, stand in solidarity with asylum seekers. The common rhetoric of migrants 'stealing jobs' is in fact inverted and employment for non-citizens who are present in Britain is framed as beneficial for *everyone*. This is also within the context of deep-rooted historical narratives of Britishness and otherness in which even subjects of the British Empire who had good reasons to claim British citizenship were excluded ideologically and practically from claims of membership (Hampshire 2005). Mobile solidarities in this context take the form of worker solidarity (promoted by trades unions) and human solidarity (promoted by refugee-supporting organisations). Despite some shortcomings, I will argue that the campaign entailed acts of citizenship and through the articulation of mobile solidarities the hierarchical regime of rights is challenged not from above (from international institutions) but from below.

Let Them Work

'Let Them Work' was a campaign, led by the Refugee Council and the Trades Union Congress (TUC)[1] which ran 2008–2010. Below is a brief overview of the timeline of the campaign, which is given to show the breadth, scale and tactics used by campaigners at various levels. The campaign was launched at the TUC Black Workers Conference in April 2008 and introduced by Donna Covey, Chief Executive of the Refugee Council, and Brendan Barber, General Secretary of the TUC. The campaign involved these and many other organisations, including Student Action for Refugees (STAR), Liberty and Refugee Action. This was a campaign with a very focussed aim: to get the law changed so that asylum seekers would again be granted the right to work while they awaited a decision on their claim. The tactics were clear and consistent across organisations: educate people about the issue, persuade them to write to their MP about it, and encourage MPs to sign a pledge to support the right to work.

In May 2008, the TUC Commission on Vulnerable Employment produced a report which suggested that denying asylum seekers the right to work while limiting welfare benefits can force them into informal (illegal) work. In June 2008, the most prominent regional campaign, based in the north-east region of England, was set up. The northern branch of the TUC, led by a refugee, joined with the Regional Refugee Forum (RRF) as part of its strategy to support vulnerable workers, to 'organise a vibrant campaign in the region for the Right to Work for Asylum Seekers' (Northern TUC leaflet, October 2008). In October, this campaign group met with the Chairman of the Asylum Working Group of the Centre for Social Justice to contribute to its report on asylum policy (published in the December) and the campaign had started to appear in the national media, with The Politics Show (a BBC's weekly politics programme) airing a 3-min film made by members of the campaign. At the (then in government) Labour Party Conference in September 2008 Jack Dromey, Deputy General Secretary of the UNITE trade union (which represents workers across many sectors) spoke at a fringe meeting on LTW and called on Ministers to take notice of the support of the unions. Jon Cruddas MP said the right to work was 'one of the most important issues to be debated at the conference'.

Throughout 2009, presentations were made at trades union branch meetings, at the Trades Council and at Student Union meetings (often via STAR). The aim was to raise awareness amongst potentially sympathetic publics. In February 2009, the Church of England Synod joined the campaign (Beckford 2009). Campaign leaders again spoke to the TUC

Black Workers Conference in April 2009. In March 2009, the campaign, with Lynne Jones MP as primary sponsor, brought an Early Day Motion (EDM) to parliament with 105 MP supporters (EDM 2009).

In July 2009, The Refugee Council and the Zimbabwe Association published a report on wasted skills and enforced dependence among Zimbabwean asylum seekers in the UK (Doyle 2009). In the same month, Communities Minister Shahid Malik committed publicly to raise the issue of the right to work for asylum seekers with the Immigration Minister, Phil Woolas. In the September, he spoke at a special debate at the Labour Party conference titled 'is asylum policy damaging community cohesion?' and the TUC staged a rally to help raise union support for LTW. In October, the Churches Regional Commission publicly reiterated their support for the campaign at an event in the North East marking 'World Day for Decent Work' and in December the Bishop of Newcastle also spoke out on the subject. Building up to the May 2010 general election, Lord Morris hosted a reception in the House of Lords in December 2009 on the LTW campaign which included speakers from The Refugee Council, the TUC, the Confederation of British Industry and the Regional Refugee Forum North East.

A second EDM in March 2010 on the topic of asylum seekers and the right to work was brought by Fabian Hamilton MP (EDM 2010). Ahead of a general election it garnered only 40 signatures and the Conservative/Liberal Democrat coalition government formed following the May 2010 election did not restore the right to work to asylum seekers and made clear that it was not even considering this policy change (Home Office 2010). Since then, the focus of campaigning has moved on to destitute failed asylum seekers, whose situation is extremely precarious and urgent, and efforts to realise the right to work for asylum seekers have thus been subsumed under a larger umbrella. The LTW campaign disbanded and campaigning on this issue has largely come through Still Human Still Here, a coalition of over 60 organisations whose main focus is ending destitution amongst failed asylum seekers.

What I have briefly laid out here is a large-scale and multifaceted campaign which, though ultimately unsuccessful, did present the opportunity to change the script on asylum seekers and citizenship at a high level of politics. The next section develops an analysis of the campaign focusing on representations of citizenship and invocations of mobile solidarity.

The 'Let them Work' campaign: troubling the exclusive privileges of citizenship

Representations of citizenship

This section discusses two representations of citizenship that appeared across campaigning materials. The discursive (re)framing of citizenship – as struggle and as an inclusive social project – through texts and speeches entailed acts of citizenship which made it possible to reimagine asylum seekers as citizens.

Citizenship as struggle

The idea of citizenship as struggle is not new, but it does go against dominant political and policy discourse in the UK and elsewhere that frames citizenship as something to be earned through demonstrating the characteristics of 'the good citizen' (Anderson 2013). The expanding of access to citizenship, and expanding some of the rights and privileges of citizenship, to non-citizens is something which has historically been hard won by marginalised groups and their advocates. However, this is not the message that dominates public discussion of citizenship.

In the LTW campaign, 'struggle' was at the centre of the discursive framing of the issue. The right to work is something to be won in battling injustice, not simply in proving one's worth. In 2009, a Refugee Council Campaigns Team blog stated

> everyone acknowledges that this is a difficult issue to be working on but one we're all committed to. We'll be continuing to put pressure on the government to change the rules and give all asylum seekers of working age permission to work. ('Labour Party Conference Update' 22nd September 2008)

This idea of the right to work as something to be struggled for is interesting because in the dominant script the modern citizen is often depicted as the 'worker citizen', defined by the qualities and moral capacity to 'work'. Those who fail to fulfil this duty are often represented as 'failed citizens' (Anderson 2013). The 'benefit scrounger' is one of these failed citizens. However, by drawing attention to the *exclusion* of asylum seekers – non-citizens – from work, they immediately become implicated in a common struggle with other marginalised (citizen) groups. Therefore, as well as being a site for scripting the dominant mode of political subjectivity tied to the 'good'/rightful citizen, struggles around work can also provide multiple sites of political contestation which bridge the citizen/non-citizen divide.

For LTW campaigners, this struggle follows on from previous struggles for employment rights. For example, in her speech to the TUC Black workers conference in April 2008 Donna Covery (Chief Executive of the Refugee Council) discussed asylum seekers in relation to women, black people and gay people – groups united in the long struggle for justice:

> The last time I came to the TUC Black workers conference was in the 1990s. The equality agenda – in the UK and the rest of the world has moved on since then. We live in a world where women sit in Government across Europe, civil partnerships are celebrated, and a black man may become the next president of the United States. But one group of people are still discriminated against in the UK – not just through ignorance, but also as matter of active government policy. Asylum seekers.

As people of colour and homosexuals have historically been marginalised and criminalised by the British state, and their achievement of 'good citizen' status was hard won (and the struggle in many ways continues), the linking of this with the struggle of asylum seekers bridges the non-citizen/citizen divide. Indeed, the struggles of people of colour in Britain have also been implicated in histories of immigration and successive generations have moved from the status of 'outsider' to 'insider', making this connection all the more pertinent.

The work of campaigning organisations such as the Refugee Council who work on publicly unpopular issues such as the rights of asylum seekers is always an exercise in struggle. And struggle within this context is discursively associated with the challenges faced by asylum seekers both in their countries of origin and in the UK. Yet, by partnering with the TUC the reference to struggle immediately taps in to another discourse around struggle which involves a history of fighting for the economic, social, civil and political rights of workers. For example, Donna Covey stated:

> All of us in this room are used to fighting hard campaigns. For causes we believe in, that others think are pie in the sky [...] Because you have always stood up for the most vulnerable in our society. That's why the trades unions have campaigned successfully for equal pay and a minimum wage. You know 'and injury to one is an injury to all' – that's why British trade unionists have always been at the forefront of global solidarity (Refugee Council 2008)

In this sense, the act of citizenship is one in which asylum seekers become citizens through speaking of them as *already* in possession of the right to claim economic rights (to paraphrase Hannah Arendt), as already equal to citizens, and the fact of their exclusion from the labour market therefore being one of straightforward injustices. The effect is to create a new script in which already present asylum seekers belong here and are entitled to the same right to work as citizens. The boundary between citizens and non-citizens is not just blurred but is transformed. The asylum seeker is no longer excluded; she is, in effect, a citizen.

Citizenship as a liberal social project

The second representation was of citizenship as a liberal social project. This representation of citizenship at first glance follows the dominant script of the liberal 'worker citizen'. Indeed, Tyler and Marciniak (2013, 144) have argued that 'in order to effect material changes, protestors are [often] compelled to make their demands in the idiom of the regime of citizenship they are contesting'. Throughout the campaign asylum seekers were represented as model citizens within a discourse of liberal citizenship which emphasises working to support oneself and one's family, and not relying on the state, as both morally desirable on an individual basis, and at the level of the collective. This representation relies on the inversion of the notion of the non-citizen as also 'failed citizen' (undeserving, workless), but equally the inversion keeps the distinction between asylum seekers and failed citizens alive.

Asylum seekers are, in all campaign materials, speeches and press releases, consistently represented as hard working, highly skilled and keen to work in order to support themselves and their family, as well as to contribute to society through paying taxes. In a sense, then, they are implicitly pitted against 'failed citizens'. A 2008 TUC leaflet, for example, stated 'many asylum seekers are well qualified. 57% are educated to A-level standard, and 24% have higher level qualifications' and later provided the following quote from a Zimbabwean asylum seeker living in Middlesborough:

> I've been in the UK for more than 5 years and I'm still waiting for a decision. I've not been able to work as I am an asylum seeker. But I have managed to do a lot of volunteering in the community and at my local refugee centre. It is my culture that I work, so instead of wasting time lying around at home doing nothing I volunteer' (Northern TUC and Regional Refugee Forum North East 2008)

This example is typical of campaign materials and the statistics cited are repeated across genres, and by a diversity of organisations. In their speeches at the campaign launch event Donna Covey and Brendan Barber both spoke of Aisha from Ethiopia, a primary school teacher with eight years' experience who speaks six languages (Refugee Council 2008; TUC 2008). The denial of Aisha, as a purportedly typical example of an asylum seeker, denies the collective opportunity to benefit from, rather than support, such individuals within society. A LTW leaflet produced by the Regional Refugee Forum North East encapsulated this representation of citizenship as a liberal social project when it stated 'when people say "I want to work", they are saying "I want to look after myself" There is dignity to that' (Regional Refugee Forum North East 2008).

While following the government script by allying asylum seekers with 'good citizens' rather than 'failed citizens', this model liberal citizen, which is embodied in the asylum seeker (as represented by the campaign), is nevertheless included *within* the collective of society. A Refugee Council blog from December 2009 points out that 'in times of economic difficulty, we must allow everyone in society to work and contribute to the economy'. And yet, government policy on the stratified right to work does not include all migrants within the category of 'everyone in society'. It is precisely by excluding asylum seekers from such duties as contributing to the economy if they are able, in times of economic difficulty or otherwise, that the government maintains the distinction between citizen and asylum seeker, and in doing so protects citizenship as a reward and a privilege (Tyler 2010). By including asylum seekers within this national project of liberal subjecthood, then, the campaign performs an act of citizenship when it attempts to elide official distinctions and follow a narrative of 'rightful presence' (Squire and Darling 2013). By their very presence, asylum seekers are thus a part of society, and should be permitted to perform the duties demanded by the collective.

Citizenship as a liberal social project is similarly invoked by reference to integration and community cohesion. For example, a TUC leaflet stated 'it is well documented that employment is the best way for a person to integrate into society – yet asylum seekers are denied this chance' (Northern TUC and Regional Refugee Forum North East 2008). Reference was consistently made to 'people in *our society*' (e.g. see TUC 2008), again discursively including asylum seekers within, rather than outside of, the citizen collective. A STAR leaflet suggested that 'engaging in work can help people seeking asylum to improve their English; meet new people; make friends and contribute to the community; helping to instil a feeling of acceptance and inclusion into British society' (STAR, n.d.-b). As noted above, acceptance and inclusion are precisely what the government wants to avoid. This avoidance is undertaken through reinforcing clear distinctions between citizens as rightfully and permanently present (and therefore entitled to work), and particular groups of non-citizens (here, asylum seekers) as (potentially) not rightfully present, as temporary, and therefore not yet (if at all) entitled to integrate.

When Donna Covey stated that 'we would all benefit from giving them [asylum seekers] the right to work', she encapsulates the two arms of this representation of citizenship (Refugee Council 2008). The message being communicated is that it would be good for the collective because full members would not have to pay financially for these non-members, but they would also not have to pay the social costs created by a policy of social exclusion through economic exclusion. If asylum seekers have rights and privileges, they will also have duties, and in fulfilling them it will be good for the community as a whole. Yet, in policing the boundaries of the community, the idea of citizenship as a set of privileges is protected. Asylum seekers have been purposefully *excluded* as undesirable and labelled non-citizens, outsiders or 'others', accordingly. Therefore, in making claims that asylum seekers should have recourse to the privileges of citizenship in order that the whole *community* benefits, the campaign both rhetorically creates a community in which asylum seekers are members, and draws attention to the reality of the situation: asylum seekers are present, they live among us, and in the absence of territorial exclusion every effort is made to exclude them economically, socially and politically. Such a policy is thus made to appear untenable when the idea of citizenship as a collective social project amongst those living in the same place is invoked.

Mobile solidarities

This section describes the two main mobile solidarities that were invoked in campaigning materials and speeches. By conceptualising these invocations of solidarity in terms of mobility, the intention is to draw attention to the ways in which these discursive strategies elide divisions based on citizenship status. In doing so, they make acts of citizenship possible.

As workers

The involvement of trades unions brought to the campaign a discourse of worker solidarity which is unlikely to otherwise have been present. Much of the evidence of this articulation of mobile solidarity can therefore be found in TUC literature and speeches made to trades unionists. It is interesting that a trades union, whose remit is to work for the rights and protections of workers, would pursue a campaign such as this for a group who are not currently workers. Asylum seekers were, for the TUC, would-be workers, and they came into the organisation's populations of concern through their 'Vulnerable Workers' programme. Vulnerable workers are those in 'precarious work that places people at risk of continuing poverty and injustice resulting from an imbalance of power in the employer-worker relationship' (TUC 2007). This includes workers who do not have a legal right to take paid employment and as such the idea of a worker within this context is something which stands apart from legalistic conceptions of citizenship or immigration status. Trades unionists are well placed, then, to undertake 'enactments of solidarity in which cultural categories and legal distinctions disappear or are relatively unimportant' (Squire 2011, 292) as worker solidarity does not require the *right* to work.

In part, the association between trades union activity and struggle against the government was invoked by drawing attention to these would-be workers as trade unionists. For example, a leaflet for TUC members suggested that 'many asylum seekers have survived war, rape and torture – often as punishment for trade union activity or opposition to oppressive regimes' (Northern TUC and Regional Refugee Forum North East 2008). However, even more pertinent to this article were the solidarities invoked between asylum seekers and citizens as rightful workers in the UK. Asylum seekers were assumed already to be workers, and to be in need of activation. For example, 'it's time to end a situation where skilled people who want to work are forced to live in poverty and destitution' (Regional Refugee Forum North East 2008). Connections were made by Donna Covey in her campaign launch speech between the situation of workers denied employment as a consequence of government policy, and the situation of asylum seekers:

> As trades unionists, we know the impact that unemployment has on the lives of individuals, families and communities. We saw the way that mass unemployment under the Tories in the 1980s destroyed our towns and cities and wrecked the self-esteem of a generation (Refugee Council 2008)

Here asylum seekers are not 'other'. Their position is reimagined, they are vulnerable and excluded workers:

> I am proud [...] that we can go together to the Government so they know that British workers want asylum seekers to have the right to work [...] Because you have always stood up for the most vulnerable in our society. That's why the trades unions have campaigned successfully for equal pay and a minimum wage (ibid.)

Based on the assumption that asylum seekers are would-be workers, solidarity was further built through the use of personal narrative and 'imagine if' scenarios. For example:

> IMAGINE being told that you can not work for a living. Not because you are not up to the job but because if you do you are breaking the law. This is the situation that many refugees living on Wearside face, having to rely on benefits instead to survive (Foster 2008)

> I cannot describe the amount of stress that comes from not being allowed to work. If you expect to spend the rest of your life working and then suddenly you are told 'no just sit there, don't work' it is so stressful (Zimbabwean refugee, Teesside) (Northern TUC and Regional Refugee Forum North East 2008)

These mobile worker solidarities, alluding to the Marxist conceptions of worker solidarity which have traditionally informed trades union debate, thus foreground a common sub-jecthood at the expense of citizen and asylum seeker distinctions. Once the boundaries are blurred, asylum seekers are no longer 'other'; they are rights-holding individuals who are rightfully present, and the case for excluding them from work is weakened. Of course, this discourse of workers-in-waiting falls foul of similar challenges facing the 'activation' of unemployed citizens: some asylum seekers are elderly, disabled, have health issues which prevent them from working or face other structural barriers to entering employment. Nevertheless, this solidaristic reframing of the issue came at the same time as other voices, including the Prime Minister, were calling for 'British Jobs for British Workers' (Summers 2009). Such a slogan clearly couples citizen and worker and links the right to work with British citizenship. Yet this campaign, co-led by the TUC, elided such distinctions and sought to forge a new politics of citizenship, albeit within the terms of the neoliberal state.

As human beings

If the trades union arm of the campaign largely focussed on mobile solidarities based upon asylum seeker's status as would-be workers, Christian organisations and activists in the migrant and refugee advocacy sector spoke more to a human solidarity which tran-scends borders, cultures and legalistic distinctions. For example, Martin Wharton, Bishop of Newcastle launched a public attack on the government's treatment of asylum seekers in December 2009, five months before the general election, stating that asylum seekers were treated as 'less than human' (Aitken 2009). He referred to the Parliamentary Committee on Human Rights' finding that the asylum system inflicted 'inhuman and degrading treat-ment' on asylum seekers and asked 'how can we treat people today in a way which is even less humane than the Victorians and their work-houses'. By using the word 'humane', the Bishop not only draws attention to the fact that asylum seekers are human beings, but also to the mutually degrading effects of treating others as less than human.

Ten months earlier, the Synod (the governing body of the state religion) had voted over-whelmingly in favour of allowing asylum seekers to work. Reverend Ruth Worsley, a priest in the diocese of Southwell and Nottingham who tabled the motion on the subject said,

> with the arrival of the credit crunch, the subsequent loss of jobs, the recent call for British jobs for British people, there is a danger that we become inward-looking and even xenophobic. But the Gospel tells us that we are not a tribal nation but a global family (Beckford 2009)

This idea that 'we are not a tribal nation' draws on a religiously inscribed idea of humanity as a family which is at odds with the contemporary system of states, borders and legally distinct categories of people. But this solidarity is also similar to the cosmopolitan virtues of human rights. Indeed, activists drawing on discourses of human solidarity sometimes invoked human rights as a legitimising frame for humanitarian interventions. Bishop Whatron (of Newcastle) said, 'in the UK we have one of the worst human rights records in Europe. This is something of which we should be truly ashamed' (Aitken 2009). The Reverend William Raines, of Manchester diocese, said in February 2009 that 'the asylum system could have been designed by King Herod after reading Kafka' (Beckford 2009). Human rights law aspires to universal human equality, despite its limitations, which chimes with Bishop Wharton's statement that 'as a Christian [...] I have the basic belief that every single human being is unique and precious'.

Campaigners also invoked human solidarity on a smaller scale. It is common for charities, particularly those who work with vulnerable and marginalised groups who are not necessarily viewed in a positive light by the general public, to use personal narratives to add persuasive value to their messages. Following this approach, stories of individual asylum seekers were invoked in all campaigning materials and TUC representatives were encouraged to invite refugees and asylum seekers to their meetings to talk about their experiences (Northern TUC and Regional Refugee Forum North East 2008). Personal narratives which appear in campaigning materials range from simple statements of circumstance: 'I am living on £41 a week for everything, which is very limiting and at times feels less than human' (STAR, n.d.-a); to more emotive narratives:

> but not being able to work is degrading to me. It is something that has been taken away from me, something that I believe is a right nobody should lose. This position is a crippled life. It's a degrading situation. You feel useless in a place that sings democracy.

Humanity was also used to suggest 'normality'. A number of asylum seeker quotes provided in campaign materials sought to persuade their audience that not only are asylum seekers deserving of basic human dignities, but also that they are 'normal people', with 'normal' hopes and aspirations. These ideas of 'normality' are a re-scripting of the dominant heteronormative frame: 'I hope our situation gets better and they let us work and let us get married. We are normal people, nothing different' (Iraqi asylum seeker Hartlepool, Northern TUC and Regional Refugee Forum North East 2008). Yet, as Darling (2014) has argued, it is the art of identification and the making politically visible that accrues through acts of citizenship that are the essence of their power. Indeed, making migrant experiences visible, and perceptible, is a common aim of activism in this field. Tyler and Marciniak (2013, 152) dub these approaches 'affective technologies of the "close up"' and their aim is explicitly to humanise migrant subjects and transform them into subjects who matter.

These enactments of human solidarity therefore problematize both legalistic and culturalist conceptions of citizenship and belonging. Yet, this campaign does not wholly overlook distinctions created by the stratified regime of rights; it challenges them in attempting to affect legislative change within the parameters of existing categories. Nevertheless, divisive legalistic conceptions of citizenship are troubled through mobile solidarities which create collective political subjects outside of the bounds of either a homogenising or an exclusionary discourse of subjecthood. Such collective mobilisations necessitate the blurring, even disavowal, of legally inscribed status labels, and as such entail creative acts of citizenship.

Conclusion

This article has discussed the 'Let them Work' campaign in order to demonstrate the ways in which the stratified regime of citizenship rights in the UK is contested from marginalised spaces. It has explored how such contestation troubles the exclusive privileges of citizenship by enacting mobile solidarities through acts of citizenship. The actions of the activists involved in the campaigns have bridged the divide between the domestic politics of work and the cosmopolitan ideals necessitated by mobile solidarities. In doing so, two conceptions of citizenship were drawn on: citizenship as a suite of rights which have to be struggled for, and citizenship as a liberal social project which asylum seekers are well placed to contribute to. The solidarities which are invoked in order to mobilise around more expansive conceptions of citizenship than the state presents are worker solidarity and human solidarity. Two quite distinct groups of activists mobilised around these differing solidarities, which reflect their differing world views and the discursive resources upon which they were able to draw.

Acts of citizenship, to paraphrase Isin (2008) produce citizens and their 'others' and the campaign discussed here sought to make 'others' less 'other'. Processes of exclusion are not accidental and clearly the designation of asylum seekers as a group who are 'other' in the UK is deeply entwined with longer histories of exclusion, not least colonialism (Mayblin 2014b). By looking at acts of citizenship, we draw attention to not only those exclusions, but also attempts to re-inscribe citizenship with new ideas of rights and belonging, to blur existing boundaries between citizens and non-citizens, and ultimately to dismantle established categories of entitlement. What we see, then, is the incorporation of asylum seekers into the worker frame, and the humanity frame, in order that the activists might resist the strategies and technologies of non-citizen exclusion.

Through LTW, activists rethought citizens and their 'others' – here non-citizen asylum seekers – but they also reproduced citizens and others. Legal categories were not ignored; the aim in this campaign was to draw attention to a more expansive understanding of the right to asylum. The central paradox that emerges here is that LTW has to utilise the existing script of 'good citizens' and 'failed citizens' (in Anderson's terms) to claim rights, but this strategy clearly bears the potential for creating further boundaries of exclusion. In other words, if you only demand more inclusion based on the existing script of the rightful 'worker citizen' then what other forms of marginalisation do you re-enact? As Tyler (2013, 146) has pointed out in another context, 'although these forms of legal and political advocacy are necessary, important, and can be effective, they inevitably reproduce the inclusive/exclusive logic of citizenship, which has been designed to fail specific groups and populations'.

If successful, asylum seekers become workers and so they are produced as citizens, or more citizen than before, through what Isin (2008) describes as acts of citizenship. But in the face of failure, the distinction produced by technologies of control between citizens and non-citizens continues. This burst of activism – an insurrectional moment in Balibar's (2012) terms – ended without a positive result. Denied the right to work and living with the consequences of this policy, asylum seekers in the UK today have not reaped the potential benefits, in terms of rights and material betterment, that the acts of citizenship articulated through mobile solidarities in LTW suggested were possible.

The campaigning work continues through, most prominently, the 'Still Human Still Here' campaign. If the acts of citizenship entailed within such activities continue to build solidarities which elide official distinctions between citizens and asylum seekers, then a transformational moment *may* come in the extending of the right to work. Whether successful or not, it is clear that asylum seekers' ambiguous position vis-à-vis citizenship rights will not go unnoticed, and that injustices in this sphere will continue to be challenged from marginal political spaces.

Note

1. The Refugee Council is the largest national charity working with and on behalf of refugees and asylum seekers in the UK. The TUC is an umbrella organisation for 54 different unions in the UK.

Acknowledgements

The author would also like to thank Joe Turner, Michael Farrelly and the anonymous reviewers for their helpful comments.

Disclosure statement

No potential conflict of interest was reported by the author.

Funding

This work was supported by the research grant from the ESRC [grant number ES/L011468/1].

References

Aitken, B. 2009. "Bishop Hits out at How We Treat Asylum Seekers." *Christian Newspaper*. December 12, 2009.

Anderson, B. 2013. *Us and Them? The Dangerous Politics of Immigration Control*. Oxford: Oxford University Press.

Balibar, E. 2012. "The 'Impossible' Community of the Citizens: Past and Present Problems." *Environment and Planning D: Society and Space* 30 (3): 437–449.

Beckford, M. 2009. "Church of England General Synod Calls Asylum Seeker Amnesty." *The Telegraph*. February 13, 2009.

Crawley, H. 2010. *Chance or Choice? Understanding why Asylum Seekers Come to the UK*. London: Refugee Council.

Darling, J. 2014. "Asylum and the Post-Political: Domopolitics, Depoliticisation and Acts of Citizenship." *Antipode* 46 (1): 72–91.

Dembour, M.-B., and T. Kelly. 2011. *Are Human Rights for Migrants? Critical Reflections on the Status of Irregular Migrants in Europe and the United States*. London: Routledge.

Doyle, L. 2009. *"I Hate Being Idle" Wasted Skills and Enforced Dependence among Zimbabwean Asylum Seekers in the UK*. London: The Refugee Council.

Dwyer, P. 2005. "Governance, Forced Migration and Welfare." *Social Policy and Administration* 39 (6): 622–639.

EDM. 2009. *960 Let Them Work, 2008/2009*.

EDM. 2010. *1103 Right to Work of Asylum Seekers, 2009/2010*.

European Commission. 2003. "Reception Conditions for Asylum-seekers." *Directive 2003/9/EC*. OJ 2003 L 31/18.

Foster, J. 2008. "Asylum Seekers Claim Right to Work." *Sunderland Echo*. June 22, 2008.

Hampshire, J. 2005. *Citizenship and Belonging: Immigration and the Politics of Demographic Governance in Postwar Britain*. Basingstoke: Palgrave Macmillan.

Home Office. 2010. *IA HO0017 Impact Assessment: Permission to Work for Asylum Seekers and Failed Asylum Seekers*. July 26, 2010.

Isin, E. F. 2008. "Theorizing Acts of Citizenship." In *Acts of Citizenship*, edited by E. F. Isin and G. M. Nielsen, 15–43. London: Palgrave Macmillan.

Isin, E. F., and B. S. Turner. 2007. "Investigating Citizenship: An Agenda for Citizenship Studies." *Citizenship Studies* 11 (1): 5–17.

Marfleet, P. 2006. *Refugees in a Global Era*. Basingstoke: Palgrave Macmillan.

Marshall, T. H. 1950. *Citizenship and Social Class*. Cambridge: Cambridge University Press.

Mayblin, L. 2014a. "Asylum, Welfare and Work: Reflections on Research in Asylum and Refugee Studies." *International Journal of Sociology and Social Policy* 34 (5/6): 375–391.

Mayblin, L. 2014b. "Colonialism, Decolonisation, and the Right to Be Human: Britain and the 1951 Geneva Convention on the Status of Refugees." *Journal of Historical Sociology* 27 (3): 423–441.

McNevin, A. 2006. "Political Belonging in a Neoliberal Era: The Struggle of the Sans-papiers." *Citizenship Studies* 10 (2): 135–151.

Middleton, D. 2005. "Why Asylum Seekers Seek Refuge in Particular Destination Countries: An Exploration of Key Determinants." Global Migration Perspectives Working Paper 34. Geneva, GCIM.

Morris, L. 2002. "Britain's Asylum, and Immigration Regime: The Shifting Contours of Rights." *Journal of Ethnic and Migration Studies* 28 (3): 409–425.

Morris, L. 2009. "Asylum, Welfare and Civil Society: A Case Study in Civil Repair." *Citizenship Studies* 13 (4): 365–379.

Morris, L. 2012. "Rights, Recognition and Judgment: Reflections on the Case of Welfare and Asylum." *The British Journal of Politics and International Relations* 14 (1): 39–56.

Northern TUC and Regional Refugee Forum North East. 2008. *Rights for all (Leaflet)*.

Nyers, P. 2010. "No One is Illegal between City and Nation." *Studies in Social Justice* 4 (2): 127–143.

Refugee Council. 2008. TUC Black Workers Conference 2008, Donna Covey: Chief Executive, Refugee Council (Speech), Eastbourne, April 2008.

Regional Refugee Forum North East. 2008. *Let Them Work (Leaflet)*.

Rigby, J., and R. Schlembach. 2013. "Impossible Protest: Noborders in Calais." *Citizenship Studies* 17 (2): 157–172.

Sales, R. 2002. "The Deserving and the Undeserving? Refugees, Asylum Seekers and Welfare in Britain." *Critical Social Policy* 22 (3): 456–478.

Squire, V. 2009. *The Exclusionary Politics of Asylum*. Basingstoke: Palgrave Macmillan.

Squire, V. 2011. "From Community Cohesion to Mobile Solidarities: The *City of Sanctuary* Network and the *Strangers into Citizens* Campaign." *Political Studies* 59 (2): 290–307.

Squire, V., and J. Darling. 2013. "The 'Minor' Politics of Rightful Presence: Justice and Relationality in City of Sanctuary." *International Political Sociology* 7 (1): 59–74.

STAR. n.d.-a. *Let Them Work: The Campaign for the Right to Work for Asylum Seekers (Leaflet)*.

STAR. n.d.-b. *STAR Info: The Right to Work for Asylum Seekers*.

Summers, D. 2009. "Brown Stands by British Jobs for British Workers Remark." *The Guardian*. January 30, 2009.

TUC. 2007. *Hard Work*. Hidden Lives: The Short Report of the Commission on Vulnerable Employment.

TUC. 2008. "'Let Them Work' Campaign Launch Speech, Brendan Barber, the TUC General Secretary." Eastbourne, April 2008.

Tyler, I. 2010. "Designed to Fail: A Biopolitics of British Citizenship." *Citizenship Studies* 14 (1): 61–74.

Tyler, I., and K. Marciniak. 2013. "Immigrant Protest: An Introduction." *Citizenship Studies* 17 (2): 143–156.

UKBA. 2013. "Tier 2 Shortage Occupation List." Accessed October 25, 2013. www.ukba.homeoffice. gov.uk/sitecontent/documents/workingintheuk/shortageoccupationlistnov11.pdf

Governing the domestic space of the traveller in the UK: 'family', 'home' and the struggle over Dale Farm

Joe Turner

Department of Politics, University of Sheffield, Sheffield, UK

ABSTRACT

This article contends that domesticity and processes of domestication maintain a central role in the (re)production of British citizenship. Domesticity provides a template for living that shapes the raced, classed, gendered and sexed boundaries of Britishness. Drawing upon William Walters' concept of 'domopolitics', the article specifically explores how norms of familial domesticity are used in the marginalisation and regulation of Traveller groups in the UK. Focussing on the eviction of Irish Travellers from the Dale Farm site in Essex, 2011, the article argues that the eviction relied upon the historical mobilisation of Travellers as 'failing' norms of domesticity. However, whilst the destruction of 'home' (domicide) at Dale Farm represented a form of domestication that is enacted in the name of the 'true' domos or the home of the citizen, this did not go unchallenged. The struggle and resistance to the state-led eviction at Dale Farm unsettled the boundaries of contemporary domopolitics by providing alternative claims to belonging and 'home'. By examining the politics of domesticity in the production of marginality, we see how family and home not only act as means of stratifying and governing subjects but also emerge as sites of contestation.

Introduction

In October 2011, the UK high court approved the eviction of 83 Irish Traveller families from the Dale Farm site in Basildon, Essex. In her account of the eviction, Imogen Tyler describes how the 'Essex police, in full riot gear, employed taser guns, a battering ram, iron bars, batons, sledgehammers and shields to enter the site' (2013, 1). For those present post-eviction, Dale Farm was described as an abject space: 'a place of muddied remains and scars'; 'on par with an asylum seeker-centre, a prison or wind turbine' (Barkham 2011). The authorities' *legal* justification for the removal of nearly 500 hundred people from the long-established site was based on the failure of a planning application – a civil rather than criminal violation. Whilst evictions have emerged as a contemporary technique for regulating both the settlement and mobility of Traveller communities (Kabachnik 2012; Vanderbeck 2005), what is significant about Dale Farm is both the scale and level of violence enacted by the state (and its proxies) in the act of eviction but also the extent of its contestation by protest groups, activists and residents. Over the course of the build-up to the eviction, protests amassed on the site in solidarity with the residents, constructing barricades to protect caravans and articulating a counter-narrative to the representation of Dale Farm in the British tabloid Press which sought to describe the site as a place of illegality, squalor and disorder.

Whilst the eviction was legally justified by the sites encroachment on London's 'green belt' (the land was actually formerly a scrapyard), the rationale for the eviction also hinged on the historic representation of Travellers as 'troubling' the order of set-tled communities through their familial and social difference (Ciaschi, forthcoming; Hellenier 2003; Sibley 1981). During the eviction, there was a mobilisation of images of Travellers as anti-citizens, welfare scroungers, present social dangers. They were represented through tropes of criminality, dirt and a fixation on the caravan as an improper form of 'home' (also see Vanderbeck 2005). Just as the authorities sought to actively destroy the homes that Travellers had built at Dale Farm, the eviction relied on the (unfulfilled) promise that families could be 're-housed' in council properties. This reflects a key aspect of the modern push to regulate Traveller mobility and settlement (Kabachnik 2012). What was prevalent in the events surrounding the eviction was how domesticity became a means of both explaining the 'problem' of Traveller lifestyles and providing a set of solutions to it. 'Home', 'family', 'belonging' all became central concerns around which the struggle for Dale Farm was articulated and fought.

What I argue in this article is that Dale Farm and the regulation of Traveller groups more widely provide us with a vital insight into the contemporary politics of 'home' in the UK, a politics which is premised on a fundamental relationship between domesticity, family and citizenship. Drawing on Walters (2004) work on 'domopolitics', I set out how domesticity and domestication have formed a central part of the architecture of (post)colonial citizenship in the UK. This reveals how an imaginary of familial domesticity stratifies marginal groups (such as Travellers) from the national 'home' – and relies on certain raced, classed, gendered and sexualised co-ordinates to do so. I then explore how the policing of Travellers through anxiety over failed domesticity was actively contested in the acts of protests over the Dale Farm evictions. Whilst domesticity and family have been used as ordering principles in Britain, I suggest that they also provide sites through which the dominant logic of home citizenship can be challenged. In the case of Dale Farm, the counter-narrative of 'home' provided by the protests worked to refuse the existing codes of sedentary citizenship and the violent process of domestication enacted in its name. This explores how marginality is configured through norms of domesticity but equally the political struggles over home and family life that this also engenders.

As I have begun describing, the home or 'domos' provides a historically contingent assemblage between intimacy, territory, belonging and the state which is frequently drawn upon in the production and regulation of marginal groups. As Walters (2004) argues, what is powerful about the emotional imagery of home is that has come to refer to norms of the inti-mate, private, familial domestic space in the same instance that it enacts a sense of belonging to the nation-state, domestic sovereignty and the 'homlie' nation (also see Darling 2014). Whilst domesticity relates to a series of historical, spatial, cultural and economic practices (LeBaron 2010; McKeon 2005), it is also formulated through a specific relationship to a model of family life – with the 'white', heteronormative and gendered ideals this also relies upon. Domesticity and the familial are thus wrapped up together in the symbolic order of home. From the late nineteenth century, a vision of home or homliness has frequently played a role in the configuration of national belonging (McClintock 1993; Yuval-Davis 1996), just as modes of family life, moral behaviours, habitation and reproduction are upheld as the active responsibilities/expectations of *citizens* (Turner 2008). Through this assemblage, the emotional image of familial intimacy has been mobilised in the regulation of subjects who appear to reject, deny or fail the ideals of 'family life'. Travellers' and 'Gypsies[1] have been viewed as social problems, especially throughout the twentieth century, because they present the wrong type of 'home' and 'household'. This has explicitly referenced (ir)regular mobility, nomadism, caravans, black market labour, criminality, cultural rituals. The manner in which Travellers are marginalised connects them to the historical treatment of other problem groups who are viewed as 'not belonging' because they appear to 'fail' the contingent norms of familial domesticity i.e. migrant families, colonial subjects, the 'underclass', vagabonds, homosexuals. In the case of Travellers such as those at Dale Farm, the 'failure' to follow the cultural script of 'bricks and mortar' home has led to multiple strategies of regulation, from welfare, education policy, policing methods, enforced mobility, containment and equally forms of 'domicide'; the violent destruction of home.

This article contributes to debates in citizenship studies concerning the politics of family (Turner 2008; Yuval-Davis 1996), intimacy and reproduction (Hanafin 2013) by exploring how domesticity provides both a normative arrangement for forms of social control and marginalisation but also a distinct site of political struggle through which different modes of belonging are disrupted and claimed. What previous studies have tended to focus on is the capacity for the diagram of family domesticity to act as an oppressive institution (Poster 1978; Thorne 1992) or ideology (Card 1996). Those scholars studying the relations between domesticity, family (Turner 2008), natality (Roseneil et al. 2013; Yuval-Davis 1996), reproduction (Halsaa, Roseneil, and Sümer 2012; Lee 2008) and citizenship have also tended to stress the exclusory nature of this relationship. The fetishisation of the family as the ultimate social and political 'unit' is viewed as providing the conditions for the denial of political, cultural social rights: through norms of gender (Fraser 2009; Orloff 1993; Walby 1994), sexuality (Evans 1993; Richardson 2000; Roseneil et al. 2013; Weeks 1998), class (Bertone 2013) and race (Lewis 2000; Stoler 1997). To certain Feminist-Marxists, the quest for emancipation hinges on the active rejection of family life, domestic arrangements, marriage and motherhood (see Card 1996). Whilst post-Marxist accounts have attempted to reveal the complex tension between the desire for family intimacy and oppression (Barrett and McIntosh 1982), studies which appreciate how family also acts as a site for disruption, resistance and alternative claims to citizenship remain underdeveloped (see Hanafin 2013). Speaking to the special issue theme, the article explores how citizenship works as ambivalent process – even in the marginalisation of certain 'others' from regimes of British citizenship, there emerges new political possibilities, resistance, denial. The contemporary politics of 'home' reveals how familial domesticity works as a site through which the boundaries of citizenship are reconstituted and also interrupted (Isin 2008, 20). Exploring the marginalisation of Travellers provides a significant case for the themes of this special issue, precisely because Travellers in the UK are often formal citizens but normative, cultural and legal codes of citizenship persist to differentiate their way of life as problematic.

Domesticity, family and citizenship

The mobilisation of familial domesticity is not new; running through modern nationalism are norms of heteronormativity (Evans 1993; Hanafin 2013; Levine 2006), reproduction (Roseneil et al. 2013; Turner 2008) and home-making (Baxter and Brickell 2014; Porteous and Smith 2001). The nation has been historically imagined through appeals to the familial (Yuval-Davis 1996). Kinship, intimacy, blood-ties, fertility are used as imaginaries of the cohesive nation (McClintock 1993); just as masculine sovereignty is tied to the protection of the 'motherland', the sanctuary of the hearth, the innocence and vulnerability of maternity and child rearing (Dowler 2012; Rofel 2002, 185–186). Exploring the metaphorical connections of domesticity and the nation is vital but it is also important to recognise the relationship between domesticity and social control.

A reading of Walter's approach to 'domopolitics' (2004) provides a way to navigate this terrain. To Walters what defines contemporary liberal regimes of government and social ordering (security) is how the state is governed as a 'home' or 'domos'. The relationship between citizen, community and state is configured through a diagram of home which emphasises the nation as a domestic(ated) space of intimacy, emotional ties and familiarity (Darling 2008). This relies on a particular historical depiction of home as: family, sanctuary, land and place; a depiction that calls upon an unquestionable/ commensensical desire or 'will to domesticate the force which threaten the sanctity of home' (Walters 2004, 242). The form of social ordering linked to the domos produces strategies which filter, classify and monitor subjects through their imbrications, ties and familial connections to an imaginary of home, and/or their disturbance of it. Thus regulating 'circulations of "good" and "bad"' (Darling 2008, 265) means monitoring and fostering the correct morals, behaviours, forms of intimacy, social relations that could emerge in the 'family home'.

Domestication

The relationship between domopolitics and family is defined by two interlinking processes – one concerns a mode of domestication (Darling 2008, 264), the other concerns the relationship between reproduction and domesticity (McClintock 1995, 42; Stoler 1997). The emergence of a western bourgeois model of family 'home' in the eighteenth and nineteenth century has been well documented (Hareven 1991; LeBaron 2010; McKeon 2005; Rose 1990). Home was configured as the site of family life, a private space of inner sanctuary, leisure, consumption (McKeon 2005, 101). Whilst feminist scholar has long problematised this persistent ideal (Anderson 2000; Beechley 1977), what is important for this study is how the 'cult of domesticity' (McClintock 1995, 35) has been central to the management of subjects and groups who exist in tension with this social formation. The bourgeois household evolved through the integration of different groups into its gendered and class arrangements (domestic work, cleaners, nannies); however, throughout the nineteenth century, this model of domesticity was increasingly imposed upon and used to manage certain 'undomesticated' groups: the street poor (Donzelot 1980), vagabonds (Dean 1991), elements of the working class (Rose 1990; Steedman 2007, 221–224), Amerindians (Kotef 2015, 102–103), 'colonised' subjects (Amadiume 1987, 121–123) and Irish Travellers or Gypsies (Hellenier 2003). McClintock's (1995) seminal work *Imperial Leather* highlights the centrality of domesticity and *domestication* to British colonialism and the knowledge(s) and practice(s) of gender, race and class. As McClintock (1995, 35) argues:

> Through rituals of domesticity, increasingly global and more often than not violent, animals, women and colonized peoples were wrestled from their putatively 'natural' yet, ironically, 'unreasonable' state of 'savagery' and inducted through the domestic progress narrative into hierarchal relation to white men.

Thus domestication the promotion of domesticity across a territory and across a population is inherently tied to the 'conquest, taming and subduing' of different 'uncivilised' groups who 'fail' familial domesticity (also see Amadiume 1987, 119, 121–125). Reading Walters work through these histories means recognising how domopolitics mobilises a certain (post)colonial arrangement of familial domesticity and a certain conception of sedentary or 'domestic' citizenship. Whilst dominant modes of familial domesticity are imagined through claims to universal inner sanctuary and privacy, these are always etched with a certain ethnocentric, bourgeois and colonising logic. In the case of the regulation of problematic populations within Britain, we can still read this as part of a colonial project or what Foucault termed an expansion of 'internal colonialism' (Foucault 2004).

Reproduction

Domopolitics works to foster the domestic space (both national and private) of the citizen. What is absent in Walters' original analysis, is how domopolitics relates to an ideal of family life and questions of reproduction. Drawing upon the recent turn towards reproduction, sexuality and intimacy in citizenship studies (Halsaa, Roseneil, and Sümer 2012; Roseneil et al. 2013; Turner 2008; but also Stoler 2002), it is possible to suggest that what is ultimately at stake in the regulation of domesticity is the moral and biological (re)production of subjects who may be citizens. Reproduction and citizenship presents a complex assemblage. Social recognition, rights and reproduction are tied together: on one hand, rights and social legitimacy are accorded through the expectations to fulfil the heteronormative ideals of 'family life' (tax breaks, healthcare, education); on the other hand, as formal citizenship is often inherited, the family as a site of reproduction becomes targeted by fears over 'who' will have access to rights (see Tyler 2010). Racist ideologies are thus very carefully woven into questions of sexuality; anxiety over the 'health', characteristics and composition of the political community is manifest in this site of reproduction (Young 1995). To Roseneil et al. (2013, 901), this means we have to recognise:

> The biological, sexual and technological realities of natality, and the social realities of the intimate intergenerational material and affective labour that is generative of citizens, and that serve to reproduce membership of, and belonging to, states, nations, societies and, thus of 'citizenship' itself.

Recent studies of reproductive citizenship (Bertone 2013; Halsaa, Roseneil, and Sümer 2012) have focussed on how norms of reproduction problematise 'non-procreative' groups (homosexuals, transgender, single people, the infertile). However, by exploring how domopolitics works to marginalise Travellers, this recognises how the modern British state has been concerned with promoting the reproduction of certain groups, whilst simultaneously intervening in the reproduction of others. Recognising that domesticity has moral, classed as well as sexed, raced and gendered components means we need to see the monitoring of domesticity along a broad continuum through which the social and political status of multiple subjects and groups is both made possible and denied. In the context of (post)colonial Britain, subjects can emerge as 'different' by failing norms of family domesticity (the 'problem' families, homosexuals, Traveller groups); equally, 'difference' becomes disturbing precisely because it is reproduced in the site of the family (again Traveller families, migrant-families, mixed–raced couples, the intergenerational 'workless'). This creates demarcations over who has access to state protection and resources which equally complicates the distinction between citizen/ non-citizen. This is because, as with the case with 'failed citizens' such as Traveller and the 'workless', states seek to actively manage such problem groups even though they have formal access to rights (see Anderson 2013).

Having set out some of the historical and conceptual links between domesticity, family and citizenship, I now turn to how the marginalisation of Traveller provide one manifestation of the will to *domesticate*. After providing some historical context surrounding the emergence of a governmental focus on domesticity, I explore some of the strategies that have targeted Travellers in the UK. This recognises that the regulation of Travellers is racialised but this works through the mobilisation of class, gender and sexuality. In Britain, the contemporary neoliberal mobilisation of 'home' (the dwelling of the citizen) is presented as both a space of sanctuary and productivity, which corresponds to a certain composition of fixed territory, intimacy and belonging. This is symbolised in the 'bricks and mortar' family home or the abode of the 'working family'. By looking at practices which target Travellers, I argue that there is a constant fixation on Travellers as failing this particular domestic order. That is by living in unsuitable conditions, the use of land, a fixation on hygiene, household governance, child rearing. Whilst Travellers are marginalised through strategies of forced mobility (such as eviction), containment and settlement, the target of these practices is arguably a push towards domestication – fostering the rhythms of a sedentary, 'bricks and mortar' home, or a denial of 'improper' domesticity. As with other historical examples of failed domesticity (problem families, 'welfare scroungers', migrants families), what authorities are often anxious about is the (re)production of certain forms of difference in the family 'home'.

This history of marginalisation is important to detail because it also helps us recognise how political struggles also emerge. The last section of the article explores the evictions/ protests which occurred at Dale Farm in more detail. Whilst the activism to protect large parts of the caravan site were ultimately unsuccessful, it offers insights into the presence of counter-claims to domesticity and family life and the complex threads of resistance within contemporary domopolitics. The protest formed temporary solidarities which were not only orientated towards existing 'rights' claims but focussed on contesting the destruction of alternative form of family life and home.

Travellers, 'problem families' and domopolitics

The events surrounding Dale Farm in 2011 hold a significant place in the recent history of neo-liberal Britain. The eviction has been heralded as the largest mass eviction by the British state. It is also revealing of the UK authorities' human rights record towards Traveller communities, who constitute one of the most discriminated ethnic minority group in the UK (Hellenier 2003; Tyler, 2013, 133). However, the event mirrors other evictions of Traveller sites and other unwanted 'neighbours' which have taken place in recent years (Flint 2004).

Equally, the practice of eviction itself relies on a longer history of discrimination which works to make Travellers 'evictable', alongside a string of regulatory strategies which have intensified the regulation of Travellers since the 1960s. By exploring these links, we can see that whilst the regulation of Travallers is historically specific, the focus on 'improper' domestic arrangements which is used to define Travellers parallels the treatment of other 'problem groups' such as migrants and different renderings of the 'underclass' or 'workless' poor.

Estimates put the 'nomadic' population of Britain between 45 and 100,000. This reflects the problematic nature of defining 'nomadism' along with the varied composition of different groups who have been identified or identify as 'Traveller' or 'Gypsy'. Some individuals and groups travel occasionally or throughout the year, others choose to live in a caravan rather than a 'bricks and mortar house', others have settled (or have been settled) into more sedentary housing arrangements. In Britain, nomadic or semi-nomadic ways of life have been increasingly controlled post-World War Two but equally so has the conditions for living semi/permanently in a caravan (Kabanchnik 2012, 212). Planning legislation, policing practices, environmental policy have all amassed to limit the stopping places for caravans, this is paralleled by campaigns to domesticate certain groups into the cultural practices and physical spaces of the 'settled community' (Greenfields and Smith 2010). Since 1994, the most pervasive measure to deal with semi/permanent Traveller sites has been eviction; after the 2010 Decentralisation and Localism Act, the legal aspects of eviction were strengthened making it easier for the local councils to deny planning applications and bolstering police and private security services to destroy 'illegal' dwellings (Ciaschi, forthcoming). So whilst state practices have also increasingly attempted to the assimilate Traveller and Gypsy groups in to sedentary life, this is paralleled with the criminalisation of caravan sites and stopping places thus enforcing movement. As one Dale Farm resident declared in frustration, revealing the ambiguity and misconception of the label of Traveller: 'People say we are Travellers and we should travel but the world is changing, our kids need to go to school. They keep pushing us on the road, but where does the road end?' (Topping 2011).

Whilst a body of critical scholarship has argued that modern states control 'nomadism' through a will to monitor mobility (see Basaran 2008; Deleuze and Guttarri 1987; Friese and Mezzadra 2010, 302; Kotef 2015; Procacci 1991), Kabachnik suggests that Travellers are problematised through their perceived inferior emotional attachment to, and 'civilised' use of, place (2012, 222). Under contemporary domopolitics, Travellers are often represented as threatening because of how they 'impact' on a place. Racist tropes of pollution, animalism, degeneracy, criminality and invasion are often used to *reveal* the absence of domesticity, care and civility towards both land and household (Kotef 2015, 104).

Domesticity, social control and citizenship

To understand the relationship between domesticity and Traveller marginality, it is worth considering how domesticity emerged as a target of government practice, its connection to the ideals of family and citizenship. As I have noted, to McClintock (1995), the management of domesticity and intimacy was central to how colonial authorities produced and sustained racial claims to European superiority in the late nineteenth century. A particular configuration of white, bourgeois family life became defining of the 'European self' (see Mills 2005; Stoler 2002; Turner 2014). This draws upon the imagined failed domesticity of other social groups. Across the British Empire in the early twentieth century, loose family structures, lack of formal lodgings, uncleanliness were all used as examples of social and moral failure of the colonised and lower classes. In Britain especially, welfare authorities began to target the domestic arrangements of the poor specifically because they saw this as the way of improving the 'stock' of the British race (see Soloway 1990). As Stoler (2002, 200) argues:

> At the turn of the century, in both metropole and colony, the liberal impulse for social welfare, representation and protective legislation focussed enormous energy on the preparatory environment for civic responsibility: on domestic arrangements, sexual morality, parenting, and more specifically on the moral milieu of home and school in which children lived.

This focus on domesticity was justified by both progressive and conservative reforms alike (Cruikshank 1998, 54). The nuclear family household was presented as *the* site for proper and necessary socialisation of children who would be British citizens (Rose 1990). Thus, expanding welfare provisions were focussed on fostering and promoting the domestic arrangements of bourgeois households, especially onto the poor but later on commonwealth citizens, migrants and Travellers (Lewis 2000; Stoler 1997; Welshman 1996). A central feature of this push towards domestication was the discovery of 'problem families' who failed to conform to the domestic ideals of the white, middle-class family and were 'held back' by their inability to govern their households. As Welshman argues, they were defined by 'their inability to benefit from education, by the dirt and chaos of their homes, and the high number of children' (Welshman 1996). Through such a script, we can see how the raced and classed borders of true 'Britishness' were in part constituted and played out through representations of failed familial domesticity: errant fathers, overcrowded housing, poor hygiene, chaotic lives of the poor and 'non-whites' (Webster 1998).

Amidst the persistence focus on domesticity as a mode of belonging, authorities in the mid-twentieth century became increasingly concerned with the 'living conditions' of Traveller settlements as well as the economic relations and forms of governance apparent in Traveller families. This formed as part of the wider dynamics of domestic welfarism but took on its own unique trajectory. Authorities anxious about Travellers modes of domesticity frequently focussed on the caravan as a form of failed household, in need of active governmental intervention. For instance, in the 1960s, authorities began a programme for the formalisation of traveller sites to be provided by Local Councils in England. As Sibley argues, such sites where specifically designed to create an architecture of Traveller life in keeping with the rhythms, rituals and spatial order associated with sedentary domesticity (Sibley 1981, 26). In the contemporary discourse on Travellers, in both governmental and media accounts, the Traveller caravan, the stopping place, the semi-permanent site are persistently cast as spaces of disorder: defined by dirt, litter, poor sanitation – foremost lacking the proper practices and domestic rituals of cleanliness, order and household governance (Sibley 1981, 31). Judith Okely (Okely and Houtman 2011, 26) discusses in her ethnographic work with Travellers how local councils and officials have been historically obsessed with an imagined lack of hygiene at Traveller sites, fixating on the (lack of) provision of bathing facilities over any other amenity. Traveller children in particular are the target of this obsession with dirt, often depicted as grubby, unkept, or in a feral state (Okely 2014) – thus both constituted as victims and sites of future social anxiety (Image 1).

Image 1. 'Gypsies and other Travellers': Ministry of Housing and Local Government report 1967.

This focus on dirt is significant in the regulation of Travellers. Following Douglas (2002, 41) if cleanliness is the defining feature of order, care and correct use of place, then dirt corrupts and pollutes. This symbolic register is apparent when Travellers are treated as an 'invasive' presence; 'polluting' a place and threatening its true inhabitants (settled citizens) thus demanding government intervention to be moved on, evicted – thus preventing contamination (Kabachnik 2010). The failure to live up to imaginaries of hygiene and order was central to the constitution of Dale Farm residents as 'evictable'. In the lead up to the eviction of Dale Farm, the Secretary of State for Communities and Local Government (2011) talked of how Travellers were being allowed to encroach on London's green belt, which is often depicted as a rural idyll of 'middle England' – the heart of the British domos (Bhopal and Myers 2008, 150–153). In the 2005 run up to the general election, *The Sun* newspaper ran a prominent campaign called 'Stamp out the Camps' which called upon the government to evict Traveller sites without initial planning permission. The iconography of the campaign was significant, focusing on Dale Farm as the 'largest Gypsy camp in Europe' the paper utilised blurry images of young Traveller men standing round camp fires, roaming dogs, rubbish strewn pitches, as telescopic lenses focused on residents at a 'animal photographer' distance. Tyler (2013) suggests that the campaigns significance was how it was taken up by elites in the Conservative Party; the promise to 'control' Travellers access to land was central to Michael Howard's election pledge and influenced the Conservative-Liberal coalition position in 2011. For *The Sun* (2005), 'Gipsies' presented a form of intolerable 'lawlessness', dirt and filth which carefully recoded racism through the prism of domesticity. It argued that: 'Communities do not want people setting up illegal sites in their midst because the camps are dirty, cluttered, insanitary and an eyesore.' Dale Farm was 'a squalid eyesore – blighting the lives of villagers … each morning gallons of sewage over flows into the roads. Stray dogs roam in packs feasting on rats in the makeshift estate' (cited in Tyler 2013, 136).

Domesticity and cleanliness frequently function to stratifying Travellers as failed families and thus failed citizens who needed to be regulated for the good of the domos (the 'villages', 'tax payers' and 'communities' who belong). This also links to questions of economic productivity. In similar ways that the late Victorian cult of domesticity focused on economic relations of the nuclear family, in neo-liberal Britain, the normative claim to citizenship is often presented through the ideal of the 'working family'. This Fetishisation polices numerous swathes of social life from the access to welfare benefits, the criminal justice system (Waquant 2009), visa applications (Turner 2014) and the naturalisation process. Whilst Dale Farm was presented as a place of squalor and chaos in the lead up to the eviction, this was equally linked to further moralising questions of dependency, of 'feckless' and 'idle' individuals (Fairbairn and Snell 2011; O'Shea 2011). As with historical representations of the problem family and underclass, 'primitivism' and backwardness were revealed by an apparent absence of wage labour. The moral failure to care for *place* (dirt, trash, chaos) was paralleled to a lack of work ethic and the historical link with Travellers surviving through the black economy and petty crime (Okely 2014). As the patriarchal management of home is composed around and in relation to the responsibility of 'hardworking' and breadwinning parents, the symbolic economy of the caravan appears to deny these norms of proper domesticity. It is cast as beyond the norms of the liberal relationship between ownership, property and production (Kotef 2015). Travellers are thus made evictable through failing the responsibilities of the 'good', 'working' and property owning citizen (Garrett 2007).

The representation of Travellers as failing to live by proper domestic codes is keenly highlighted in authorities' focus on children as the bearers and victims of Traveller life. Mobility is often narrated as problematic because it disturbs the 'natural' and healthy rhythms of family life and child rearing. So are the spatial and domestic arrangements of living in a caravan. The 'deviant' lifestyles of Travellers have sometimes lead to state social service intervening and removing children from their parents (Vanderbeck 2005, 78). Education policy similarly reflects an anxiety surrounding Traveller children who are frequently treated as 'victims' in need of saving (Vanderbeck 2005, 79). In this context, school is often treated as an opportunity to socialise Traveller children into 'mainstream society' (Sibley 1981, 41–42) – just as settlement in a 'bricks and mortar' house is viewed as in the 'interest of children'. When Traveller parents refuse to send their children to school, this is frequently presented as a sign of incivility rather than resistance to cultural assimilation (Kabanichnik 2010, 220). As Vanderbeck (2005, 73) argues, 'child rights discourses are often employed to construct Traveller parents as obstacles to their children's development and well-being and thus serve to legitimize various forms of state intervention.' The mainstream discourse of 'child rights' does this whilst equally silencing the damaging effects that institutional racism, forced mobility, evictions and coercive settlement practices have on children (Greenfields and Smith 2010; Tyler 2013, 128). Casting Travellers as failed parents is equally tied to anxiety over the risk that problem children pose to future society order through: anti-social behaviour, crime, delinquency – all at the cost to the 'public purse' (Gardener 2008, 59). In the absence of proper domesticity, schooling is viewed as the last hope for future social order (Cabinet Office 2008). This is because as Gardener (2008, 59) argues:

> Not only is problem behaviour stable across the life course, it also affects the next generation. There is compelling evidence from intergenerational studies showing that problem behaviour is one of the key ways in which disadvantage is transmitted across generations.

Disadvantage here is addressed as a moral question that is passed on and learnt through family structures and socialised through the child's intimate environment (also see Foster and Cemlyn 2012).

The targeting and representation of Traveller children (as both victims and threats) illustrates how anxiety around reproduction is re-assembled in the contemporary domestication of Travellers. Contemporary liberal policy still treats the Traveller family as the site of social reproduction which can create the conditions for 'intergenerational disadvantage', linked through lack of wage labour and hygiene (Cameron 2011). This is revealed again in the prioritisation of Traveller families to be housed in council properties. Akin to other policies which have historically restricted the possibility of reproduction, the Traveller family remains a site for the transference of morality, behaviours and culture (which again are linked to the environment of the caravan). Through the persistent representation of dirt, poverty, informal work is viewed as culturally determined, rather than seen in terms of Traveller group's marginal position in regards to, say, the structures of late capitalism or the active destitution brought about by historical state policy. The anxiety surrounding Traveller difference and strangeness is found in their proximity and intimacy to those 'citizens' they are said to threaten; articulated through a concern regarding 'un-neighborliness' and invasion (see Fortier 2007). Marking out Travellers through their failed domesticity articulates their otherness through a link to both private and national conceptions of home. Viewed through the lens of contemporary domopolitics and the wider history of domesticity, events such as Dale Farm can be seen as acts of violent domestication which herald both the return of *place* to proper domesticity and care (the green belt, the protection of the property and rights of citizens), whilst guiding Travellers towards sedentary forms of spatial and cultural practice through the removal of alternatives.

Protesting the eviction

The events at Dale Farm are remarkable in terms of the activation of state violence, of which they form part of a much longer history, but the protests against eviction are equally significant in terms of their performance of activism (Isin 2008). Dale Farm was rendered a space of incivility by the authorities, removed from the dominant familial and domestic conceptions of British citizenship (relating to my analysis above). However, this was directly challenged by the protests against eviction. I argue that the protestor's counter-narrative reveal the multiplicities of claims over 'home' which disturb the rigid understanding of domesticity and family life. If ultimately unsuccessful in stopping the evictions, these 'acts' opened up space for the contestation over a more ambiguous form of citizenship (Ní Mhurchú 2014).

Under the label of 'Dale Farm Solidarity', protesters from both within the Traveller and settled communities descended on the site throughout October 2011 to show support for those threatened with eviction. Significantly, non-resident activists were drawn from organisations such as No-borders which linked the Travellers predicament to other struggles over 'home' and belonging at various border sites. As part of the emergence of what activists would call 'Camp Constant' protestors and residents erected extensive barricades against the private bailiff company who, under the protection of the police, intended to seize the site. Importantly, what the protest relied upon was the construction of a powerful counter-narrative, made possible through an online media presence (see https://dalefarm. wordpress.com/), which disturbed claims that Dale Farm represented failed domesticity. In the same way that the authorities relied on a vision of illegality and disorder, the counter-narrative relied on central appeals to the history of the Dale Farm site: the caravans and the relationships constructed over a 10-year period as a different rendering of home and belonging. This described family as a space of extended communal affiliations, of the warmth and close-knit ties that transcended the ideal of an autonomous family household. Denying the co-ordinates of the 'working/wage labour family', this activated a claim to home which was described as networked through trust. As one resident put it: 'This is a safe community. When my baby gets bigger I'll know that if he goes outside someone will bring him back'. Kathleen McCarthy, a resident and campaigner speaking to the *Guardian* Newspaper described the eviction notice in similar terms – ending the possibility of networked affiliations of family life:

> My whole family is here, and just about everyone here is family. There's my children, grandchildren, my sisters and brothers, my mother, my aunts, my uncles. How can we all live together again? Would they do this to any other group of people? Any other community wouldn't be treated the way we are being treated (Walker and Barkham 2011).

The claim that 'just about everyone here is family', posits a different conception of the boundaries of family than the norm of contemporary rule. It performs different codes of affiliation and solidarity which work in a different register of space and intimacy. Such a discourse relied on a central tension; between upholding a heteronormative and gendered narrative of familial relations, whilst rejecting claims of the 'bricks and mortar' diagram of home. What vexed so many observers of Dale Farm was that whilst upholding an indentification to forms of nomadism, the residents protested *being moved*, as Leo McKinistry commented in the *Daily Express* 'if they are travellers, then they should travel'. Whilst this shows a blatant disregard of historical and often violent re-appropriation of land, practices of enclosure and legal restrictions on temporary stopping places, it actively misconceives the claim of Travellers to multiple sites of occupancy and to multiple spaces of cultural and social significance (which *could* be called 'home'). Significant, those resisting eviction did not purely make a claim to Dale Farm through the territorial links of ownership/private property definitive of liberal citizenship but instead because eviction represented the state sanctioned death of Traveller life itself – because there was 'nowhere to go'. The spaces and possibility of traveller life was being enclosed and destroyed. It represents a form of what Porteous and Smith (2001) call 'domicide'. Barkham (2011) described this effect:

> Life in a house is a claustrophobic prospect when all you have known is a caravan. The children sleep at one end, their parents at the other; everyone worries they won't be able to sleep in bedrooms. More importantly, the plots allow the Travellers to live in extended families. Everyone feels safe. The children bounce between aunties and grandparents, roaming free, playing among friends; their mothers knowing that they are among friends and someone is looking out for them.

The utilisation of the narrative of family, security and paternal care not only appealed to the existing register of (gendered) family life and citizenship (which the Travellers were described as 'outside' of) but in doing this opened up space to embolden resistance to the eviction. However, it is important to note how this networked deployment of family and community emerged precisely *because* the Traveller's site was rendered as an abject failure of home and domesticity. In doing so, the domopolitics provided both the scope and the possibility of resistance. Tellingly, the acts of counter-narrative which troubled the idea of Dale Farm as a failure of home actively sought out the claims of 'community' central to the broader appeal of British citizenship idealised in the politics of the 'working family'. To some protestors, Dale Farm represented the promise of communal citizenship and caring which was supposedly absent in the rest of 'Broken Britain': As Barkham (2011) again argues:

> Dale Farm's residents gave a glimpse of the kind of community that everyone living in houses and flats in towns and cities bemoans the loss of. Now it will be smashed up by bailiffs and bulldozers.

The multiple strategies employed by those resisting eviction utilised the norms of family and citizenship but, through opening up the claims of home, activated the possibility of different forms of familial life. Rather than a claim to territory, or to reclaim a strict ideal of familial domesticity, the protests acted as a struggle against the *destruction* of a way of life. The enclosure of Traveller mobility and its criminalisation which the Dale Farm eviction represents, reveals the contemporary shape of domestication, the taming and subduing of those forces that 'threaten' the domos. However, rather than merely controlling the dangers of mobility, this represented a will to unmake and destroy alternative forms of home (domicide) – committed in light of the need to foster and protect the historical ideal of the heteronormative, settled home of the citizen. One of the most haunting photographic images that came to define the last day of the protest and the process of eviction was that of a burning caravan, with the word 'our home' etched out across rubber tyres strung out across the barricade in front of it (Image 2). This image arguably became the aesthetic of a different claim to home which was made even in the presence of its destruction.

The politics of home articulated in the protests was continued in the memorialisation of Dale Farm. Artistic projects such as Soil Despositions (SD) actively sought to highlight the (im)possibility of a nomadic claim to home in contemporary Britain (https://soildepositions. wordpress.com/). A year after the eviction of the site, artist-activists began the project which used soil donated by former female residents collected from their one-time caravan pitches. The soil was then 'deposited, framed and documented' at other sites which held cultural and political significance for the evicted women and for practices of nomadism. This dispersal was international, from the Westway Traveller Site in London (also threatened with eviction), the former protest site in Parliament Square, to other places of dispossession/displacement such as favelas in Rio de Janiero and Palestine (McCarthy 2015). By removing and dispersing the soil, the project sought to reveal the ambiguity around territorialised and fixed notions of home and the materiality of the 'dispossession and liquidation of property' that Travellers continue to experience. In the temporal dispersal of the soil connections where made with global struggles for land and movement but equally, this dispersal revealed a central paradox, as McCarthy (2015) argues 'the person who drops the soil is operating through a mobility and a freedom of movement that is assumed to be attributed to Travellers' lifestyles (nomadism) but which has largely been curtailed' (81). In this way, the project set to highlight the extreme marginalisation experienced by Travellers through the government of domesticity, but equally, the multiple directions and movement of the soil symbolises the 'diffuse' possibility and desire for different forms of home and belonging which Dale Farm also presented.

'Acts' and disturbances of domopolitics

Speaking of 'activistic' citizenship, over active citizenship, Isin (2008, 22) suggests that moments of 'activism' that disturb and make possible new sites and scales struggle cannot be reduced to a totality of 'success' or 'failure'. We should instead read interruption, disturbance and resistance as the emergence of others ways of *being political* (White 2008, 44). The Dale Farm activism failed to stop the eviction; however, it reveals the extent to which the contemporary government of the domos remains contestable and contingent. Whilst heavily limited through relations of power, the process of marginalisation that we see in Dale farm was 'interrupted' by alternative claims to home and this produced openings in the composition of domopolitics.

In its appeal to a different form of home, outside of the neo-liberal focus on autonomy, internal governance and wage labour, the acts of protest and memorialisation reveal a different claim to 'belonging' in contemporary Britain, one based on fractured appeals to solidarity and temporality. Furthermore, what is significant is that the central claim to affiliated family life rescripts the territorialised sovereign notion of home through the struggle over keeping *the possibility* of nomadic movement and different cultural affiliation *alive*. The protests created new assemblages between Traveller and settler groups and the 'Traveller Solidarity Network' which emerged out of the resistance, and although not unproblematic, this did provide an agonistic space to challenge the dominant notions of 'domesticity' and citizenship. Equally, networks of international activist across Europe have shown solidarity with the eviction by appropriating the symbol of 'Dale Farm' as a call to arms and, as the SD project articulated, making connection with other forms of violent dispossession of homes and the control of movement globally. What these solidarities and the counter-narrative of Traveller claims to home does is disturb the smooth operation of domicide. In doing so, such 'acts' can be read, in the words of Ranciere, as 'represent(ing) ongoing effort(s) to create forms of the common different from the ones on offer' (Ranciere, 2011, 80).

Viewing the protests as acts which disturb the fabric of violent domestication and domicide allows us to see these struggles as alternative claims to home without treating the counter-narrative of the protesters as fully emancipatory or utopian (Darling 2014, 83). Instead, they remain interruptions and openings. The counter-narrative of home remained firmly grounded within a heteronormative and highly gendered register of the family (which may account for some of its emotive traction in parts of the media). The tragedy of the eviction was precisely represented through the horror of the destruction of a family life: 'there are families here' read one banner (see Barrett and McIntosh 1982). In understanding the politics of the Dale Farm, we need to avoid romanticised and the idealisation of the 'Traveller home' as a site of further resistance. Firstly, this risks homogenising the Traveller community and covering up many problems with the protest movement itself. For example, the organisation of the protests tended to operate around male figures in the solidarity movement, often denying both female voices and, ironically, residents themselves (see Anon 2015). Equally, many Travellers have criticised the conduct of the media campaign which tended to focus the protest on the 'politics of identity' and cultural preservation rather targeting the active destitution which has lead from historic state practice. To idealise the Traveller home as a site around which new co-ordinates of domesticity can be configured could also risk obscuring power relations within Traveller families, for instance, obscuring high levels of domestic abuse – which are in no way isolated to Traveller communities (Allen 2011, 7). Instead, exploring the co-ordinates of the protests reveals an event of contestation and contestability, the interruptions of Dale Farm need to be read as part of the ongoing struggle over domopolitics, not its zenith.

Conclusion

By exploring the struggle over Dale Farm, I have sought to understand one way in which domesticity and home is central to strategies of regulation and the politics of citizenship in contemporary Britain. Rather than viewing the regulation of Travellers as linked to the question of mobility, this needs to also be understood in relation to domesticity, the apparent failure of Travellers to follow norms of domestic practice – 'home-making', household governance and wage labour, hygiene, use of place and territory. Situated in a wider history of domopolitics, there is a push for authorities to domesticate Travellers into the rhythm and life styles of the settled community or protect areas from their 'invasive' presence. This links to other acts of domestication which have historically targeted the underclass, poor and racialised migrant, 'problem families'. The case of Traveller families reveals how both disciplinary (eviction) and empowering (education) strategies coalesce to monitor domesticity. In that anxiety regarding improper domesticity is focussed on children and the familial this reflects the persistence of fear regarding reproduction of difference within the national domos. Domestication in this sense works to both deny certain forms of life whilst equally protecting the dominant link between citizenship and home. The fabric of these shifting re-deployments are draw from historical legacies of the raced and sexed assemblage of British nationhood and its ideal of white, bourgeois, family life.

However, this is never exhaustive. Domopolitics is shaped by the enduring presence of difference which reveals the overdetermined nature and uncertainty of the dominant claim to home. The example of the Dale Farm protests brings to the fore how the need to regulate and restrict are conditioned by the enduring presence of others. The temporality and nomadism that disturbs the sedentary claim to home is targeted in attempts to transform and discipline it, yet the activism around the Dale Farm protests reveals how this is always, in part, a failed project. As I illustrated with the counter-claim to family life in the protests, this provides (limited) space for the emergence of political challenge from spaces of marginality and the ever present possibility of disruption and alternative claims to citizenship. Ultimately, the continual presence of Traveller ways of life, cultural forms and their resistance to following the dominant script of the domos has led to increasing levels of state violence (as revealed in the intensification of evictions). However, rather than seeing this as the strength of contemporary domopolitics, we can perhaps view this in terms of its weakness. The marginalisation of certain groups provides the grounds for different claims to belonging, care and home; but this actively rests on de-centering the model of white heterosexual familial home and its attachments to nationhood. If neoliberal citizenship, as a racialised assemblage, focusses on domesticity, then this also provides material for thinking through and keeping *alive* different ways of living.

Note

1. I use the word Traveller more frequently here as a term which refers to different semi/nomadic groups in the UK: Travellers, Irish Travellers, Romanis and Scottish Traveller. I have designated a specific affiliation when it appears relevant. As Vanderbeck (2005) suggests, the term 'Traveller' has been rejected in favour of 'Gypsy', whilst others find 'Gypsy' a pejorative term. This follows the distinctions made by Traveller rights organisations and solidarity groups. The prevalence of the term Gypsy or Gipsy in negative portrayals in the tabloid press also influences my inclination towards the label Traveller, this by no means suggests that the term is unproblematic.

Acknowledgements

I would like to thank the two anonymous reviewers of this article for their in-depth feedback, as well as Helen Turton and Cristina Dragomir for their constructive comments on earlier drafts. Versions of this article were presented at the Government of Postcolonial Citizenship and Migration symposium at the University of Sheffield and the Postcolonial Governmentalities workshop at Cardiff University. I would like to thank the participants and fellow panellist at these events for their erudite questions and discussion.

Disclosure statement

No potential conflict of interest was reported by the author.

References

Allen, Mary. 2011. "Domestic violence within the Irish Travelling Community: The Challenge of Social Work." *British Journal of Social Work* 42 (5): 1–17.

Amadiume, Ifi. 1987. *Male Daughters, Female Husbands: Gender and Sex in African Society*. London: Zed Books.

Anderson, Bridget. 2000. *Doing the Dirty Work?: The Global Politics of Domestic Labour*. London: Zed Books.

Anderson, Bridget. 2013. *Us and Them?*. Oxford: Oxford University Press.

Anon. 2015. "How I think we should have resisted the Dale Farm eviction." *Rabble*, January Article History 15 . Accessed July 1, 2015. http://rabble.org.uk/how-i-think-we-should-have-resisted-the-eviction-at-dale-farm/

Barkham, Patrick. 2011. "Dale Farm: The Final Days." *The Guardian*, September Article History 18. Accessed March 15. http://www.theguardian.com/uk/2011/sep/18/dale-farm-final-days-photographs

Barrett, Michele, and Mary McIntosh. 1982. *Anti-social Family*. London: Verso.

Basaran, Tugba. 2008. "Security, Law, Borders: Spaces of Exclusion." *International Political Sociology* 2 (4): 339–354.

Baxter, Richard, and Katherine Brickell. 2014. "For home unmaking." *Home Cultures* 11 (2): 133–143.

Beechley, Veronica. 1977. "Some Notes on Female Wage Labour in Capitalist Production." *Capital & Class* 1: 45–66.

Bertone, Chiara. 2013. "Citizenship Across Generations: Struggles Around Heteronormativities." *Citizenship Studies* 17 (8): 985–999.

Bhopal, Kalwant, and Martin Myers. 2008. *Insiders, Outsiders and Others: Gypsies and Identity*. Hatfield: University of Herefordshire University Press.

Cabinet Office. 2008. *Think Family: Improving the Life Chances of Families at Risk*. London: Cabinet Office.

Cameron, David. 2011. "Troubled Families Speech." *Cabinet Office*, December Article History 15. https://www.gov.uk/government/speeches/troubled-families-speech.

Card, Claudia. 1996. "Against Marriage and Motherhood." *Hypatia* 11 (3): 1–23.

Ciaschi, Patrick. Forthcoming. "Domo/Politics – A Diagrammatic View of 'Home as Resistance' in the Dale Farm Traveller Site Evictions." Unpublished Paper, The New School. Accessed February 1, 2015. https://www.academia.edu/2402716/Domo_politics__A_Diagrammatic_view_of_Home_as_Resistance_in_the_Dale_Farm_Traveller_site_evictions

Cruikshank, Barbara. 1998. *The Will to Empower: Democratic Citizens and Other Subjects* New York, NY: Cornell University Press.

Darling, Jonathan. 2008. "Domopolitics, Governmentality and the Regulation of Asylum Accommodation." *Political Geography* 30 (5): 263–271.

Darling, Jonathan. 2014. "Asylum and the Post-political: Domopolitics, Depoliticisation and Acts of Citizenship." *Antipode* 46 (1): 72–91.

Dean, Mitchell. 1991. *The Constitution of Poverty*. London: Routledge.

Deleuze, Gilles, and Felix Guttarri. 1987. *A Thousand Plateaus: Capitalism and Schizophrenia*. Minneapolis, MN: University of Minnesota Press.

Department for Communities and Local Government. 2011. "Time for Fair Play for all." 13th April. Accessed June 2015. https://www.gov.uk/government/news/time-for-fair-play-for-all-on-planning

Donzelot, Jacques. 1980. *The Policing of Families*. London: Hutchinson.

Douglas, Mary. 2002. *Purity and Danger: An Analysis of Concepts of Pollution and Taboo*. London: Routledge.

Dowler, Lorraine. 2012. "Gender, Militarization and Sovereignty." *Geography Compass* 6 (8): 490–499.

Evans, David T. 1993. *Sexual Citizenship*. London: Routledge.

Fairbairn, Emily, and Snell, Andrew. 2011. "The Sun Goes Undercover for Dale Farm diary." *The Sun*, October, Article History 22 . Accessed March 19. http://www.thesun.co.uk/sol/homepage/features/3887347/The-Sun-goes-undercover-for-Dale-Farm-diary.html

Flint, John. 2004. "The Responsible Tenant: Housing Governance and the Politics of Behaviour." *Housing Studies* 19 (6): 893–909.

Fortier, Ann-Marie. 2007. "Too Close for Comfort: Loving Thy Neighbour and the Management of Multicultural Intimacy." *Environment and Planning A* 25 (1): 104–119.

Foster, Brian, and Sarah Cemlyn. 2012. "Education, Inclusion and Government Policy." In *Gypsies and Travellers*, edited by Joanna Richardson and Andrew Tsang, 61–81. Bristol: Polity Press.

Foucault, Michel. 2004. *Society Must be Defended: Lectures at the Collège de France 1975–1976*. London: Penguin.

Fraser, Nancy. 2009. "Feminism, Capitalism and the Cunning of History." *New Left Review* 56: 97–117.

Friese, H., and Sandro Mezzadra. 2010. "Introduction." *European Journal of Social Theory* 13 (3): 299–313.

Gardener, Frances. 2008. "Effective Parenting Interventions – Breaking the Cycle of Disadvantage by Helping Troubled Families." In *Getting in Early: Primary School and Early Interventions*, edited by Jean Groom, 58–68. London: The Smith Institute and the Centre for Social Justice.

Garrett, P. M. 2007. "'Sinbin' Solutions: The 'Pioneer' Projects for 'Problem Families' and the Forgetfulness of Social Policy Research." *Critical Social Policy* 27 (2): 203–230.

Greenfields, Margaret, and David Martin Smith. 2010. "Housed Gypsy Travellers, social segregation and the reconstruction of communities." *Housing Studies* 25 (3): 397–412.

Halsaa, B., S. Roseneil, and S. Sümer, eds. 2012. *Remaking Citizenship In Multicultural Europe: Women's Movements, gender and diversity. Citizenship, Gender and Diversity*, 1–20. Basingstoke: Palgrave Macmillan.

Hanafin, Patrick. 2013. "Rights, Bio-constitutionalism and the Politics of Reproductive Citizenship in Italy." *Citizenship Studies* 17 (8): 914–927.

Hareven, Tamara K. 1991. "The History of the Family and the Complexity of Social Change." *The American Historical Review* 96 (1): 95–124.

Hellenier, Jane. 2003. *Irish Travellers: Racism and the Politics of Culture* Toronto: University of Toronto Press.

Isin, Engin F. 2008. "Theorising Acts of Citizenship." In *Acts of Citizenship*, edited by Engin Isin and Greg Neilsen, 15–44. London: Zed Book.

Kabachnik, Peter. 2010. "Place Invaders: Constructing the Nomadic Threat in England." *Geographical Review* 100 (1): 90–108.

Kabachnik, Peter. 2012. "Nomads and Mobile Places: Disentangling Place, Space and Mobility." *Identities* 19 (2): 210–228.

Kotef, Hagar. 2015. *Movement and the Ordering of Freedom*. Durham, NC: Duke University Press.

LeBaron, G. 2010. "The Political Economy of the Household: Neoliberal Restructuring, Enclosures, and Daily Life." *Review of International Political Economy* 17 (5): 889–912.

Lee, Hye-Kyung. 2008. "International Marriage and the State in South Korea: Focusing on Governmental Policy." *Citizenship Studies* 12 (1): 107–123.

Levine, P. 2006. "Sexuality and Empire." In *At Home with the Empire*, edited by C. Hall and S. O. Rose, 122–142. Cambridge: Cambridge University Press.

Lewis, Gail. 2000. *'Race', Gender, Social Welfare: Encounters in Post-colonial Society*. Cambridge: Polity Press.

McCarthy, Lynne. 2015. "Aesthetics at the Impasse: The Unresolved Property of Dale Farm." *Research in Drama Education: The Journal of Applied Theatre and Performance* 20 (1): 74–86.

McClintock, Anne. 1993. "Family Feuds: Gender, Nationalism and the Family." *Feminist Review* 44: 61–80.

McClintock, Anne. 1995. *Imperial Lather: Race, Gender and Sexuality in the Colonial Contest*. London: Routledge.

McKeon, Michael. 2005. *The Secret History of Domesticity*. Baltimore, MD: The John Hopkins University Press.

Mills, Sara. 2005. *Gender and Colonial Space*. Manchester, NH: Manchester University Press.

Ní Mhurchú, Aoileann. 2014. *Ambiguous Citizenship in an Age of Global Migration*. Edinburgh: Edinburgh University Press.

Okely, Judith. 2014.' Recycled (mis)Representations: Gypsies, Travellers or Roma Treated as Objects, Rarely Subjects', *People, Place and Policy Online* (2014): 8/1, pp. 65–85.

Okely, Judith, and Gustaaf Houtman. 2011. "The Dale farm eviction: Interview with Judith Okely on Gypsies and Travellers (Respond to this article at http://www.therai.org.uk/at/debate)." *Anthropology Today* 27 (6): 24–27.

Orloff, Ann Shola. 1993. "Gender and the Social Rights of Citizenship: The Comparative Analysis of Gender Relations and Welfare States." *American Sociological Review* 58 (3): 303–328.

O'Shea, Gary. 2011. "Gypsies 60k benefits for illegal Dale Farm camp." *The Sun*, September Article History 23 . Accessed March 19. http://www.thesun.co.uk/sol/homepage/news/3830534/Gypsies-60k-benefits-for-illegal-Dale-Farm-camp.html

Porteous, Douglas, and Sandra Smith. 2001. *Domicide: The Global Destruction of Home*. Montreal: McGill Queen's University Press.

Poster, Mark. 1978. *Critical Theory of the Family*. London: Pluto Press.

Procacci, Giovanna. 1991. "Social Economy and the Government of Poverty." In *The Foucault Effect*, edited by Colin Gordon, Graham Burchell, and Peter Miller, 161–169. Chicago, IL: University of Chicago Press.

Ranciere, Jacques. 2011. "Democracies against Democracy." In *Democracy in What State*, edited by Giorgio Agamben, Alain Badiou, Daniel Bensaid, Wendy Brown, Jean-luc Nancy, Jacques Ranciere, Kristin Ross, and Slavoj Zizek, 76–82. New York, NY: Columbia University Press.

Richardson, Diane. 2000. "Claiming Citizenship? Sexuality, Citizenship and Lesbian/Feminist Theory." *Sexualities* 3 (2): 255–272.

Rofel, Lisa. 2002. "Modernity's Masculine Fantasies." In *Critically Modern: Alternatives, Alterities, Anthropologies*, edited by Bruce Knauft, 175–194. Bloomington: Indiana University Press.

Rose, Nikolas. 1990. *Governing the Soul: The Shaping of the Private Self*. London: Free Association Books.

Roseneil, Sasha, Isabel Crowhurst, Ana Cristina Santos, and Mariya Stoilova. 2013. "Reproduction and Citizenship/Reproducing Citizens: Editorial Introduction." *Citizenship Studies* 17 (8): 901–911.

Sibley, David. 1981. *Outsiders in Urban Societies*. Oxford: Blackwell.

Soloway, Richard. 1990. *Demography and Degeneration: Eugenics and the Declining Birthrate in Twentieth-Century Britain*. Chapel Hill: University of Carolina Press.

Steedman, Caroyln. 2007. *Master and Servant*. Cambridge: Cambridge University Press.

Stoler, Ann Laura. 1997. "Sexual Affronts and Racial Frontiers: European Identities and the Cultural Politics of Exclusion in Colonial Southeast Asia'. In *Tensions of Empire: Colonial Cultures in a Bourgeois World*, edited by Frederick Cooper and Ann Laura Stoler, 198–238. Berkeley: University of California Press.

Stoler, Ann Laura. 2002. *Carnal Knowledge and Imperial Power: Race and the Intimate in Colonial Rule*. Berkeley: University of California Press.

The Sun. 2005. "Rights, Wrongs." Accessed August 1, 2015. http://www.thesun.co.uk/sol/homepage/news/sun_says/113776/Rights-wrongs.html

Thorne, Barrie. 1992. 'Feminism and the Family: Two decades of thought'. In *Rethinking the Family: Some Feminist Questions*, edited in Barrie Thorne and Marilyn Yalom, 3–31. Boston, MA: Northeastern University Press.

Topping, Alexandra. 2011. 'Dale Farm Residents and Supporters Plan to Leave', *The Guardian*, October Article History 20 . Accessed March 12, 2015. http://www.theguardian.com/uk/2011/oct/20/dale-farm-residents-supporters-leave

Turner, Bryan. 2008. "Citizenship, Reproduction and the State: International Marriage and Human Rights." *Citizenship Studies* 12 (1): 45–54.

Turner, Joe. 2014. 'The Family Migration Visa in the History of Marriage Restrictions: Postcolonial Relations and the UK Border', *British Journal of Politics and International Relations* 17 (4): 623–643. doi:10.1111/1467-856X.12059.

Tyler, Imogen. 2010. "Designed to Fail: A Biopolitics of British Citizenship." *Citizenship Studies* 14 (1): 61–74.

Tyler, Imogen. 2013. *Revolting Subjects: Social Abjection and Resistance in Neoliberal Britain*. London: Zed Books.

Vanderbeck, Robert. 2005. "Anti-Nomadism, Institutions, and the Geographies of Childhood." *Environment and Planning D: Society and Space* 23: 71–94.

Walby, Sylvia. 1994. "Is Citizenship Gendered?" *Sociology* 28 (2): 379–395.

Walker, Peter and Patrick Barkham. 2011 "Dale Farm Prepares for its Final Battle." *The Guardian*, September Article History 18 . Accessed March 19, 2015. http://www.theguardian.com/uk/2011/sep/18/dale-farm-travellers-eviction-basildon

Walters, William. 2004. "Secure Borders, Safe Haven, Domopolitics." *Citizenship Studies* 8 (3): 237–260.

Waquant, Loic. 2009. *Punishing the Poor: The Neoliberal Government of Social Insecurity*. Durham: Duke University Press.

Webster, Wendy. 1998. *Imagining Home: Gender, 'Race' and National Identity, 1945–64*. London: Routledge.

Weeks, J. 1998. "The Sexual Citizen." *Theory, Culture & Society* 15 (3–4): 35–52.

Welshman, John. 1996. "In Search of the 'Problem Family': Public Health and Social Work in England and Wales 1940–70." *Social History of Medicine* 9 (3): 447–465.

White, Melanie. 2008. "Can an Act of Citizenship be Creative?" In *Acts of Citizenship*, edited by Engin F. Isin and Greg Neilsen, 44–56. London: Zed Books.

Young, Robert. 1995. "Foucault on Race and Colonialism." *New Formations* 25: 57–65.

Yuval-Davis, Nira. 1996. "Women and the Biological Reproduction of 'The Nation'." *Women's Studies International Forum* 19 (1–2): 17–24.

Between safety and vulnerability: the exiled other of international relations

Amanda Russell Beattie

Department of Politics and International Relations, University of Aston, Birmingham, UK

ABSTRACT

Inspired by the idea of safe citizenship this article queries the possibilities of safety in an age of securitization. It challenges the cosmopolitan worldview and its iteration of a global cosmopolitan citizen. It champions an account of affective citizenship, narration and attends to the trauma of exile. It offers an account of exile before suggesting an institutional design premised on politicization. This design, it is argued, facilitates moments of storytelling fostering individual empowerment. This unorthodox rendering of agency allows the traumatized exile to negotiate the world as it is, not as it could be, as a potential 'safe' citizen.

Introduction

Writing in *Citizenship Studies* Weber (2008) suggests the possibility of safe citizenship under-pinning the task of institutional design. She suggests three different angles to understand citizenship; a Hobbesian, a Foucualdian, and a networked account of citizenship. She is clear that her understanding of citizenship reflects legal membership to a community that outlines the rights, obligations and a sense of belonging between the individual and the community that she or he is a part (Weber 2008, 129). As her discussions of Hobbesian citi-zenship deepens, she interrogates the possibility of safe citizenship noting that this particular understanding of citizenship fails to engage with the problems of allegiance and belonging. While scholars of both politics and IR have grappled with these particular problems, I sug-gest that a turn to affect, drawing on the lived experiences of exile, provides an alternative means of attending to such challenges. Affective knowledge, rooted in the lived experiences of exiled persons, provides a personal and emotional quality to discussions of citizenship. It is a form of subjectivity that displays unique forms of criticality. Such criticality, I suggest, can help scholars and activists attend to the trauma of exile, and mobility politics in general.

I draw on Weber's account of Hobbes in order to challenge cosmopolitan iterations of citizenship, envisioning in turn what citizenship, informed by lived experience, might become. I question the bounded nature of citizenship that emerges within a state and its boundaries. Within these boundaries, I discover two inter-related relationships. The first relationship is that between the government and its people. The second relationship is that between the citizens themselves. Safety, if we accept Weber's suggestions, ought to feature in both of these relationships. Yet, I suggest throughout this paper that while we can begin to understand a modicum of safety between citizens, it is difficult to envision the sought after safety in the relationship between the governed and the government simply because it is premised upon the legitimate use of violence, sovereignty and negative liberty. Values, I suggest, which inform a particular reading of the securitized state. This article focuses on the later relationship in order to attend to the potential for harm and trauma that can emerge in the absence of safety, or, I suggest, vulnerable framings of the citizen.

Aware of the various accounts of citizenship (racial, sexual, denationalized, neoliberal, flexible, neurotic, bionic and accidental) this paper engages with two interpretations of citizenship. It challenges the cosmopolitan agent's ability to attend to the lived experience of the exiled other. It suggests that cosmopolitan citizenship, in its critical iterations fails to understand the lack of a voice, or the silence, experienced by the exile. Moreover, it identifies a particular role that the cosmopolitan agent, cum universal ethicist, plays in furthering this silence. The lived experience of exile is a form of trauma. The fact that the cosmopolitan agent contributes to this experience, rather than attending to it in its various guises is deeply problematic if, as cosmopolitan scholars suggests, there is a universal vulnerability shared amongst a global population that are all equally deserving of the rights and obligations outlined by Weber.

One area where this trauma is most overtly evidenced and simultaneously ignored is within the practices of migration, and in particular, deportation. Deportation, as Nyers (2003) writes, is one of the last domains where states can legitimately display traditional forms of sovereign power. It allows the government to overtly display both its legitimate domination of power and its ability to delivery security to its domestic population. Deportation policies frame a discussion that outlines the good democratic citizen while removing those from within the state that fail to live up to such expectations. Yet, it is this very act that demonstrates just how unsafe citizenship actually is and the precarious power imbalance that exists between the state and its domestic population. I suggest this precariousness exists because of the wider framing of securitization, discussed in the first and final sections of this article. I do not engage in a robust critique of deportation. I touch on it briefly at this point to highlight the vulnerability of the citizen vis-a-vis its government in light of the criminalization of those that challenge the public good and are, in turn, deported in order to enhance the safety of the domestic population.

Overt displays of powers, like deportation, can be traumatic. They can rupture our world-view rendering the experience incommunicable to a wider audience. Individuals become isolated. Such isolation may have a geographical quality, but it can also have a relational quality. Both experiences reflect an inability to communicate with others. This is what it is to experience trauma. As Edkins (2002) writes, trauma occurs when 'it involves an exposure to an event so shocking to our everyday expectations of how the world works are severely disrupted' (245). Trauma involves a loss of trust, a breakdown of everyday patterns, and an inability to make sense of the various worlds we are a part. I argue in this article that exile, the counterpoint to citizenship, is a traumatic experience because it does just this. It silences the individual, denies them access to the political, and renders their vulnerability explicit. Bounded accounts of citizenship, that unfold within in institutional design of the contract, like that found in the works of Hobbes, cannot attend to the trauma of the exile because they are designed within a bounded notion of securitization that criminalizes threats and situates them outside the status quo. Bounded accounts of citizenship are tied to descriptions of the exile as criminal and thus a threat to the public good. They suggest that in order to manage our vulnerability the state must be securitized. Securitization enhances the silence of trauma. It isolates those deemed criminal and denies the opportunity to tell their stories.

This article seeks out the space within which the exile can tell his or her story. It champions a narrative methodology in order to emphasize the value of lived experience in the construction of an affective account of citizenship. In order to achieve this goal part one interrogates the cosmopolitan citizen. It contends that critical iterations of cosmopolitan citizenship lack the necessary reflexive capacities needed to engage with the knowledge that emerges when stories are told. It moves into affective notions of citizenship to understand the origins of trauma and links this trauma to discussions of security and safety. I turn, in the second section, to a discussion of exile to demonstrate how it is an isolating experience that forecloses discussion and in turn, enhances the experience of trauma. The exilic state cannot sustain the necessary working through of the experience if we understand citizenship as bounded, and emerging from within an institutional design of securitization. In the third section, I turn to different framings of the political. I suggest, drawing on Edkins (2002) that an institutional design premised on politicization offers a glimpse of the type of space that affords storytelling a prominent role in the understanding of affective citizenship. Ultimately, this article concludes by demanding a more personal, emotive, form of citizenship that welcomes the exile, and the stories they tell, into the political.

Part one: citizenship

Cosmopolitanism should be the appropriate framework to acknowledge a lack of safety within IR, and in particular, citizenship. Cosmopolitanism in its ethical, moral and legal iterations makes overt claims of a shared human vulnerability. This vulnerability should motivate agents to achieve a sense of safety for domestic and international populations in their daily lives. Moreover, this vulnerability ought to attend to the problems that emerge when citizens' experiences are marginalized and set outside the political. For example, Lu (2009) writes of a world informed by friendship and perpetual peace that eschews universal claims of personhood. Yet, her writings do not offer any means of achieving a kinder world that welcomes the particularities of everyday experiences in a global world. Other cosmopolitan scholars have sought to explain this problem. For example, Waldron's (2000) iteration of cosmopolitanism suggests intersecting communities where multiple identities emerge and relationships are formed. Yet, this account, while offering an antidote to the problems of time, space and distance that are otherwise absent in Lu's imaginings, still sits firmly within bounded accounts of statehood. Lu's cosmopolitanism, I suggest, demands more than a bounded concept of order. Herein, lies its appeal, a call to a future better world. Yet, the possibility of a future better world is co-opted, as Hutchings (2013) writes, because the cosmopolitan agent, cum universal ethicist, lacks the necessary reflexivity to attend to the suffering of others. Such agents cannot grapple with the personal, emotive knowledge that can, in Lu's words, 'eschew the universal'.

A cursory engagement with critical cosmopolitanism's iterations of citizenship reveals why this is the case. Such scholars suggest that the spread of democratic values will attend to the problems of universal vulnerability. Democratic practices, so the story goes, will enhance participation amongst a global population inviting those outside such institutional designs into the conversation. Yet, the focus on structural and political change, and the absence of reflexive practices, evidenced in such iterations, negates the possibility of listening to such voices. For example, Linklater (1998) draws on the dialogical potential of the cosmopolitan international citizen to enact structural and political change. He contends that the dialogical act in and amongst political agents can compel a much needed democratic overhaul of various global structures thereby compelling global actors to avoid instances of harm (Linklater 2001). Likewise, Benhabib (2004) frames an account of global cosmopolitan citizenship suggesting a democratic iteration which prompts discussion and negotiation among agents in order to entrench equality and justice throughout global political structures. Both Benhabib and Linklater focus their accounts of citizenship on the assumption of an empowered agent who already has a strong and compelling voice to add to the conversation. Where, in this conversation, I wonder, is the space for the vulnerable, or perhaps the exile, to speak? Moreover, who is listening if they do? I suggest that the empowered agent cannot owing to the particular design of the political.

Within the political, the space within which dialogic politics and democratic iterations begin, we can begin to find evidence of the underlying norms and values that deny a voice to certain segments of the population. The political, drawing on Dallmayr (1996, 196), reflects an ethereal space where agents come together and create 'a constitutive, quasi-transcendental setting or matrix of political life'. It is within this space that the ideals and values informing politics emerge. It is to note, as Lang (2002) does, that politics is a highly personal endeavour. I draw on such statements in order to propose that the political can be a dynamic space that, like Benhabib's iterations, can contest, challenge and discuss the underlying norms and values that inform politics. I am all too aware, however, that such spaces, for the most part, reflect an assumed stasis championing universal assumptions of personhood that are supported by technical and rational knowledge claims (Beattie and Schick 2012). These values emerge from within the social contract tradition, and the writings of Thomas Hobbes. It is this framework that sustains the idea of a safe citizen, as discussed by Weber, and within which a particular hierarchical relationship between the government and the governed emerges.

While the cosmopolitan citizen, in its various incarnations, remains wedded to such assumptions, it will remain difficult, if not impossible, to address the particularities of human vulnerability. Yet, it is possible to find evidence of an emerging trend focused on the particularities of being human. In 2002, Roland Bleiker published his now groundbreaking article that suggested an aesthetic approach to international relations. He challenges the mimetic practices of IR suggesting an alternative, more personal approach, was needed. The influence of his work remains and, in the writings of Solomon (2012) we can find evidence of the use of emotional engagements with security discourses of IR as well as the emerging discussions of micro politics. An affective, or emotional turn, has much to offer the discourses of citizenship studies and in the works of Isin (2004) we begin to understand the point of origin for an affective account of citizenship. Isin's notion of the neurotic citizen is framed in a Foucauldian understanding of power. His work attends to a lack of safety on the part of the citizen as he interrogates the desire for those ever present desires of predictability and stability within the political. He begins to discuss the idea of insecurity and neuroses felt by domestic population in a contemporary age. In his discussions of the neurotic citizen Isin reveals some of the insecurities that arise when domestic subjects are imagined as rational, and unilateral beings, capable of making cost/benefit decisions on a daily basis. He suggests that the neurotic citizen emerges at that point when he or she understands the tensions that surround the rational renderings of citizenship in the face of the emotional, more personable, rendering of the human being.

I am all too aware of this particular challenge. I was ordered deported from the UK because my presence in the country was deemed contrary to the public good as described by the UK Home Office and Border Agency. I was internally exiled within the UK as I fought to stay in the same country as my husband and children, all of whom are British by birth. (I am Canadian). An exile, I soon learned, lacks the traditional recourse to agency and cannot participate in the discussions proposed by Linklater and Benhabib. I had to rely on others to make my voice heard, yet I had lost the words to describe what I was feeling and experiencing. I was living through a traumatic episode that challenged the iterations of ethical, moral and philosophical agency and cosmopolitanism that I had encountered, and even lectured on, as a scholar of IR (Beattie 2014). While I acknowledge that my experience of state deportation was experienced in a supportive and entitled framework, it revealed the distance between my own understandings of self, of who I was and what I offered to the community, and the way the government understood the idea of me. In short, they did not align, and the values of democracy, good citizenship, and participatory government that I identified with gave way to a shattered world view. This dissonance, and the absence of any effective mode of agency, contributed to a daily sense of insecurity and an ongoing trauma.

According to Isin, this dissonance is the origin of neurosis. Such neurosis can, I suggest, tend particular individuals towards traumatic experiences. Unfortunately, such renderings of the citizen, as a rational and technical being are difficult to challenge as they are tightly interwoven into the contract design of the modern state and the relationship of hierarchy and violence that sustain the tradition. This is deeply problematic because an approach to design that fosters securitization not only denies the space within which narration can emerge, it further entrenches the experience of trauma. Edkins (2002) suggests that for those that experience trauma, the turn to securitization heightens the structures that contributed to the unfolding trauma in the first place. What is more, for an account of securitization to seem to be working there must be a scape goat, or an exile, to blame for the security threat. Shildrick (2000) has commented on this phenomenon throughout history noting that in the face of threats, fear and insecurity, that which does not align with the status quo is set outside the boundaries of the political.

Isin's neurotic citizen may begin to locate the source of the neuroses. His writings do not, however, offer his reader an understanding of what affective citizenship might look like. In the writings of Zembylas (2009), an understanding of affective citizenship begins to emerge. Like Isin he suggests a turn to the emotional qualities of being human in order to understand the identities, individual and communal, that sustain human relationships. He suggests that an interrogation of conviviality and hospitality might begin to inform an alternative critical pedagogy of citizenship. What Zembylas makes clear is that living together is not always comfortable, yet this discomfort need not render the political hostile. It need not tend towards exclusion and exile as the account of securitization requires. Rather, he suggests, that the emotional criticality afforded to the affective individual allows citizens to attend to the fear of difference and reimagine the relationships of us/them, or 'other' that inform politics. For Zembylas, hospitality and conviviality offer the reader an enriched affectivity.

Zembylas goes much further the Isin in his description of affective citizenship. Before such interrogations begin, I suggest that an understanding of the exile might afford some insight into the nature of the traumas endured by those who sit outside the peripheries of citizenship. Moreover, I wonder if, rather than drawing on theoretical and philosophical works, a turn towards lived experience might generate a greater understanding of the emotional experiences, and trauma of the vulnerable, or indeed, the exile. I suggest that an awareness of the lived experience of the individual and the dynamic iterations that emerge when individuals engage with one another has a compelling potential to achieve a valuable understanding of affective citizenship, especially when such ends are framed within an understanding of narrative politics. An appreciation of what it is to be an exile, and the ability to listen and reflect on the lived experience of the exile can only begin when they are allowed the space to author, and re-author, their own experiences of citizenship, or a lack thereof. Such narrative practices, I suggest, enhance the reflexive potential of the cosmopolitan agent while simultaneously empowering the exile. They could, potentially, open up the required space within the present to attend to the traumas of a vulnerable population and heed the calls of Schick (2011). As the ensuing sections reveal, narrative politics and the move towards individual empowerment in the face of trauma, present one way of imagining an affective account of citizenship.

Part two: exile

Exile is the counterpoint of citizenship. We can understand it from a wide variety of perspectives: historical, political, legal, anthropological or even philosophical. Writing in 1993 Shklar interrogates the relationship of political obligation, loyalty, and exile. She provides a basic, and helpful, definition. She wonders, 'What is an exile?' arguing that 'An exile is someone who voluntarily leaves the country of which he or she is a citizen' (Shklar 1993, 187). That being said there are already distinctions and differences to this particular definition – in some cases an individual may not leave voluntarily but instead may be forced out. Likewise, it might not be an individual who needs to move. Large communities can also find themselves exiled from their native lands. Shklar is pragmatic. She notes it is almost impossible to generate an exhaustive list of exiled experiences. Consequently, the concept of exile is dynamic and evolving. But, at its most blunt, exile demands an understanding that for whatever reason one, or many, find themselves alienated and outside the formal boundaries of 'the political'.

An exiled being, while denied access to the political, may still live out their daily lives within its confines. Shklar points out that some individuals may be internally exiled, in essence, a non-territorial form of exile.

> Official illegality may also create a non-territorial form of exile, internal exclusion from citizenship, which affects slaves, unwelcome immigrants and ethnic groups, and morally upright people trapped within the borders of tyrannical states. The excluded, or internal exiles as they have sometimes been called, even sometimes appear in constitutional regimes on those occasions when these engage in exceptionally unjust and immoral policies. The morally isolated individual may be reduced to living in accordance with no rule other than his private conscience, and I shall try to say something about the arguments that such people make, as part of my review of the obligations and loyalties to excluded persons. (Shklar 1993, 190)

Shklar's essay is interesting on multiple fronts. She is clear that political theory, in 1993, had not paid much attention to the idea of the exile, or his or her plight. But following on from this claim she wonders if the plight of the exile is any more special then the plight of others who decide whether or not to obey the state and its laws. The different lies in the reaction to unjust laws, deciding ultimately if such laws can be changed or if policies are, in her words, 'manifestly unjust' (Shklar 1993, 193). The different, I believe, is for those who find themselves in exile with no community to support them there is nowhere to go. Shklar notes this point. It is one thing to be an internal exile fighting to achieve institutional change (if you disagree with a political policy). It is another thing to lack empowerment and be unable to leave a country or fight for change, in the absence of representation. Finally, it is another situation altogether when you leave the state that persecutes you and it continues on an overt path of aggression be it at an individual or communal level.

At the end of the day, the exile has nowhere to go. If they must leave their state, they rely on the goodwill of another to allow them entry, and if they cannot leave, they require the help of an empowered agent to achieve institutional change that may not address the original vulnerability that lead to their internal exile. In essence, the structures of the political generate dependency while at the same time foreclosing the possibility of reflection and listening. We simply cannot be, we must do, but what we do is a highly scripted engagement of conformity, acceptance, and denial as it relates to promoting state security at the cost of human representation.

Said (2001) provides an alternative, but no less interesting, departure for discussions of exile. Exile, he writes, 'is a condition legislated to deny dignity-to deny an identity to people' (Said 2001, 139). He speaks of the role of nationalism in the quotidian, constructed as an antidote to the experience of exile. 'Nationalism is an assertion of belonging in and to a place, a people, a heritage', he writes. 'It affirms the home created by a community of language, culture and customs; and, by so doing, it fends off exile, fights to prevent its ravages' (Said 2001, 139). While nationalism is experienced in common exile is assumed to be a solitary experience that occurs outside the community. It draws on the historical antecedent of banishment, the ultimate punishment.

Said stresses the negative side of exile. To be alone and to be outside, he wonders, does it create a sense and need to belong? He wonders if the experience of exile helps in creating a hyper-nationalism to overcome the insecurity and jealousy that can surface in the absence of solidarity. He writes that exile is a jealous state. It is also, he writes, a state of resentment.

> Exiles look at non-exile with resentment. They belong in their surroundings, you feel, whereas an exile is always out of place. What is it role to be born in a place, to say and live there, to know that you are of it, more or less forever? (Said 2001, 139)

Said distinguishes categories of exile drawing a line in the experiences of those he labels refugees and those expatriates who he associates with an intellectual lifestyle born out in choice and not in the absence of agency. While refugees connote a political and historical problem, the need for assistance in the face of innocent rupture and bewilderment, an exile and his or her experience, according to Said is both solitary and spiritual. But within this distinction Said notes that exile is an alternative mode of being political that stands in contradistinction from the state.

> Exile is not, after all, a matter of choice: you are born into it, or it happens to you. But, provided that the exile refuses to sit on the sidelines nursing a wound, there are things to be learned; he or she must cultivate a scrupulous (not indulgent or sulky) subjectivity. (146–147)

In this way we can begin to envision how an exile might inform an affective account of citizenship. The exile enjoys a subjective positioning that allows them to query to status quo, to wonder, in the absence of key political relations, if the institutional design, alluded to by Weber (2008) can provide the necessary safety and security envisioned within a liberal, international, world order. He or she is able to do so aware of the emotional impact of feeling unwanted, of being that other. It highlights the emotional impact of hostility and fear discussed by Zembylas.

Said (2001) turns to Adorno to show this exact point. In Adorno we see exile as the means of interrogating the nature of the world 'as it is'. For Said, Adorno reflects a worldview that acknowledges the contingent nature of the world and the provisional nature of security and its constructs. 'Borders and barriers', he writes, 'which enclose us within the safety of familiar territory, can also become prisons, and are often defended beyond reason or necessity. Exiles cross border, break barriers of thought and experience' (Said 2001, 147). Yet, this very act, of intervention if you will, is silenced for fear of rupturing the fragile act of securitization. The exile, removed from the political, highlights the precarious position of the citizen vis-a-vis the government. In revealing the permeable nature of boundaries and borders, and the impossibility of complete safety the citizen is vulnerable. They are vulnerable because, if they are found wanting, they are criminalized and removed in a bid to acquire a modicum of safety.

Shklar (1993) and Said (2001) both reflect on the silencing of the exile. This silencing, I suggest, is the way in which the state, as legitimate wielder of violence, forecloses any possibility of vulnerability and insecurity. As Shildrick (2000) has demonstrated in her work individuals who do not align with the status quo, or force questions relating to categories of belonging within the political, are silenced. Such silencing is produced through the erection of a cordon sanitaire that hyper-securitizes the status quo label of the in group, while maligning the threat of the outsider. For example, she notes, in ancient history, how the image of the feminine was denied access to the political and forbidden from participating in public life, simply due to the dominance of the masculine. She traces this unfolding separation not only through the treatment of disabled throughout history, but also at the contemporary example of the HIV/AIDS hysteria in the 1980s when to be homosexual was to stand outside the status quo. It speaks to the problematic nature of boundaries, and borders, within any construction of the political and the complicit role they play in security provision premised on infallibility and a lack of vulnerability.

This separation as silencing indicates a problem with boundaries and labels. It suggests a faith in the permanence of human creations and a lack of awareness of their dynamic nature. It is also, I suggest, a silencing that denies the ability of the agent to develop, to be a genuine person. I wonder if this is what Said was attending to when he argued that exile is an undignified experience. In short, silencing denies traditional forms of agency premised on a relational account of the political. It denies the expression of the self within the political, and does not engender the safety of citizenship alluded to by Weber (2008). It is a silencing enacted by the state as it seeks permanent secure structures in a dynamic and changing account of the political. This silencing is a form of exile. It exiles the person from a secure state of being and denies the possibility of development on the part of the person as an autonomous and creative force. It highlights the problematics of a state/individual relationship premised on violence and sovereignty as articulated by Weber (2008). I propose it is indicative of one way that a liberal world view maintains its hierarchical and universal institutional design. In short, exile is the overt controlling of individuals whose life experiences and subjectivity call the status quo into question.

In her 1996 fieldwork in Rwanda and Burundi, Lissa Malkki provides compelling evidence of this type of silencing in her accounting of the liberal humanitarian development regime. As she was listening to those living in exile it became apparent to her that the stories of who they were, as people, the notion of identity, and personality, did not fit within the defined categories of expected and accepted knowledge. When discussing this phenomenon with the aid workers on site, she was quick to learn that this phenomenon was an accepted reality, one that she struggled to comprehend. In the end, she wrote about this exact phenomenon labelling the experience of denied personhood one of corporeal anonymity. Herein, lies her parallel with Said (2001). In essence, to live in exile is to be unable to engage as a whole person. The structures that guide international politics; namely the human rights regime, a subsidiary of the universal rights project, demands one particular notion of being human; namely, a rights bearing subject. To enhance, or even challenge, this image is to render the larger story problematic and reveal the inherent vulnerability of being human and the ensuing narrative that each and every person can, if allowed, author.

Exile, I suggest is a symptom of the underlying relationship of violence and power described by Weber and discussed in the Introduction of this article. It suggests the effective management of the relationships that guide the daily interactions of human beings and their government. What it does not attend to is the relationship of the powerful over the un-empowered. Here, I am suggesting that in the relationship of citizen and government it is the later that holds the power and is able to dictate the relationship between the two. This power imbalance is not limited to the various framings of citizenship discussed by Weber (2008). It is likewise evident in cosmopolitan framings of moral agency. I suggest that until such a time that this particular relationship is unpacked and there is a space for the exiled to author their story, on their own terms, in a safe political structure, it will remain impossible to truly work through the trauma of exile in a way that renders the individual within, or outwith, the state truly safe.

Trauma and the institutional design of exile

How might we begin to make sense of this need to exile and begin to work through trauma? I turn to the writings of Edkins (2002) who offers an alternative means of being political in order to interrogate this claim. Writing in the aftermath of 9/11 Edkins interrogates the decision by the American Government to enact a series of policies that reified boundaries of us and them, create a series of boundaries that reinforced the promotion of anarchy and survival within the international and failed to attend to the opportunities for alternative institutional design. Edkins is highly critical of this political framework. She notes how such an approach cannot attend to the vulnerabilities of being human. In fact, the turn to securitization, is precisely done to avoid such discussions altogether. Vulnerability is denied by a call to arms, quite literally, the use of military prowess in order to safeguard the well-being of the domestic population in times of uncertainty.

The enactment of exile is, I suggest, a direct response to the uncertainty posed by mobile peoples that challenge boundaries within the political. The institutional design of securitization, at the outset, assumes human stasis. Anyone who challenges this assumption and migrates beyond his or her original state is considered out of the ordinary. Writing on the problems of human stasis, and complimenting her work on corporeal anonymity, Malkki (1995) probes this very assumption and argues that mobile peoples, either forced or voluntary, are considered pathologically ill. The underlying assumption of order, Malkki contends, is that individuals remain in the same place for their whole life and it is the geographical location, and the relational elements it promotes, that provide a moral education. People who are seen to leave this environment cannot acquire the necessary moral knowledge to be good citizens, either domestic or international. It is necessary to curtail their action, interrogate their entire subjectivity, prior to potentially admitting them into the community.

When the arguments of Malkki (1995, 1996) are situated alongside the critique of securitization offered by Edkins (2002), some interesting ideas emerge. Edkins highlights the inherent insecurity of a securitised regime that fails to overtly tackle the problems of instability cum vulnerability. One way to attain this level of sought after predictability is to establish boundaries that demarcate who is, and who is not, a legitimate citizen. This, I suggest, leads to situations of exile, both internal and external alike. This exilic state not only stands in direct opposition to the underlying assumptions of a cosmopolitan worldview, it is a direct challenge to the agent's, cum global citizen, ability to affect change. In essence, it denies the space where stories can be told, or re-authored. It is focused on a future better world and cannot provide the space for the exile to work towards a particular form of empowerment. How might we begin to envision such a space that goes beyond the named safety of Weber (2008) that does not rely on the universal cosmopolitan ethicist or agent that cannot attend to the particularities of trauma?

Once again the writings of Edkins (2002) are exceptionally helpful. At the opposite end of a securitization approach rests the notion of politicization. She proposes to her readers that the ensuing quiet, both psychical and aesthetic, of 9/11 offers an alternative for institutional design. A design which, I contend could sustain the desires of safe citizenship proposed by Weber, because it allows us, as human beings, to admit, engage, and work through a shared vulnerability within the community. Politicisation demands that agents be attuned to the quiet that emerges in situations of trauma and insecurity. It seeks out the human, the relationships that can prompt action of an altogether different sort. Such acts seek reconciliation, prompt communication that fosters understanding, and imagine the possibility of unity and not separation.

Politicisation offers an alternative to the teleological orientation of a cosmopolitan worldview. It is attuned to the present and does not focus the ends of agency understood as a future sought after, and at times elusive, end goal. Politicisation situates the agent within the daily framework of unfolding events aware of the vulnerabilities associated with a relational ontology. It allows for unpredictability, creativity and a dynamic human nature that engages with otherwise previously unknown outcomes that can be simultaneously positive and negative alike. This, I suggest, is a subjectivity that does not accommodate a cosmopolitan ethic or moral agent, but is one account of being human that fosters politicization. The temporality of policization attends to the dislocation of the exile. Moreover, it suggests a thoughtful working through of trauma like that hinted at within Isin's notion of neuroses. It recognizes the creative potential of a subjective critique of the status quo discussed by Said (2001). Likewise it understands the powerful drive of quiet and the unique opportunity it presents to the exile to recreate themselves, and the worlds in which they are a part.

This creative tendency within politicisation facilitates an alternative form of human agency. It is an account focused on empowerment not social or political change. This is an absent, but much needed discussion that emerges at the intersection of citizenship discourses and institutional design that engages with the challenges of exile. Traditional forms of agency suggest empowered individuals (MacIntyre 1999; O'Neill 2001) that engage with institutional design (Erskine 2003) or, focus on states as the primary agents of IR (Wendt 1999). The exile, on the other hand, is unable to access the political. Thus while he or she can reason and deliberate, their ability to affect change as articulated by O'Neill or MacIntyre is impossible. Likewise, any institutional change, as suggested by Erskine rendered impossible. The exile lacks that teleological quality assumed within a cosmopolitan ethic. Consequently their lived experience reflects the realities of dislocation, separation and loss. The exile must work within this story and, as Said has proposed, cultivate a scrupulous subjectivity (2001). I suggest that we, as scholars, ought to champion a narrative framework to citizenship and draw on the emerging methods of autobiography and autoethnography, in order to generate the space for the exile subject, or solitary agent, to embark upon such a task.[1] There is a space within storytelling that affords the exile the opportunity to work towards a form of personal empowerment.

I suggest that storytelling is that particular act that brings together the notion of traumatic exile, discussed in the introduction of this article, the possibilities of an institutional design premised on politicisation as proposed by Edkins (2002) and the ability to frankly and openly discuss exile within the political. If exile, as I contend, is a traumatic rendering of the individual subject, and is a product of an abusive and violent relationship between the government and the governed, there is a need for such individuals to tell their stories, in essence, to reclaim back their personhood and their identity in the face of securitization. Storytelling, understood as a form of therapy, may in fact provide such an instance. If we turn to the works of Crossley (2000) we can begin to see how important storytelling, as a form of empowered agency, nay therapy, may prompt alternative understandings of the worlds of which we are a part. It attends to the insecurity that follows on from a traumatic episode and allows individuals to reimagine both their subjectivity and positionality in the world aware of an ever-present ontological vulnerability.

Crossley (2002) situates her account of therapy within the works of Carr (1986), who suggests temporal and spatial parallels in the lived experience of traumatized subjects and the unfolding narratives of fiction. He argues on behalf of a relational account of human action which, I suggest, has implications for how we think through not only individual subjectivity and identity formation, but any form of agency that ensues. The works of Crossley are important because they show, very simply, the mirroring of lived experience and narrative and how that plays out within therapy.

> Literary stories such as fiction and autobiography do not in any sense 'impose' a structure and order on human action and life. Instead, they tend to reinforce and make more explicit the symbolisation that is already at work within a culture at the level of practical human action. The function of narratives such as autobiographies, then, is simply to reveal structures or meanings that previously remained implicit or unrecognised, and thus to transform life and elevate it to another level. (2000, 537)

Storytelling does two things. It allows individuals to negotiate the vulnerability of trauma. Individuals can reconcile the traumatic events that have unfolded while simultaneously reenvisaging their role in the world. Here, the distinction between world and the political is important. Storytelling, and the ensuing empowerment that can occur during this process, need not happen within the relational structure of the political, what it does allow for is a reimaging of the individual and their abilities, aware of their particular temporal and spatial displacement. Empowerment, the second aspect of storytelling, is achieved simply by reconstructing the human narrative that assigns renewed understanding and acceptance in the face of the labelling imposed on the self, by others. In essence the subject is recreating the relationships that sustain their sense of personhood but doing so in such a way that does not reinsert them into the world as it was, hoping for a better future. Instead, this form of empowerment allows the agent to develop an inner strength that enables them to take on the world as it is. In essence, storytelling as agency reflects the temporality of politicisation and not the cosmopolitan ethic emerging within a securitized institutional design.

As I read through Weber's notion of safe design, I find a synergy within its hopeful future to the teleological assumptions of a cosmopolitan ethic. The notion of a 'safe' institutional design mirrors, in subtle ways, the idea of a better future world. But in focusing on the creation of the future better, we forget about the harmful present, a point well noted and reflected upon by Schick (2009). Imagining the benefits of Adorno's work on ethical international relations Schick reminds scholars and practitioners alike of the attendant harm that comes when the immediate present is overshadowed by future potential design. She poignantly argues on behalf of the concrete other of the universal rights project so central to ethical discourses of IR and suggests that only when harm is negotiated in the present, and the traumatized subject is given recourse to negotiate this harm on their own terms, can ethical encounters within the international begin to realistically grapple with the outcomes of trauma. For we must recall, as was made clear in the introduction of this article that trauma is idiosyncratic and so to must the recourse to trauma be multivariate and personal. Cosmopolitanism, in its universal, technical cum rational approach to the world, cannot accommodate this much-needed personableness.

There is no universal approach to rectifying harm and suffering and so, to fully mediate its unfolding and its impact, securitization as an approach to institutional design must be abandoned. It must be abandoned because it cannot accommodate the inherent vulnerability of being human, a vulnerability that sits at the core of trauma. Yet, this vulnerability has always, in the ethical discourses of IR, been something to avoid rather than embrace. An account of agency that rests upon storytelling, of finding one's place within the world, embraces this vulnerability and thus poses questions for the institutional designs of Linklater and Benhabib. Likewise it pushes us to go beyond the safety desired by Weber, but facilitates a thoughtful understanding of the affective citizen. It asks us to recognize individuals, as they truly are, not subjects, but persons with stories, histories and identities that enrich the various worlds of which they are part. It suggests how scholars can begin to imagine the lived experience of affective citizenship.

Conclusion

This article was inspired by the ideas of Weber (2008) and her desire to frame an account of citizenship that is safe. Normative ethical discourses of International Relations, in particular Cosmopolitanism, envision how this safety might come about, if it is understood as a protection from suffering, and an access to the basic rights of security and subsistence, by all members of a global population. Yet, as this article has stressed, cosmopolitanism, in its various guises, while focused on the vulnerable subject, has been unable to attend to the emerging harms evident within an institutional design that adopts the ideas of securitization.

This article suggests an engagement with the idea of politicization outlined by Edkins. Such a framing of International Relations provides the requisites space within which to understand the possibilities of affective citizenship and what this might mean for empowerment of exiled individuals. As Zembylas (2009) has suggested in his engagement with affective citizenship education emotional relationships sustain both individual and communal identities. This type of knowledge can, and does emerge, when stories are authored and re-authored and the lived experience of the exile is allowed to come through. Yet, such stories will only emerge in an institutional design that challenges the need to securitize the state in the face of otherness.

Until such a time arrives when the ends of politicization are realized, individuals must negotiate the world as it is. It is only very recently that a turn to micro-politics has shifted the focus of IR scholars allowing the aesthetics turn in IR to deepen its understanding of the individual affective experience. It remains a peripheral area of study and thus open to criticism. Indeed, many scholars of IR would suggest a focus on storytelling as empowerment is not needed if, by nature, the focus of the discipline is the state. Indeed, safe accounts of citizenship reify the state as primary actor within bounded accounts of citizenship. Likewise, scholars engaged in the task of institutional design will possibly struggle to align the temporal needs of institutional change with the non-linear renderings of traumatic experiences. As Schick has suggested it is easier to pass over traumatic pasts in order to attend to a possible better future. Consequently, scholars engaged with moral and ethical accounts of agency may struggle with an individual focus on agency that addresses the idiosyncratic nature of trauma rather than a universal scripted engagement with exiled others.

Storytelling is an unorthodox form of agency. It empowers individuals in the face of inequality and injustice. As a method of therapy storytelling can help the individual reinsert him or herself in the world aware of its precarious and unpredictable nature. Storytelling, as autobiography, Inayatullah (2010) suggests, reveals the structures and institutions that frame our everyday experience. He also notes, much like Crossley (2000) that such revelations disclose affinities and dissonance within the stories of others. In this way, storying is part of affective citizenship. As Zembylas has suggests it informs an understanding of how best to live with others in a complicated and unpredictable world. This is part of the narrative process, or storytelling. As Crossely notes, this process allows individuals to reconnect with the relationships that matter, and helps individuals to make sense of the worlds they are a part. In this way, individuals can find a sense of inner security, despite the labels, boundaries and projections that are associated with the exilic state. Consequently, the exiled storyteller can imagine alternative subjectivities that understanding that status quo while simultaneously reimaging the particular form it takes in their daily lives.

Note

1. This methodological approach is only now emerging in International Relations and does remain on the peripheries of the discipline. For a cursory overview of this approach see the writings of: Dauphinee (2010, 2013), Doty (2004, 2010), Neumann (2010), and finally, Inayatullah (2010).

Acknowledgements

I would like to thank Joe Turner for the opportunity to produce this article. Equally, I am grateful for the insight offered from my colleagues at Aston University where I presented this paper and received valuable feedback, in particular the insights from my conversations with Graeme Hayes. The paper has benefitted from positive feedback and insight from two anonymous peer reviews which greatly enriched the arguments of this paper.

Disclosure statement

No potential conflict of interest was reported by the author.

References

Beattie, A. R. 2014. "Engaging Autobiography: Mobility Trauma and International Relations." *Russian Sociological* 13 (4): 137–157.
Beattie, A. R., and K. Schick, eds. 2012. *The Vulnerable Subject: Beyond Rationalism in International Relations*. Basingstoke: Palgrave Macmillan.
Benhabib, S. 2004. *The Rights of Others: Aliens, Residents, and Citizens*. Cambridge: The Press Syndicate of the University of Edinburgh.
Carr, D. 1986. *Time, Narrative, and History*. Bloomington: Indiana University Press.
Crossley, M. L. 2000. "Narrative Psychology, Trauma and the Study of Self/Identity." *Theory & Psychology* 10 (4): 527–546.
Dallmayr, Fred. 1996. *Beyond Orientalism: Essays on Cross-cultural Encounter*. Albany: State University of New York Press. 193.
Dauphinee, E. 2013. *The Politics of Exile*. New York: Routledge.
Dauphinee, E. 2010. "The Ethics of Autoethnography." *Review of International Studies* 36 (3): 799–818.
Doty, R. L. 2010. "Autoethnography – Making Human Connections." *Review of International Studies* 36 (04): 1047–1050.
Doty, R. L. 2004. "Maladies of Our Souls: Identity and Voice in the Writing of Academic International Relations." *Cambridge Review of International Affairs* 17 (2): 377–392.
Edkins, J. 2002. "Forget Trauma? Responses to September 11." *International Relations* 16 (2): 243–256.
Erskine, T. 2003. "Embedded Cosmopolitanism and the Case of War: Restraint, Discrimination and Overlapping Communities." *Global Society* 14 (4): 569–590.
Hutchings, K. 2013. *A Place of Greater Safety? Securing Judgement in International Ethics*. London: Palgrave Macmillan.
Inayatullah, N. 2010. *Autobiographical International Relations: I, IR*. London: Routledge.
Isin, E. F. 2004. "The Neurotic Citizen." *Citizenship Studies* 8 (3): 217–235.
Lang, Anthony, Jr. 2002. *Agency and Ethics: The Politics of Military Intervention*. Albany: State University of New York Press. ix.
Linklater, Andrew. 2001. "Citizenship, Humanity, and Cosmopolitan Harm Conventions." *International Political Science Review* 22 (3): 261–277.
Linklater, A. 1998. "Cosmopolitan Citizenship." *Citizenship studies* 2 (1): 23–41.
Lu, C. 2009. "Political Friendship Among Peoples." *Journal of International Political Theory* 5 (1): 41–58.
MacIntyre, A. 1999. "Social Structures and their Threats to Moral Agency." *Philosophy* 74 (3): 311–329.
Malkki, L. H. 1995. "Refugees and Exile: From 'Refugee Studies' to the National Order of Things." *Annual Review of Anthropology* 24: 495–523.
Malkki, L. H. 1996. "Speechless Emissaries: Refugees, Humanitarianism, and Dehistoricization." *Cultural Anthropology* 11 (3): 377–404.
Neumann, I. B. 2010. "Autobiography, Ontology and Autoethnology." *Review of International Studies* 36 (4): 1051–1055.

Nyers, P. 2003. "Abject Cosmopolitanism: The Politics of Protection in the Anti-deportation Movement." *Third World Quarterly* 24 (6): 1069–1093.

O'Neill, O. 2001. "Agents of Justice." *Metaphilosophy* 32 (1–2): 180–195.

Said, E. 2001. *Reflections on Exile: And Other Literary and Cultural Essays.* London: Granta Books.

Shklar, Judith N. 1993. "Obligation, Loyalty." *Exile. Political Theory* 21 (2): 181–197.

Schick, K. 2009. "'To Lend a Voice to Suffering is a Condition for All Truth': Adorno and International Political Thought." *Journal of International Political Theory* 5 (2): 138–160.

Schick, K. 2011. "Acting Out and Working through: Trauma and (in) Security." *Review of International Studies* 37 (4): 1837–1855.

Shildrick, M. 2000. "Becoming Vulnerable: Contagious Encounters and the Ethics of Risk." *Journal of Medical Humanities* 21 (4): 215–227.

Solomon, T. 2012. "'I wasn't Angry, because I Couldn't Believe It Was Happening': Affect and Discourse in Responses to 9/11." *Review of International Studies* 38 (4): 907–928.

Waldron, J. 2000. "What is Cosmopolitan?" *Journal of Political Philosophy* 8: 227–243.

Weber, C. 2008. "Designing Safe Citizens." *Citizenship Studies* 12 (2): 125–142.

Wendt, A. 1999. *Social Theory of International Politics.* Cambridge: Cambridge University Press.

Zembylas, M. 2009. "Affect, Citizenship, Politics: Implications for Education." *Pedagogy, Culture & Society* 17 (3): 369–383.

Ethiopianism, Englishness, Britishness: struggles over imperial belonging

Robbie Shilliam

School of Politics and International Relations, Queen Mary University of London, London, UK

ABSTRACT

In this article, I problematise a tendency to situate concerns for citizenship and belonging via what might be called 'narratives of settlement'. In these narratives, the chronology of settlement begins with the visceral and institutional racism met by non-white immigrant peoples of the commonwealth post Second World War, and the tempo of settlement is marked by the problem of integrating into and within UK society. Such narratives occlude a broader and deeper contextualisation of struggles over citizenship within struggles over imperial belonging. To substantiate this critique, I examine various actors across the British empire who struggled over Englishness and Britishness – connected but discrete imperial cultures of belonging – during the Italy/Ethiopia war of 1935–1941. These actors variously problematised belonging to British empire via an ethical commitment to Ethiopia's independence. Unlike narratives of settlement, the tempos and chronologies of these Ethiopianist narratives are fundamentally global-colonial in their framing of the problem of belonging in so far as their tempos are determined by the pursuit of African redemption and their chronologies are structured around the enslavement, colonisation and prospective liberation of African peoples. The benefit of undertaking an historical examination of the Italy/Ethiopia conflict is to bring into sharper relief struggles over imperial belonging wherein the moral and political compass of protagonists is oriented to resolutions that exceed an equitable national settlement.

Introduction

> This country is honoured by the emperor having taken up his residence here. Ten righteous men would have saved Sodom; I feel the emperor is one of the comparatively few who may save Britain. (*New Times and Ethiopia News* 1937d)

These are the sentiments of one anonymous letter writer to Sylvia Pankhurst's *New Times and Ethiopian News*, on the seventh anniversary of Haile Selassie I's coronation as emperor of Ethiopia, which he spent in exile in Bath. In October 1935, Fascist Italy had violently invaded Ethiopia – fellow sovereign members of the League of Nations – as part of its colonial project for Africa. Yet subsequently, the British government did nothing to support Ethiopia except to grant permission for its Emperor and his small retinue to live incognito in England. The response from the public was damning and questioned the very integrity of race and empire: 'Can Britain look in the face of her many million coloured subjects and call herself a just nation?', considered one Una Brown (1937) in Pankhurst's newspaper as she reflected that 'to preserve Ethiopia's freedom is to preserve Britain'. More precisely, the British government's response to Italy's aggression severely tested Englishness and Britishness, entangled cultures of imperial belonging that, by the *fin de siècle*, had become central to maintaining the normative integrity of the empire in an era of increased imperial competition. In this article, I examine the struggles over Englishness and Britishness which threatened to dissolve the complex lattice of imperial loyalties and racial exclusivities that constituted these cultures of belonging.

The subject matter of this historical episode speaks directly to the British provenance of the Cultural Studies tradition. Oftentimes the work of Stuart Hall et al. are mobilised as part of a broader postcolonial approach to unpacking the relationship between citizenship, race and colonialism (see, e.g. Sajed 2010). This can be a very productive practice. However, for the aims of this argument, the diverse approaches that are nowadays registered under 'postcolonial studies' are too diffuse to make for an effective interlocutor. Instead, I want to speak specifically to the engagement by Cultural Studies with the imperial lineages of British citizenship. Before the arrival of postcolonial studies, Hall and his colleagues had done much to establish the premise that the culturally mediated relationship between nation and belonging in Britain was congenitally colonial and hence necessarily racialised (Hall et al. 1978; Centre for Contemporary Cultural Studies 1992; see also Baker Jr., Best, and Lindeborg 1996).

Indeed, following in the wake of Cultural Studies, a voluminous literature has excavated in some detail the colonial constitution of Englishness and Britishness (see Baucom 1999; Langlands 1999; Rush 2002; Wellings 2002; Lawrence 2003; Blackstone 2005; Gorman 2006; Gikandi 2007; Young 2008; Bell 2014). Through this scholarship we now know that 'Englishness' came to denote an inclination towards liberty, respect for the law, fair play, compromise and impartiality – all of which were considered core competencies for enlightened imperial governance.[1] Englishness, a culture of belonging that owed much to the white Diaspora for its development, was racially exclusive for the most part. However, 'Britishness', as enunciated by the Earl of Balfour at the height of the Italy/Ethiopia crisis in 1936 (Wellings 2002, 5–6), set aside such exclusivity so that even colonial subjects to the crown could, by vicarious association and at a secure distance from the metropolis, find a place off belonging in an empire normatively guided by the cultural competencies of Englishness.

Additional to this influence, I would also suggest that the Cultural Studies tradition – and the political milieu in which it developed in the UK – has fostered a tendency to situate concerns for citizenship and belonging primarily in the post-war, post-colonial era via what might be called 'narratives of settlement'. In these narratives, the chronology of settlement begins with the visceral and institutional racism met by non-white immigrant peoples of the commonwealth post Second World War, and the tempo of settlement is marked by the problem of integrating into and within UK society (see e.g. Favell 1998; Turner 2001, 12; Hansen 2002; Hampshire 2005; Stevenson 2010, 286). In these stories of immigration and settlement, Britishness comes to clash intimately with Englishness. However, by occluding a broader and deeper history of struggles over imperial belonging narratives of settlement tend to marginalise or occlude the self-conceptions of those for whom an equitable national settlement was not – and is not – always the sole reason for such struggles (see Lockward 2013). In other words, while these struggles might not necessarily eschew an inclusion into the polity in order to enjoy the full range of citizenship rights, such an inclusion does not mark the final resolution to the struggle over belonging.

In what follows I work with the self-conceptualised narratives of those struggling over Englishness and Britishness in the context of the Italy/Ethiopia war of 1935–1941. These narratives all share an orientation towards Ethiopia which has been termed 'Ethiopianism' (see Shepperson 1953; Nelson 1994; Price 2003). I should make it clear that Ethiopianism was less so developed and/or enunciated by Ethiopians themselves – at home or abroad – but more so by peoples of African descent in British colonies (and in the US). However, in this article, I also introduce the differential use of Ethiopianism by white subjects of Britain who invested in Englishness. Unlike narratives of settlement, the tempos and chronologies of Ethiopianism are fundamentally global-colonial in their framing of the problem of belonging. That is to say, the question of settlement – whether within an empire or a nation – is never divorced analytically or prescriptively from the more fundamental colonial and racial ordering of the world. Therefore, rather than domestic integration, the tempos of Ethiopianism are determined by the pursuit of African redemption; and instead of a post-war point of departure, the chronologies are structured around the enslavement, colonisation and prospective liberation of African peoples. The benefit of undertaking an historical examination of the Italy/Ethiopia conflict is to bring into sharper relief struggles over imperial belonging wherein the moral and political compass of protagonists is oriented to rearrangements that exceed an equitable national settlement.

The archive that I use to explore these hermeneutical struggles over imperial belonging consists primarily of Sylvia Pankhurst's papers, her newspaper *New Times and Ethiopia News,* as well as the wider British newspaper press of the era. I proceed by first clarifying the different but conjoined challenges to Englishness and Britishness that resulted from the conduct of the British government vis-à-vis Italian aggression towards Ethiopia in the lead up to Second World War. I argue that this conduct severely undermined the racially exclusive competencies of imperial governance that framed Englishness. At the same time, I argue that the government's conduct also severely undermined the inclusivist pretensions of Britishness by demonstrating to Black subjects of the British empire the abiding differential treatment of peoples based on race which underwrote its cultures of imperial belonging. Subsequently, I explore two related responses to these challenges: what I shall term 'Euri-centric Ethiopianism' and 'Afri-centric Ethiopianism'. While both responses entangled the fate of Englishness and Britishness with the deliverance of justice for Ethiopia they differed in terms of their broader commitment to the liberation struggles of African peoples worldwide. I finish with an extended conclusion that, by looking at the emergence of and reaction to the RasTafari movement in the UK in the 1970s, brings forward the Ethiopianist narrative to suggest continuities in struggles over imperial belonging pre- and post-war/empire.

In making this argument, I acknowledge the seminal importance of the British cultural studies tradition in exposing the conjoined nature of national belonging, colonial legacies and their racial schemas. Nevertheless, I do believe that this tradition became entrapped by the wider obsessions over post-war settlement. Perhaps, these obsessions even demonstrate a subtle attempt to domesticate the influential narratives of Ethiopianism mobilised by some African–Caribbeans resident in the UK from the 1960s onwards to address the strictures of race and nation. This might seem a strange critique given that the most influential work arising out of the cultural studies tradition has been Paul Gilroy's global-diasporic investigation of the *Black Atlantic*. However, I find Simon Gikandi's recent suggestion quite provocative when he proposes that Gilroy turned from a cultural study of British nationalism to the modernity of North America in order to find clues as to how a Black minority (African–Americans) could become acknowledged, albeit begrudgingly, as citizens through their cultural production (Gikandi 2014, 242). In this respect, the *Black Atlantic* could be seen as a critical pedagogy of settlement. Ultimately, then, I wish to suggest that there are narratives other than that of settlement that frame struggles over belonging through abiding global racial and colonial coordinates (see also Yuval-Davis 2004). Their imperial genealogies are far longer, deeper and complex than those that make up the problematique of national citizenship. They survive, and will not disappear anytime soon.

Englishness, Britishness and the Italian/Ethiopian war

From the very start of the Italy/Ethiopia war, the competencies of the British government to diplomatically lead on a just and enlightened settlement were put under question by the British public. Strong public support for Ethiopia is evident in the UK as early as the summer of 1935 when Mussolini began amassing an invasion force from its Eritrean colony. At this point the League of Nations Union, a London-based civic group, organised a 'Peace Ballot' wherein 11,559,165 respondents voted positively for a policy of peace and disarmament through the League, with approximately 6,750,000 voting specifically for military sanctions against Italian aggression (*Morpeth Herald and Reporter* 1935; Howell 2006, 67).

Initially the British government also expressed support for Ethiopia and the principles of the League of Nations to which Ethiopia, Italy and Britain were all full members. Foremost amongst these principles were the observance of treaties, the practice of open and just relations between members, and the obligation not to resort to war. Yet in the aftermath of the Italian invasion in October 1935, and subsequent aerial bombardment of civilians with poison gas, the British government did nothing substantial to support Ethiopia via the League's principles. Instead, the government preferred to enact a policy of appeasement towards Mussolini. In December 1935, details of a secret pact were made public wherein Britain and France had proposed to grant Italy significant territories in Ethiopia. The public outcry over rewarding fascist aggression was so vociferous that it forced the resignation of Samuel Hoare, Foreign Secretary and British author of the pact.

Responses to the Italian invasion were shaped by – and responded to – a particular nineteenth century innovation of 'standard of civilisation' jurisprudence. By the early twentieth century, the putative existence of domestic slavery provided the measure for European powers to determine the legality and morality of intervention into and colonisation of various African polities. This new standard of civilisation articulated intimately with nineteenth century abolitionist ideology that presented British imperial governance as a force for civilisation superior even to other European powers (see e.g. Miers 1998; Heartfield 2015). In this respect, the abolition tradition was assumed to demonstrate the normatively unparalleled record of Englishness on the world stage.

But Ethiopia presented a conundrum in this respect (Allain 2006): although slave-trading and slavery was practiced in its porous borders, especially in those western and southern areas recently incorporated into its empire during the reign of Menelik II, half of its peoples practiced a Christianity more ancient than that established in Britain; and Christianity was, of course, one of the hallmarks of (European) civilisation. Moreover, Selassie I was both an avowed Christian and social reformer who actively pursued the eradication of slavery in his lands. It was for these reasons that support for Ethiopia in Britain could not be decided by way of a stark racial binary of white civilised European and black savage African, but rather, through a convoluted interrogation of the degree to which Ethiopia was sufficiently tackling its domestic slavery. It was through this calculus that the degree of failure of Englishness on the contemporary world stage was assessed.

It must be said that some of the contemporary abolitionists adjudicated Ethiopia's status to be insufficiently civilised. For example, Lady Simon, a leading figure in the British and Foreign Anti-Slavery and Aborigines' Protection Society, and wife to a cabinet minister, accepted Mussolini's abolitionist rhetoric and, in Sylvia Pankhurst's assessment, took a 'very hostile attitude towards Ethiopia' (Pankhurst 1939; Høgsbjerg 2014, 90). Meanwhile, John Harris, previously the long-standing secretary of the Society, did not discount the utility of the grand development plans that Mussolini proclaimed for Ethiopia under Italian colonialism (*The Western Morning News and Daily Gazette* 1935b). Various commentators shared Harris's diffidence, chiding Selassie I for not having entirely wiped out slavery in his lands, and berating the League of Nations for admitting an uncivilised Ethiopia into its membership (see e.g. Allen 1935).

Nonetheless, it is fair to say that by far the dominant sentiment expressed by British publics was in affirmation of Ethiopia's civilised status and Selassie I's efforts at reform. In the run up to the Italian invasion, and in the succeeding years, various adventurers, travel writers and abolitionists regularly joined with their counterparts from the Ethiopian legation in London to speak publically on the specific nature of slavery in Ethiopia in contrast to its Atlantic predecessor (e.g. *Northern Daily Mail* 1935a, 1935b). More importantly, members of the Ethiopian legation and its varied supporters – learned, philanthropic, political, aristocratic, commoner and otherwise – often pointed towards the anti-slavery bureaus, set up by Selassie I and tasked with substantively supporting emancipated persons, as evidence of significant reform. They all argued that it was Mussolini's colonial project itself that had interfered with and suspended these reform efforts (e.g. *Aberdeen Press and Journal* 1935; *The Western Morning News and Daily Gazette* 1935a; *Hastings and St. Leonards Observer* 1936; *The Nottingham Evening Post* 1936).

The majority public opinion therefore considered Ethiopia to be civilised – or civilising – despite its African provenance. Ethiopian policies on the world stage could be said to even aspire to the example of Britain. The problem was that these publics' own government had given no substantive support to Ethiopia and effectively stood by while a fascist aggressor invaded and occupied. Why, then, was not Englishness and its competencies of justice, impartiality and fairplay being applied and demonstrated on the world stage at this critical juncture? And so, as Italian forces swept across the country in 1936, and Selassie I was forced to seek exile in England, the Friends of Abyssinia League of Service asked 'shall we continue to abandon Abyssinia, or shall we keep our pledged word …? Shall we lower the honour of Britain throughout the world, or maintain our high tradition for justice and fair play?' (Friends of Abyssinia League of Service 1936) Similar sentiments were expressed in September 1937 by the Dean of Winchester who confirmed that 'the real thing which moves English people is that Abyssinia has not had fair play' (*New Times and Ethiopia News* 1937c).

The normative impact upon Englishness by government (in)action is aptly demonstrated by a poetic witness to Selassie I's historic speech to the League of Nations in June 1936, wherein the exiled emperor challenged the nations present to defend the principle of collective security and meaningfully support Ethiopia's cause:

> … Our English gestures were unable, as impotent as our looks, to speak to him of our wretchedness
>
> Yet it seemed that he sensed our homage
>
> Knew that the shame of England was our own shame.

In fact, some commentators suggested that the competencies of Englishness were now being preserved by an African nation: One Isabel Bible from Devon lamented thus:

> I wonder how many people today feel hot shame mounting to their faces when they remember the GREAT BETRAYAL of 1936 in which England took such a leading part! ENGLAND, THE WORLD CHAMPION! The Guardian of freedom! HOW ART THOU FALLEN! BUT BE OF GOOD CHEER, ETHIOPIA! OUT OF THY MARTYRDOM THOU SHALT RISE UP A QUEEN! (*New Times and Ethiopia News* 1937b)

The intimacy of this relationship was signalled by Freda Collier, whose brother was a governor of the Bank of Ethiopia. Collier noted that England and Ethiopia shared the same patron saint – St George (*Sunday Post* 1935). And one poet even imagined that St George, the protector of Englishness, would perhaps now favour Ethiopia over England:

> What though beyond the seas a nation stand
>
> Called also by my name, untouched and bright?
>
> What do I care for any other land
>
> But her, but her, whose setting is my night?
>
> Let Ethiopia sink in blameless pride;
>
> But England is my own, and she has died. (Snow 1937)

To these and many other observers, the British government's unprincipled response to the Italian invasion worked to undermine Englishness and its claims to racially superior competencies in imperial rule – claims that underwrote the very standard of civilisation itself.

But so too did the British government's response undermine the integrity of Britishness, that other culture of belonging that offered a vicarious enfranchisement of subjects of African descent within the racial exclusivities of imperial rule. As one letter writer from Fareham put it perceptively on the eve of the Italian invasion,

> [b]y going back on his word to Abyssinia, Mussolini is not only letting Italy down in the eyes of the world, he is letting the white man down in the eyes of the coloured peoples everywhere, he is letting civilization down. (Evans 1935)

Two years later, notable public intellectuals and politicians such as Norman Angell, Stanley Jevons, Lloyd George and H.G. Wells wrote to the Times, warning once more of these repercussions and their impact upon the normative integrity of the British Empire (Angell et al. 1937).

They were not wrong. For the betrayal of Ethiopia was apprehended by many British subjects of African descent as an injustice personally done unto them by their own Empire.

And in these apprehensions the racially exclusivist culture of Englishness was placed in opposition – rather than in extended association – with the more democratic culture of Britishness. One writer to the *New Times and Ethiopia News* from British Guiana warned in October 1936 that 'It being always understood all over the world that an Englishman's word is his bond', yet they 'had made a gentlemen's agreement to hold Ethiopia in a state of bondage! ... the coloured race are closely watching events' (C.A.B. 1937).Another 'native of British Guiana', now resident in Bradford, wrote in the newspaper a year later that

> Africans at home and abroad have come to regard England as their Mother Country, but of late the Mother has been sadly neglecting her African children and has done them a cruel wrong in allowing Ethiopia to be ravaged by Italy. (*New Times and Ethiopia News* 1937e)

These protestations continued and, as Europe mobilised for world war, began to articulate with a critique of the martial sacrifices that Empire required from its colonial subjects. In 1938 I.T.A. Wallace Johnson, a trade unionist and social reformer, organised a resolution by the West African Civil Liberties and National Defence League that, in light of its recent recognition of Italian sovereignty over Ethiopia, chided the British government for betraying 'the confidence of the African people in British equity and fair play' and promised no further enjoining of Armistice Day commemorations by members of the West African League (Wallace Johnson 1938).

Alternatively, martial sympathies were increasingly extended to Ethiopia. In 1936, Trinidadian Pan-Africanist George Padmore observed that

> Blacks ... have rallied to the defence of Ethiopia, as though they were the subjects of the emperor, Haile Selassie. Everywhere one hears them proclaiming the slogan : 'Our flag is our Colour. An injury to one is an injury to all'. (Padmore 1969, 363)

Across the Empire subjects of African descent, whilst still 'proclaiming anew' loyalty to the crown, demanded the right to 'pursue steadfastly, all lawful means towards ... restoration of the sovereignty and independence of that Black empire' (*New Times and Ethiopia News* 1937a). At this point in time Leonard Howell, a Jamaican preacher and organiser, now known colloquially as the 'first Rasta', earned a number of years in Bellevue, the Kingston mental asylum, on account of his publically proclaimed service to Selassie I (on Howell see Hill 2001; Lee 2003).

In sum, Englishness and Britishness, as cultures of imperial belonging, were significantly undermined due to the British Government's conduct in the Italy/Ethiopia war. We shall now examine how an Ethiopian orientation was cultivated by white and Black subjects alike as a response to these challenges. But we shall also explore how these orientations differed significantly in terms of offering resolutions to the disturbance in imperial belonging.

Euri-centric and Afri-centric Ethiopianisms

The Ethiopianism cultivated predominantly by white residents in the UK – I will call it Euri-centric Ethiopianism – emerged from a set of travelogues by sojourners to the horn of Africa that were published at the time as books and/or serialised in newspapers, some being republished in the lead up to the war (e.g. Baum 1935). Many of these reports were ideologically consolidated into a critique of Italian colonialism through the notion of an expanded body in Christ. It is important to note that churches and church leaders of many denominations often staked a claim in the moral and spiritual leadership of the British

Empire in the Christian pursuit of peace, fairness and justice. Oftentimes, church leaders would move a resolution amongst their congregation to express sympathy with the Ethiopian Orthodox Tewahedo Church.

In this respect, the white Christian body in Britain had to (once more) distance itself from the moral and spiritual authority of the Papacy which, as one letter writer from Plymouth put it, had warned all nations of the growing Communist threat yet had said not a word about the 'wholesale murder in Abyssinia'(*The Western Morning News and Daily Gazette* 1936). Instead, white Christians would have to express solidarity with the 'native African Christian church' (the Ethiopian Orthodox Church) that often operated as a site of resistance to Italian occupation and hence had become a target of attack by fascist forces. Indeed, the very Englishness of these Christians demanded such solidarity, as Isabel Fry, influential educationalist, argued: 'In England for two hundred years we have had the blessings of complete religious toleration ... to forbid the free exercise of our religion is inevitably to penalise the noblest and most sincere part' (*New Times and Ethiopia News* 1937c).

But to link the redemption of Englishness to the fate of the Ethiopian Orthodox Church necessarily tested and complicated the civilizational hierarchies that placed African polities significantly below the European family of nations, and that positioned the competencies of Africanicity firmly below those that composed Englishness. On the one hand, it had to be acknowledged that Ethiopian Christianity had a pedigree that was not shared by the Western church; as Acts 8: 26–40 suggested, the gospel reached Ethiopia before it reached Rome (*The Essex Chronicle* 1935). Selassie I himself claimed lineage to the Old Testament Queen of Sheba and King Solomon, and such intimate biblical connections were also recognised to carry weight amongst the non-aristocratic populace (*Western Daily Press and Bristol Mirror* 1935). In light of this biblical heritage white Christians often alluded to Psalms 68:31 – 'Princes shall come out of Egypt; Ethiopia shall soon stretch out her hands unto God'. Rev Josephy Gilbert, for example, preached that 'this ancient prophecy was being fulfilled in our own day ... Ethiopia to-day is stretching out her hands in earnest supplication to all justice loving people' (*North Devon Journal* 1935; see also, for example, *The Whitstable Times and Tankerton Press* 1935).

Yet, on the other hand, such hermeneutics by and large assumed that Ethiopians were stretching out their hands to white Christians – God's children – for salvation: 'Ethiopia ... is stretching out her hands unto God', proclaimed the Missionary Service Bureau and Ethiopian Prayer League; 'will His people come to her aid regardless of personal sacrifice or inconvenience?' (Pankhurst 2003, 164) In this respect, the support that white Christians gave to Ethiopia was usually parsed through the civilisational supremacy that was encoded in Englishness. (Here, perhaps, it was the racial specificity of Englishness – as white – rather than its geographical specificity – a nation within the UK – that enabled commentators to partake of its particular sense of belonging.) Thus, white Christians often mobilised established Orientalist tropes: Ethiopia's Christianity was ancient, yes; but it did not enjoy the progressive impulse of the Western Church, had therefore fallen into barbaric torpor, and currently provided a key institutional support for slavery (e.g. *Yorkshire Evening Post* 1935; *Western Daily Press and Bristol Mirror* 1936). And if abolition work exemplified a core competency of enlightened imperial governance, then this was a competency that Ethiopia's ancient religion was still struggling to cultivate.

Moreover, most of those who staked their Englishness to the redemption of Ethiopia at the same time applied a particular racial lens to Ethiopia's peoples that questioned their

Africanicity. In the opinion of Hazel Napier, secretary general of the Friends of Abyssinia, there were a 'great many different races in the Abyssinian empire.' Indeed, for her – and for many others at the time – the etymology of Abyssinia resolved to Hebas or Habesh, 'meaning to mix' (*The Courier and Advertiser* 1935; *The Essex Chronicle* 1935). Whilst Habesha does not necessarily connote a mixing of racial types per se, such commentators racialized the meaning of the term in order to dilute the 'negroid' presence of Ethiopia. For one Miss Rouse, for example, Ethiopians 'were more Semetic Jews, only in the past they had inter-married a lot with the negroes' (*The Courier* 1935). And for others who believed that Habesha resolved to a tribal name, this tribe originated not from the continent but South Arabia (*The Yorkshire Post* 1936; for a critique of this thesis see Bekerie 1997). In fact, some commentators proclaimed that 'there are no negroes in the country, except as slaves' (*The Evening News* 1936).

So while Euri-centric Ethiopianists embraced an African polity in order to redeem Englishness, the intimacy of this embrace – the sharing, for example of the Christian St George – was enabled only on condition that Ethiopians be categorised as not properly African and certainly not straightforwardly 'negro' as was the vast majority of British subjects in the African and Caribbean colonies, and that the indigenous church of this Christian African polity was backward. Therefore, principled support for Ethiopia nevertheless sought to uphold the jurisprudential tradition of the standard of civilisation which protected the racial exclusivity of the competencies that made up Englishness. The effect, then, was to insulate support for Ethiopia from any deeper and broader commitment to African liberation, the tempo of which in any case was to be determined by white saviours.

Alternatively, the catechism for Psalms 68:31 articulated by Afri-centric Ethiopianism radically resituated and realigned the competencies of enlightened imperial governance: Ethiopia was to save herself with the aid of the Black subjects of the British empire (see in general Belgrave 1937; Mensah 1937; Shepperson 1953).This Pan-African interpretation built upon the sense of outrage that accompanied the revelation that those Black peoples who claimed Britishness were treated not as mutual subjects but rather as de facto aliens. 'This cold hard inhuman attitude which the European powers have assumed towards Ethiopia,' proclaimed Belgrave (1937), a 'British West Indian Negro', in a letter headed with Psalms 68:31, 'has taught us black men that somehow or other, there is a difference in justice. There is one kind of justice for white folk, and another kind for black'.

Some of Britain's Black subjects even began to consider the Empire that they belonged to as a willing accomplice to Italy, united not necessarily by imperial interests but certainly through a white supremacist design for global order. Kwame Nkrumah's memory of his 1935 sojourn through the UK provides evidence of this feeling. Reading a placard proclaiming Mussolini's invasion of Ethiopia, the future leader of independent Ghana felt 'as if the whole of London had suddenly declared war on me personally. For the next few minutes I could do nothing but glare at each impassive face wondering if those people could possibly realise the wickedness of colonialism' (Nkrumah 1957, 29).The feeling was far more widespread. For instance, vendors in the British Cameroons of Sylvia Pankhurst's pro-Ethiopia newspaper nevertheless found it increasingly hard to sell copies due to the fact that it was published in Britain and therefore perceived as anti-African (Ngongi 1939).

Such discrepancies and perceived discrepancies in treatment bolstered an established critique of Black belonging to Western polities and empires, the race consciousness of which had already been catalysed during the previous 20 years by Marcus Garvey and

Amy Ashwood Garvey through their extremely influential Universal Negro Improvement Association. In this respect, as the imperial belonging promised associatively by Britishness rescinded, so race consciousness was re-mobilised around the defence of Ethiopia. Thus, in contrast to the diffidence of Euri-centric Ethiopianism, Afri-centric Ethiopianists in the Caribbean and African colonies situated Ethiopia firmly in the heart of Black Africa, as professed by a 'Bantu voice' from Cape Town: 'we sympathise with Ethiopia because she is in Africa, because she is black, because we believe her to be the Cradle of Blackdom. We say so with tremendous pride' (Citashe 1936). A statement from Theo Jean, a Trinidadian, expresses the dissolving effect of Ethiopianism on imperial belonging as Britishness was put aside for Pan-Africanism:

> I claim Africa as my own because my fathers were born there. Because I happen to be born in lands known to be owned by Britain I am called a British subject; nevertheless the place of my birth has not affected my stock. I am all African. Africans at home and abroad are my bone and my flesh, and when anything is done to cause hurt to my bone and my flesh I must publish it abroad … Oh Britain; Britain! You have given us cause to make use of words to which you are no stranger; 'if we had served our God as faithfully as we served you, He would not in our times of trouble have turned His back upon us'. (Jean 1937)

But Afri-centric Ethiopianism was not just a phenomenon of the colonies; it also had a presence in the heart of British empire where, in the UK, it radicalized many Black subjects who – as would be the case for the Windrush generation – already faced issues to do with the 'colour bar' and discriminatory work practices (Fryer 1992, 325–330; Adi 2013, 278). Certainly Afri-centric Ethiopianism was promoted by resident race radicals such as Garvey (at least, until he soured towards Selassie I in 1936). But even the League of Coloured Peoples, a group that lobbied for imperial reform from within their claim to Britishness, protested against the betrayal of Ethiopia, 'the last part of Africa to have maintained its independence' (League of Coloured Peoples 1938, 2; see in general Rush 2002). In fact, as Asante (1974) identified, a clear line runs through the introduction to the UK of Afri-centric Ethiopianism in 1935 to the post-war anti-colonial Pan-Africanism that signalled the formal demise of empire in the African world.

The International African Friends of Abyssinia (IAFA) had its first public meeting in July of 1935 (Høgsbjerg 2014, 91), and was established by writers and activists of African descent including CLR James, Amy Ashwood Garvey, George Padmore, Jomo Kenyatta and Chris Braithwaite. In supporting the Ethiopian cause, CLR James was keen to tell the crowds at a pro-Ethiopia rally in Trafalgar Square on 2nd August 1935 that they were not animated by 'anti-White feeling' but more by a 'union of sentiment between black men … all over the world' (*Nottingham Evening Post* 1935).By 1937 the IAFA had morphed into the International African Service Bureau (IASB), the aims of which, as the name suggests, were to support a broader movement of self-determination amongst peoples of African descent. Nonetheless, the IASB maintained its personal links to the Ethiopian legation in London as well as its ideological support of the Ethiopia cause in general (Ras Makonnen 1973, 120). In addressing the need for such an organisation, the IASB (1937) explained that

> … never since the emancipation of the slaves have Africans and other subject races been so awake to a realisation of the wrongs and injustices inflicted upon weak and defenceless peoples as since the brutal Italian fascist war against Abyssinia.

The newspaper of the IASB put the case more bluntly in 1939: 'as the Ethiopian struggle has shown, all Negroes everywhere are beginning to see the necessity for international organisation and the unification of their scattered efforts' (*International African Opinion* 1939).

Subsequently some of the figures active in the IASB re-grouped as the Pan-African Federation under whose auspices the fifth Pan-African Conference was held in Manchester one month after the cessation of hostilities in 1945. Attended by a number of future independence leaders the eighth resolution of the conference demanded the 'withdrawal of the British Military Administration from Ethiopian soil' (Sherwood 2012, 109). For these intellectuals and future leaders, Britishness could no longer contain Pan-African designs. Afri-centric Ethiopianism had catalysed an anti-colonial politics that sought the very dissolution of British Empire. The sons and daughters of that dissolution would soon bring Ethiopianism back to the United Kingdom in the post-colonial era.

In sum, slavery emancipation and liberation framed the narratives of both Ethiopianisms, albeit in various ways. However, their tempos diverged significantly. The movement of Afri-centric Ethiopianism was determined by the self-deliverance/determination of African peoples – on the continent and in the Diaspora – against European colonial rule. In this movement the pretentions of Britishness towards imperial inclusivity were exposed as a (racist) sham. Alternatively, the tempo of Euri-centric Ethiopianism was driven by the salvation of Ethiopians by white Christians (and other white subjects of Britain). And in this movement the core competencies that made Englishness racially exclusive and culturally superior on the world stage were defended. In fine, Euri-centric and Afri-centric Ethiopianism vied to resolve in different ways the disparagement of Englishness and Britishness as cultures of imperial belonging. But only one erupted as a fundamental challenge to imperial belonging itself.

Finally, the stakes at play for both Ethiopianisms were manifested in the personage of Haile Selassie I. For Afri-centric Ethiopianists, Selassie I was, as I have already presented, the symbol and promise of Black and African independence. As the British government betrayed Ethiopia and revealed their racial prejudices and biases, many Black subjects turned away from any pretentions towards a shared imperial Britishness. Instead, they started to identify with Selassie I as his de facto Ethiopian/African subjects for whom they were quite willing to die for on the battlefield (see e.g. Wallace Johnson's testimony in *New Times and Ethiopia News* 1937c). Some, who would create a movement known by his Crown Prince name of Ras Tafari, even proclaimed Selassie I to be their God as well as King.

For Euri-centric Ethiopianists, Selassie I became the substitute incarnation of Englishness when those leaders who should have exemplified its core competencies had instead betrayed them. 'Nobody … could fail to be impressed by the quiet dignity and regal fortitude of Haile Selassie', commented one attendee to a reception at the Ethiopian Legation, 'even in the most difficult circumstances, [he] displays just those qualities we like to regard as part of the public school tradition' (*Devon and Exeter Gazette* 1936). Additionally, Selassie I was said to embody that quintessentially English tradition of impartial and civilising governance through the work of abolition (e.g. *Gloucestershire Echo* 1936). Meanwhile, Selassie I's troubling Africanicity could always be tempered by allusion to his 'mixed' Semetic heritage and the – albeit 'native' – Christian and Biblical provenance of his imperial authority.

By way of conclusion: Ethiopianism past and present

The struggles over imperial belonging that I have examined in this article began when the cultures that were supposed to provide the cognitive integrity of British empire were put into question by government (in)action over the Italian invasion of Ethiopia. These struggles were articulated by the protagonists themselves through diverse narratives of Ethiopianism that clashed over the question as to who could quicken African redemption from slavery and colonialism and to what extent. In the introduction, I suggested that narratives of settlement run the risk of domesticating struggles over belonging that are framed, by the strugglers themselves, through global racial and colonial coordinates. I also suggested that in these self-conceptualizations the division between pre- and post-war, pre- and post-colonialism is not a categorical one, and so the moral and political compass is oriented towards rearrangements that exceed an equitable national settlement – colonial or postcolonial. I would therefore like to finish by sketching out a couple of further points on an Ethiopianist narrative that join the struggles in the 1930s with those of the early 1980s and, ultimately, of today.

The demonisation of African-Caribbean youth in 1970s England constituted one of the key political reference points of the Cultural Studies tradition. Many African–Caribbean families arrived in the UK still cleaving to a certain Britishness. Yet Britishness was never meant to intimately mingle with Englishness in the metropolis: what distinguished the two cultures of belonging was that the former was supposed to be practiced at a colonial distance. With the collapse of this distance mainstream media and academicians proselytised on the inability of recently-arrived African-Caribbean families to adapt to English culture, thereby producing 'subnormal' or 'socially deficient' children that threatened the future integrity of UK society (Carby 1999; Warmington 2014, 66). The environment was ripe for the creation of a moral panic surrounding Black 'criminality', that is, the notion that Black culture was fundamentally alien to English mores (Gilroy 1982).

A loosely knitted but easily visible movement amongst Black youth took centre stage in this panic, especially in London and Birmingham. They knew themselves as RasTafari, but were described, disparagingly, as a 'muggers' mafia' or a 'black power movement on the warpath' (Cashmore 1979, 208). The movement had been intergenerationally transmitted through Caribbean family members and peers, the genealogies of which return us to Leonard Howell (the 'first Rasta') and other Afri-centric Ethiopianists from the 1930s. In Britain, however, members of the movement took the Crown Prince title of Haile Selassie I (Ras Tafari) as a claim to African belonging that stood opposed to the racist exclusions of Englishness and one which would be realised by repatriation to Ethiopia.

Yet even sympathetic intellectual responses to RasTafari refused to take such self-conceptualisations seriously and mobilised, instead, a narrative of settlement that sought to domesticate the movement into, for example, a 'subculture' that could be comfortably placed alongside other British subcultures of youthful rebellion (see Hebdige [1979] 2007; for a broad critique see Henry 2006). Len Garrison, an influential Black educationalist, did acknowledge the self-understanding of RasTafari as a Pan-African liberation movement in a path-breaking treatise on the subject. Yet Garrison still ultimately argued that any quest for an 'African personality' would have to proceed through a process of settlement facilitated by an endorsement by the British public of 'cultural plurality' (Garrison 1979, 39).

Garrison's treatise was prescient, written just before the dramatic uprisings of 1981 in Brixton and other urban areas heavily populated by African-Caribbean communities. In writing his famous report on these disturbances, Lord Scarman leaned upon the American sociology of Daniel Patrick Moynihan in order to locate the root of the problem in the dysfunctional Black family unit (Kushnick 1993, 18). In this respect, Scarman's report was framed very much by a narrative of settlement that took Englishness as the aspirational norm. But Scarman also consulted Garrison's treatise on RasTafari in preparation for his report, and he entered into a hesitant but somewhat receptive consultation with key RasTafari individuals and groups ('Note of a Meeting Between Lord Scarman and Rastafarian Representatives' 1981). Scarman was even determined that RasTafari should be allowed to have their say in public sessions (Kirby 2006, 614). True, Scarman might have been using the RasTafari movement to sidestep groups such as the Brixton Defence Campaign who were campaigning for the Black community to boycott the report; and true, too, Scarman was less concerned with entertaining the cause of repatriation and more focused upon facilitating integration and settlement of RasTafari in Britain.[2] Yet it still remains a puzzle as to why Scarman would even enter into such a principled engagement with a group that so fundamentally disavowed Englishness and even Britishness.

I wish to suggest, though, that a residue of Euri-centric Ethiopianism informed Scarman's understanding of the struggle. He would have been 25 years old when the Italy/Ethiopia war erupted in 1935, and a year later he joined Middle Temple as a Harmsworth Law Scholar. Surveying Brixton in 1981, did Scarman recall another time when the gulf between white Englanders and Black Britons had been at least partially bridged by Ethiopianism? Is this why he could at least appreciate that the question of belonging exceeded that of national settlement?

On 1 August 2014 between 5 and 6000 people of predominantly African descent marched from Windrush Square, Brixton to Downing Street, London. The first of August marks emancipation day in the British Caribbean. The marchers delivered a petition of over 65,000 signatures for a parliamentary inquiry into reparations, part of which read:

> The lack of accountability by those responsible confirms the ongoing racism which creates disproportionate detriment to the offspring of the millions of individuals that were stolen from Afrika … Today the offspring of the stolen Afrikans encounter direct and indirect racial discrimination daily. (Rastafari Movement UK 2014)

RasTafari Movement UK organised the reparations March along with active support from a number of other Pan-African organisations and its members featured heavily in the demonstration. As the invocation of African identities in the petition suggests, reparation for the Movement is part of a broader and bolder agenda for repatriation to various sites on the African continent, including within Ethiopia. Afri-centric Ethiopianism lives on in the UK.

Nonetheless, despite peacefully disrupting central London on a Saturday afternoon, no news media (save one local Brixton paper) reported the demonstration. Perhaps even the liberal media could not quite conceive of a movement that was so strangely out of time and place in multicultural Britain, especially when Englishness/Britishness was now primarily threatened by Islam and Al Qaeda. This time, no Scarman has presented himself as a bridge-builder. Do our frameworks of citizenship and race similarly occlude the global constellations within which at least some contemporary struggles over postcolonial belonging still proceed?

By concluding in this manner I hope to demonstrate that narratives of settlement can, on the one hand, enlighten us to the struggle between rights claims and culturally determined exclusions. But on the other hand they can obfuscate the way in which struggles over belonging so often work through tempos that race beyond the 'national' and enact chronologies that precede and succeed settlement and re-settlement. For Britain's Black subjects, the inter-war struggle over settlement in the empire which implicated Britishness, and the post-Windrush struggle over settlement in the UK which implicated Englishness, are not necessarily separate stories divided by world war and empire. They can, instead, be joined by an Ethiopianism that provides different cartographies of belonging leading, for some, to a Pan-African resolution of race and (post)-colonial rule.

I believe this acknowledgement is a crucial corrective to investigations of nation, culture and belonging that have framed struggle primarily though settlement. For I am arguing that sometimes struggles over belonging seek resolutions that are beyond those made possible by full citizenship. And I am making both an academic and political point. In postcolonial Britain, citizenship will always be partial if it requires enfranchisement to be parsed through cultural competency, even if the nation is painted multicultural. Let us admit, instead, that many cultures of belonging retain their long-standing racial-global coordinates and that the battleground for justice will remain similarly global in effect, affiliation and outcome. Let us also acknowledge at the same time that, at least in Britain, citizenship rights should never be framed or determined by cultural competencies at all, no matter how pluralistic the criteria might appear. Those who, in their struggles, dare to claim both citizenship rights and global justice are never easily contained.

Notes

1. On the relationship between race and competency, see Grovogui (2001).
2. For learning of these qualifications I am indebted to Cecil Gutzmore, an original member of the Brixton Defence Committee, and Ras Gabre Wolde, a RasTafari participant in the discussions with Scarman.

Acknowledgements

The research for this article was undertaken as part of the 'Rastafari: the Majesty and the Movement' project, which exhibited at the National Museum of Ethiopia in May 2014. I acknowledge my fellow members of Rastafari Regal Livity CIC who formed the UK research team. Thanks to Cecil Gutzmore and Gabre Wolde for their important insights. Thanks to Gurminder Bhambra and James Dunkerley for helpful comments, as well as two anonymous referees. And thanks, finally, to Joe Turner for his exemplary editorship.

Disclosure statement

No potential conflict of interest was reported by the author.

References

Aberdeen Press and Journal. 1935. "Efforts to Stop Slavery". July 18.
Adi, Hakim. 2013. *Pan-Africanism and Communism: The Communist International, Africa and the Diaspora, 1919–1939*. Trenton, NJ: Africa World Press.

Allain, Jean. 2006. "Slavery and the League of Nations: Ethiopia as a Civilised Nation." *Journal of the History of International Law* 8: 213–244.

Allen, E. J. 1935. "Letter to the Editor". Essex Chronicle, December 20.

Angell, Norman, Stanley Jevons, Lloyd George, and H. G. Wells. 1937. "Letter." *New Times and Ethiopia News*, March 27.

Asante, S. K. B. 1974. "The Italo-Ethiopian Conflict: A Case Study in British West African Response to Crisis Diplomacy in the 1930s." *The Journal of African History* 15 (2): 291–302.

Baker, Houston A. Jr., Stephen Best, and Ruth H. Lindeborg. 1996. "Introduction: Representing Blackness/Representing Britain: Cultural Studies and the Politics of Knowledge." In *Black British Cultural Studies: A Reader*, edited by Houston A. Baker Jr., Mantha Diawara, and Ruth H. Lindeborg, 1–15. Chicago, IL: University of Chicago Press.

Baucom, Ian. 1999. *Out of Place*. Princeton, NJ: Princeton University Press.

Baum, James. 1935. *Unknown Ethiopia: New Light on Darkest Abyssinia*. New York: Grosset & Dunlap.

Bekerie, Ayele. 1997. *Ethiopic, an African Writing System: Its History and Principles*. Lawrenceville, NJ: Red Sea Press.

Belgrave, C. C. 1937. "Ethiopia Stretches Out Her Hands to God." *New Times and Ethiopia News*, January 16.

Bell, Duncan. 2014. "Beyond the Sovereign State: Isopolitan Citizenship, Race and Anglo-American Union." *Political Studies* 62 (2): 418–434.

Blackstone, Lee Robert. 2005. "A New Kind of English: Cultural Variance, Citizenship and DiY Politics amongst the Exodus Collective in England." *Social Forces* 84 (2): 803–820.

Brown, Una. 1937. "Letter." *New Times and Ethiopia News*, July 13.

C.A.B. 1937. "Letter." *New Times and Ethiopia News*, October 2.

Carby, Hazel. 1999. "Schooling in Babylon." In Carby, H. (ed.), *Cultures in Babylon: Black Britain and African America*, 189–218. London: Verso.

Cashmore, Ernest. 1979. *Rastaman: The Rastafarian Movement in England*. London: G. Allen & Unwin.

Centre for Contemporary Cultural Studies. 1992. *The Empire Strikes Back: Race and Racism in 70's Britain*. London: Routledge.

Citashe, C. N. 1936. "A Bantu Voice from Cape Town." *New Times and Ethiopia News*, December 5.

Devon and Exeter Gazette. 1936. "A Letter from London". June 12.

Evans, J. Norris. 1935. "Letter." *The Evening News*, September 3.

Favell, Adrian. 1998. *Philosophies of Integration: Immigration and the Idea of Citizenship in France and Britain*. New York: St Martin's Press.

Friends of Abyssinia League of Service. 1936. *"Abyet! Abyet!"* WG/ITA/393. Manchester: Peoples Museum Manchester.

Fryer, Peter. 1992. *Staying Power: The History of Black People in Britain*. London: Pluto Press.

Garrison, Len. 1979. *Black Youth, Rastafarianism, and the Identity Crisis in Britain*. London: Afro-Caribbean Education Resource Project.

Gikandi, Simon. 2007. "The Ghost of Matthew Arnold: Englishness and the Politics of Culture." *Nineteenth-Century Contexts* 29 (2–3): 187–199.

Gikandi, Simon. 2014. "Afterword: Outside the Black Atlantic." *Research in African Literatures* 45 (3): 241–244.

Gilroy, Paul. 1982. "The Myth of Black Criminality." *Socialist Register* 19: 47–56.

Gloucestershire Echo. 1936. "Letters to the Editor." May 23.

Gorman, Daniel. 2006. *Imperial Citizenship: Empire and the Question of Belonging*. Manchester: Manchester University Press.

Grovogui, Siba N. 2001. "Come to Africa: A Hermeneutics of Race in International Theory." *Alternatives: Global, Local, Political* 26 (4): 425–448.

Hall, Stuart, C. Critcher, T. Jefferson, J. Clarke, and B. Roberts. 1978. *Policing the Crisis*. London: Macmillan.

Hampshire, James. 2005. *Citizenship and Belonging*. New York: Palgrave Macmillan.

Hansen, Randall. 2002. "British Citizenship after Empire: A Defence." *The Political Quarterly* 71 (1): 42–49.

Hastings and St. Leonards Observer. 1936. "Public Lecture by Anti-slavery Society", July 4.

Heartfield, James. 2015. *The British and Foreign Anti-slavery Society*. London: Hurst Publishers.

Hebdige, Dick. 2007. *Subculture: The Meaning of Style*. London: Routledge.

Henry, William (Lez). 2006. *What the Deejay Said: A Critique from the Street!* London: Nu-Beyond.

Hill, Robert. 2001. *Dread History: Leonard P. Howell and Millenarian Visions in the Early Rastafarian Religion*. Chicago, IL: Frontline Distribution International.

Høgsbjerg, Christian. 2014. *C.L.R. James in Imperial Britain*. London: Duke University Press.

Howell, David. 2006. "A Faraway Country – Abyssina and the British General Election of 1935." *Socialist History* 28: 60–75.

IASB. 1937. *Pamphlet: The International African Service Bureau*. MEPO 38/91. National Archives UK.

International African Opinion. 1939. "Editorial", February. CO 847/11/16. National Archives UK.

Jean, Theo. 1937. "Letter." *New Times and Ethiopia News*, March 6.

Kirby, Michael. 2006. "Law Reform and Human Rights: Scarman's Great Legacy." *Commonwealth Law Bulletin* 32 (4): 609–632.

Kushnick, Louis. 1993. "'We're Here Because You Were There': Britain's Black Population." *Trotter Review* 7 (2): 17–19.

Langlands, Rebecca. 1999. "Britishness or Englishness? The Historical Problem of National Identity in Britain." *Nations and Nationalism* 5 (1): 53–69.

Lawrence, Susan. 2003. *Archaeologies of the British: Explorations of Identity in the United Kingdom and Its Colonies, 1600–1945*. London: Routledge.

League of Coloured Peoples. 1938. "Seventh Annual Report." CO 318435, National Archives UK.

Lee, Hélène. 2003. *The First Rasta: Leonard Howell and the Rise of Rastafarianism*. Chicago, IL: Lawrence Hill Books.

Lockward, Alanna. 2013. "Black Europe Body Politics: Towards an Afropean Decolonial Aesthetics." *Social Text*. http://socialtextjournal.org/periscope/2013/07/black-europe-body-politics-towards-an-afropean-decolonial-aesthetics.php

Mensah, Africanus. 1937. "A Nigerian Serman." *New Times and Ethiopia News*, July 3.

Miers, Suzanne. 1998. "Slavery and the Slave Trade as International Issues 1890–1939." *Slavery & Abolition* 19 (2): 16–37.

Morpeth Herald and Reporter. 1935. "The Peace Ballot", July 26.

Nelson, Gersham A. 1994. "Rastafari and Ethiopianism." In *Imagining Home: Class, Culture and Nationalism in the African Diaspora*, 66–84. London: Verso.

New Times and Ethiopia News. 1937a. "A Voice from Africa", January 23.

New Times and Ethiopia News. 1937b. "Thou Shalt Rise Up a Queen!", March 6.

New Times and Ethiopia News. 1937c. "Speeches at Last Thursday's Conference", September 18.

New Times and Ethiopia News. 1937d. "Greetings to Ethiopian Nation", November 6.

New Times and Ethiopia News. 1937e. "Letters from a Native of British Guiana", December 4.

Ngongi, H. J. S. 1939. "Letter to Sylvia Pankhurst." ADD MS 88925/5/2, British Library Western Manuscripts.

Nkrumah, Kwame. 1957. *The Autobiography of Kwame Nkrumah*. Edinburgh: Thomas Nelson and Sons.

North Devon Journal. 1935. "Barnstaple Minister and Abyssinia", September 12.

Northern Daily Mail. 1935a. "Slavery in Ethiopia", October 25.

Northern Daily Mail. 1935b. "Slavery in Ethiopia", October 30.

"Note of a Meeting between Lord Scarman and Rastafarian Representatives". 1981. HO 266/129. National Archives UK.

Nottingham Evening Post. 1935. "Union of Sentiment", August 26.

Padmore, George. 1969. *How Britain Rules Africa*. New York: Negro Universities Press.

Pankhurst, Richard. 2003. "Pro- and Anti- Ethiopian Pamphleteering in Britain During the Italian Fascist Invasion and Occupation (1935–1941)." *International Journal of Ethiopian Studies* 1 (1): 153–176.

Pankhurst, Sylvia. 1939. "Letter to Haile Selassie I." ADD MS 88925/2/1. British Library Western Manuscripts.

Price, Charles Reavis. 2003. "'Cleave to the Black': Expressions of Ethiopianism in Jamaica." *New West Indian Guide/Nieuwe West-Indische Gids* 77 (1–2): 31–64.

Ras Makonnen. 1973. *Pan-Africanism from Within*. Nairobi: Oxford University Press.

Rush, Anne Spry. 2002. "Imperial Identity in Colonial Minds: Harold Moody and the League of Coloured Peoples, 1931–1950." *Twentieth Century British History* 13 (4): 356–383.

Sajed, Alina. 2010. "Postcolonial Strangers in a Cosmopolitan World: Hybridity and Citizenship in the Franco-Maghrebian Borderland." *Citizenship Studies* 14 (4): 363–380. doi: http://dx.doi.org/10.1080/13621025.2010.490031.

Shepperson, George. 1953. "Ethiopianism and African Nationalism." *Phylon (1940-1956)* 14 (1): 9–18.

Sherwood, Marika. 2012. "Pan-African Conferences, 1900–1953: What Did 'Pan-Africanism' Mean?" *The Journal of Pan African Studies* 4 (10): 106–126.

Snow, M. 1937. "St George, Patron of Abyssinia." *New Times and Ethiopia News*, May 8.

Stevenson, Nick. 2010. "Cultural Citizenship, Education and Democracy: Redefining the Good Society." *Citizenship Studies* 14 (3): 275–291.

Sunday Post. 1935. "In Abyssinia Today", August 18.

The Courier. 1935. "Abyssinia – Interesting Address at Lye Green", November 8.

The Courier and Advertiser. 1935. "The Emperor in the News", July 20.

The Essex Chronicle. 1935. "Abyssinia", September 6.

The Evening News. 1936. "Haile Selassie, Emperor of Ethiopia", January 30.

The Nottingham Evening Post. 1936. "Custom Almost as Ancient as Abyssinia's History", April 13.

The Western Morning News and Daily Gazette. 1935a. "Stop This Thing", December 6.

The Western Morning News and Daily Gazette. 1935b. "Peace Ballot at Plymouth", December 13.

The Western Morning News and Daily Gazette. 1936. "Letters to the Editor", May 16.

The Whitstable Times and Tankerton Press. 1935. "Bible Churchmen's Missionary Society", November 23.

The Yorkshire Post. 1936. "Words in the News", March 30.

Turner, Bryan S. 2001. "Outline of a General Theory of Cultural Citizenship." In *Culture and Citizenship*, edited by Nick Stevenson, 11–32. London: Sage.

Wallace Johnson, I. T. A. 1938. "Letter to Sylvia Pankhurst." ADD MS 88925/2/1. British Library Western Manuscripts.

Warmington, Paul. 2014. *Black British Intellectuals and Education: Multiculturalism's Hidden History*. London: Routledge.

Wellings, Ben. 2002. "Empire-nation: National and Imperial Discourses in England." *Nations and Nationalism* 8 (1): 95–109.

Western Daily Press and Bristol Mirror. 1935. "Legend and History of Dusky Dynasties", August 13.

Western Daily Press and Bristol Mirror. 1936. "The Darker Side of Ethiopia", May 19.

Yorkshire Evening Post. 1935. "The Church of 'Prester John'", August 30.

Young, Robert. 2008. *The Idea of English Ethnicity*. Maiden, MA: Blackwell.

Yuval-Davis, Nira. 2004. "Borders, Boundaries, and the Politics of Belonging." In *Ethnicity, Nationalism, and Minority Rights*, edited by Stephen May, Tariq Modood, and Judith Squires, 214–230. Cambridge: Cambridge University Press.

Beyond the nation state: the role of local and pan-national identities in defining post-colonial African citizenship

Gemma Bird

Department of Politics, University of Sheffield, Sheffield, UK

ABSTRACT

This article explores how the process of decolonisation offers a perspective on the politics of identification, solidarity and becoming. The hope is to offer a way of tracing a concept of citizenship that may not only be tied to the nation state but to other forms of political organisation. To achieve this, the article draws on the work of Engin Isin and the concept of the 'activist citizen' as a lens through which to examine how citizenship in the mid-twentieth century decolonisation movements in Africa was imagined by 'philosopher statesmen' as a way of re-establishing a sense of pride in the village and the pan-African community, as locations of citizenship beyond the nation state. In discussing this the article analyses the speeches, articles and monographs of, Julius Nyerere, and Léopold Sédar Senghor, questioning whether these texts reveal a complicated notion of the postcolonial citizen which begin to re-establish a belief in the value of some sense of African identity as a response to the dehumanising efforts of colonialism; establishing local and pan-national spaces as locations for 'acts' of citizenship intended to re-establish a sense of pride in African identities.

Introduction

Historically, from the period of Plato and Aristotle, the concept of citizenship has been associated with the democratic participation of individual members in the functioning of states. However, the recent citizenship literature (Isin 2008, 2009; Jabri 2013; Isin & Turner 2002; White 2008) focuses on processes of transformation and becoming that suggest the concept of citizenship refers to processes or acts of transformation and change rather than membership; intended 'to generate new ways of thinking about those ways of acting politically that are not easily captured by conventional socio-legal understandings of citizenship' (White 2008, 44). In her discussions of the Arab Spring Vivienne Jabri claims that 'recent events in the Middle East places into sharp relief questions relating to change and political transformation in the postcolonial world'. She argues that 'the primary call of the "Arab Spring" is for a renewed notion of political community' (Jabri 2013, 1). In ending this special issue I argue that an attempt to reimagine the concept of community and identity in the face of oppression is not a recent development in revolutionary movements in the post-colonial world. In doing so I explore the anti-colonial movement in Africa from 1940 to the 1960s suggesting the existence of a trend in the work of the post-colonial 'philosopher statesmen' towards an attempt to reimagine spaces beyond nation states as sites of transformation in response to the oppressive regimes of the colonial movement. The article feeds in to recent debates (Balibar 2012; Isin 2012; Stephens and Squire 2012b) that aim 'to uncover alternative spatialities and temporalities of citizenship' (Stephens and Squire 2012a, 434). In doing so the article suggests the importance of including previously marginalised voices in these discussions that offer a unique understanding of citizenship guided by cultural and political influences and experiences. The article draws on Engin Isin's concept of the 'activist citizen' (2009) as a vocabulary through which to discuss notions of citizenship, beyond membership of the nation state present in the work of Julius K Nyerere and Léopold Sédar Sengor. The article focuses on discussions in the work of these thinkers of imagined spaces on the local and pan-national levels as representing a political opportunity to think about citizenship in post-national terms. Whilst a literature exists around post-national and post-sovereign citizenship these scholars' views have been broadly marginalized in the past due to their origins outside Western scholarship.

Like Balibar (2004) this article critiques the arguments made by thinkers such as Schnapper (1994) who suggest that national solutions are the only 'effective one(s)' (Balibar 2004, 53) when thinking in terms of citizenship, considering instead local and pan-national spaces. The question of community transcending the nation state is one that Isin (2012) has considered and in doing so he makes reference to the work of Agamben (1993), Nancy (1991), and Esposito (2010) who 'investigate how community has been mobilised as a strategic concept invoking certain images against others in political struggles' (Isin 2012, 450). Isin himself argues that, 'to imagine citizens without nations requires a genealogy of fraternity' (Isin 2012, 465), a value that I argue is present in Nyerere and Senghor's discussions of local and pan-national spaces: in particular underpinning Senghor's discussions of Négritude. More broadly, this article intends to contribute to thinking in this area not by offering a new understanding of citizenship but rather by drawing on the experience of often excluded voices that draw on ideas of local and pan-national community as sites of political solidarity. In doing so the article contributes to the discussions of scholars such as Isin in thinking about citizenship beyond the nation state. In the past the primary focus in discussions of post-national citizenship have marginalised African voices, failing to take into account the pan-African project as relevant to discussions of post-national citizenship, focusing instead on projects such as the European Union. The purpose of this article is to bring those voices back in to discussions of post-sovereign citizens and to recognise that they were thinking in these terms far in advance of Isin, Balibar, Stephens and Squire, but that in the past their views have been excluded from the discourse because of their relationship with Western politics and scholarship.

The concepts of nationalism, localism and regionalism in Western discourses have become broadly associated with negative connotations of exclusivity and elitism, of fear and extremism (Berlin 1980). This article argues that contra to questions of domination and exclusivity these concepts have, in the context of the anti-colonial freedom struggle, been associated with the broadening out of community and citizenship: with an understanding of citizenship beyond the boundaries of the nation state. Thus, I argue lessons can be learnt from previously marginalised African discourses. Contra to the image of Africa as lagging behind, that has become common parlance in Western scholarship; this article is suggesting that analysis of African thinkers has the potential to provide new ways of thinking about citizenship as a political opportunity for transformation and becoming. The article seeks to extend the boundaries of national citizenship within this context to consider both localised and pan-national movements as being presented as legitimate sites of 'activist citizenship' (Isin 2009).

African perspectives are underrepresented in citizenship narratives and it is in this sense that this article contributes to the special issues broader themes of marginality. The article suggests that analysis of Nyerere and Senghor has the potential to offer a different perspective on citizenship, one that shares commonalities with Jabri's reading of community in the Arab Spring, one that has previously been marginalised and that has the power to disrupt our understanding of citizenship beyond the nation state.

That being said, it is important, before engaging in more detail in the analysis itself, to summarise Isin's understanding of 'acts of citizenship' that provides a conceptual framework through which to consider the views of the thinkers themselves in the analysis of this article. According to Isin, it is involvement in an 'act' that establishes an 'actor', or in his terminology, 'activist citizens'. He describes acts of citizenship as 'those deeds by which actors constitute themselves (and others) as subjects of rights' (Isin 2009, 371); without which they would merely be passive citizens living within the conditions set out for them. In contrast:

> activist citizenship relies on the disruption of the status quo, the undertaking of a process of transformation that alters the framework in which the individual exists: 'If acts produce actors (or actors are produced through acts) then initially we can define acts of citizenship as those acts that produce citizens and their others.' (Isin 2008, 37)

Thus, what it means to be a citizen according to Isin is not simply to be a member of a village, a town, a nation, a continent or even the global community. Rather, citizenship results from a transformative act; a disruptive process through which the individual not only becomes a citizen in their own right, but also has an effect on the community or space in which their citizenship is engendered: they transform it in some way.

As Isin argues 'the concept of the act of citizenship seeks to address the myriad ways that human beings organise remake and resist their ethical-political relations with others' (2008); thinking about what it means to be political in new and original ways. The philosopher statesmen considered in this article act in a way that disrupts the colonial understanding of citizenship associated with nation states and individuals. They focus, in their writings and speeches, on both local spaces and shared pan-African identities, or citizenship as a continent-wide phenomenon: a focus that has been broadly ignored by Western scholarships understanding of citizenship. Their conceptions of pan-Africanism and localism had the potential to play a transformative role in altering contemporary understandings of citizenship. As Melanie White suggests, 'acts' of citizenship attempt to:

> Foreground the transformative possibilities of politically becoming in the constitutive formation of new and innovative ways of acting politically. As such the 'act of citizenship' seeks to emphasize moments of aleatory possibility by highlighting the emergent, the new and, ultimately, the creative in becoming political. (White 2008, 44)

Through conceptualising imagined spaces on the local and pan-national levels, the statesmen discussed in this article do indeed discuss 'new and innovative ways of acting politically', new and innovative ways of thinking about identity beyond membership of the nation state, and, as such, new and innovative ways of being citizens beyond the process imposed upon them by colonialism. In doing so, I argue, they responded to the predictable political relations imposed upon them by the colonial movement with citizenship acts 'that disrupt (the predictable relations) through transformative action' (White 2008, 44).

The purpose here is not to claim that their projects were successful, but rather that they represented a political opportunity to think about identity and citizenship as something beyond individual membership of nation states and in that sense their work can be viewed through a lens of disruptive activist citizenship. Through a re-reading of a politically and culturally sensitive period in history the article intends not to consider issues of legal citizenship, but rather to analyse the normative aspect of the concept through a focus on 'acts' associated with the process of becoming citizens rather than simply members of communities beyond the national framework; instead focusing on local and continental levels. In agreement with Jabri, I make the claim that there is a distinction between 'politics, the realm of institutional arrangements, and the political, the realm of contested claims, of agonism and antagonism, all terms suggestive of action and hence of political agency in situated contexts' (Jabri 2013, 59).

The article thus focuses on African statesmen's views on the local and pan-national scales. Whilst accepting that the 'philosopher statesmen' were in a position to, and in fact did, implement the necessary legal and institutional frameworks to advocate for certain citizenship rights within the nation state, citizenship rights that remained firmly within the confines of a traditional individual state relationship, instead focuses on the marginalised processes that have otherwise been ignored by the citizenship literature. Arguably, this historical process disrupted contemporary understanding of what it meant to be African in the post-colonial condition; viewing it instead as 'a repudiation of victimhood (engendered by the colonial movement) and a robust assertion of the social and cognitive capabilities of ordinary individuals' (Young 2003, 2). Thus decolonisation offers a perspective on the politics of identification, solidarity and becoming. It offers a way of tracing a citizenship which may not only be tied to the nation state but to other forms of political organisation, notably the village and the continent.

In this context it is important to reflect upon Jabri's claim that 'the postcolonial world has not been considered as agent involved in the shaping of the international, but, rather as the recipient of its rules and normative interactions' (Jabri 2013, 9). It is possible to read the 'philosopher statesmen' as presenting an alternative conception of citizenship, and in this sense they can be read as transformative acts, very much intended to change contemporary understandings of what it meant to be African, what it meant to be a socialist, or even what it meant to be a member of a community. It is a common concern mentioned throughout this article, that what the theorists were able to put forward in theory was far removed from their abilities to achieve radical change. That being said, the article suggests that engaging with the work of Senghor and Nyerere, and their focus on local and pan-national communities as sites of citizenship led to a reimagining of these spaces, not as being exclusivist or restrictive but as valuable sites in inspiring activist engagement. These arguments, whilst they may not relate to realistic radical change remain disruptively interesting as normative discussions and it is for that reason they remain central to the discussions of this article.

The article is divided into three sections, the first and second sections focus on the concepts of localism and pan-nationalism respectively, whilst the third draws out the conclusions of the article as a whole. Marginalised perspectives are at the heart of this special issue and each of these sections refers to discussions of citizenship that have otherwise been ignored by the mainstream literature. The first section concentrates on Nyerere's villagisation programme and the conception of the village as a site of citizenship. This is followed by discussion of pan-African movements as a further example of the thinkers re-imagining spaces beyond the boundaries of the traditional nation state as having value in reimagining and disrupting the common understanding of citizenship. In concluding, the article considers broader conclusions regarding how the concepts of localism and pan-nationalism (as related and linked concepts) in the mid-twentieth century decolonisation movements were imagined by socialist 'philosopher statesmen' as a way of re-establishing a form of citizenship contrasting the restrictive regimes that de-humanised agents under colonialism.

The article turns first to a discussion of the village as representing a process of transformation and becoming responding to the African struggle.

The local community as a site for encouraging activist citizenship

This section focuses on the Ujamaa Vijinii programme implemented by the Tanu government of Tanzania under the leadership of Julius K. Nyerere. Arguing that, on analysing the origins of this policy, in both the Arusha declaration of the broader Tanu government, but predominantly in the speeches made by Nyerere himself, it can be suggested that the role of the villagisation project was to create a space in which individuals could, though their own actions, recreate a complicated notion of the post-colonial citizen; one which began to establish a belief in the value of African people as citizens, imbued with a sense of community and solidarity, specifically as a response to the de-humanising efforts of colonialism. This is not to suggest that the implementation and uptake of the policy in and of itself is an example of activist citizenship. In fact, the sense of solidarity it was intended to invoke amongst the people, and the conception of the state as providing a framework under which members of the community could become citizens have a lot more in common with previous conceptions of active citizens grounded on ideas of participation of the community with the running of the state (Hoskins and Mascherini 2009; Kearns 1992). However, this article argues that what is interesting about the Ujamaa project is that it sets out to think about the political in a new and transformative way. In doing so, Nyerere, and the Tanu government more broadly, offer a perspective on citizenship that has been broadly ignored, that to be a citizen can be a localised act separate to the boundaries of the nation state and participation within the broader state.

Before analysing the policies role in transforming our understanding of citizenship it is important first to give some background to the villagisation programme. The article focuses on the normative goals of the policy, rather than the process of failure that occurred following the policies implementation as, as previously stated, the aim of this article is to discuss the transformative ways in which these thinkers thought about citizenship, rather than to analyse the model of implementation. It is the *disruptive moment* that is important here and not the longer term project of implementation.

Ujamaa, or family hood, was the embodiment, or the political reality of Nyerere's philosophical socialist goals as being an African project: 'Nyerere's philosophy of African socialism provided the socialist project with an indigenous African identity that was grounded in African historical memories, experience, and realities' (Otunnu 2015, 19). This was not intended to be a conception of socialism borrowed from the West or established around previous structures, this was a marginalised conception of socialism intended to have Africa at its core and to maintain an often ignored African voice at its core. The model, 'demonstrated the urgency of building African socialism through the liberation and empowerment of rural and peasant production, as opposed to waiting for a possible proletarian revolution in some distant future when a "developed capitalist" state had emerged' (Otunnu 2015, 19). The focus on a distinctively African conception of a socialist state, and thus what it meant to be a socialist citizen outside of the traditional framework of the relationship between proletariat and bourgeoisie is the first indication of an act intended to transform the understanding of citizenship within a socialist framework, and in fact to transform the concept of socialism more broadly.

Nyerere was explicit and detailed in his account of the justification behind, and structuring of, the villagisation programme. Therefore, it is of value to quote this somewhat lengthy passage in full:

> People can only develop themselves … Ujamaa villages are intended to be socialist organisations created by the people, and governed by those who live and work in them. They cannot be created from the outside, nor governed from outside. No one can be forced into an ujamaa village, and no official- at any level- can go and tell the members of an ujamaa village what they should do together, and what they should continue to do as individual farmers … An ujamaa village is a voluntary association of people who decide of their own free will to live together and work together for their common good. (Nyerere 1973, 67)

The passage not only indicates Nyerere's vision for how the project would work in reality, but also supports the claims made above building on Ogenga Otunnu's work, that Ujamaa was a rural project that did not rely on the failings of capitalism to pave the way for its socialist ideals. On this argument, what it means to be a socialist citizen for Nyerere, in comparison to what it means for Western models originating in the work of Marx and Engels is somewhat different, and the project itself can be viewed as a transformative act: transforming the way in which we think about, and respond to, conceptions of socialism.

As a policy the Ujamaa project was set forth in the Arusha Declaration on 29 January 1967 which *formally* announced that Tanzania's economic and political goals were to follow a socialist path. The policy involved the (what became forced) relocation of Tanzania's rural population into socialist communities or Ujamaa villages, in which they could work together to provide for the needs of the community, whilst also defining the rules by which the village, and its people, lived and worked; the original intention of which was to respect the agency of the citizens of the newly defined space to make their own decisions about their roles as citizens of the village. The model relied on villagers being responsible for all decision-making in the villages, as well as food production, both for the village and to sell, (although as the state became more heavily involved production became directed toward state aims). It was at the discretion of the villagers how much of this was achieved through communal farming and how much remained in private hands. Schneider observed that the role of the Arusha Declaration was to:

> Set out the broad parameters of this new approach. It famously elevated 'ujamaa', which translates literally as family hood and is generally rendered as denoting Nyerere's particular version of 'African socialism', to be the guiding principle behind Tanzania's new approach to development. (Schneider 2004, 348)

The programme embodied Nyerere's belief that the goal of government was to enable the people, as citizens of the village, and the state more broadly, to develop themselves without the imposition of external forces and actors. This model stepped outside the traditional conception of citizenship as membership of a nation with both rights and duties, focusing instead on the individual's membership of local spaces. Thus, I argue that, in making this claim, Nyerere transformed understanding of what it means to be a citizen through a focus on a site smaller than a bounded nation state. Instead of talking in terms of what citizens owed the state, he spoke in terms of the community working together for themselves as being the real meaning of citizenship.

For him, at the heart of the programme was the concept of the people as playing an active role in their own development. The 'act' of development itself was viewed as an internal process: 'the people will have begun to develop themselves as dignified and confident human beings, in a way which is impossible if they simply take orders from someone else' (Nyerere 1973, 60). As previously discussed, Isin suggests that it is the 'act' that transforms the 'actor'. An act in this sense is 'those deeds by which actors constitute themselves (and others) as subjects of rights' (Isin 2009, 371). My argument here is twofold. Firstly that Nyerere believed a central tenant of his own philosophy was the need for the individual to transform themselves, and, secondly, that Nyerere's description of the individual developing themselves within the village is an example of an 'act' transforming not only the 'actor' but also the site of citizenship: the village. The Ujamaa village as imagined by Nyerere, therefore, can be viewed through this lens as an example of activist citizenship: as Nyerere himself undergoes a process of transformation and reimagining in his discussion of the village, altering the ways in which both himself, and others, interact with the site in the future, bringing to the fore often ignored ideas of community and citizenship.

To further emphasise this second argument, he saw no role for external experts in setting up the villages, or developing the necessary farming techniques. In fact, as previously stated, he claimed that the fundamental goal was that 'the people will have begun to develop themselves' (Nyerere 1973, 60). This conception of citizenship has far more in common with Jabri's (previously discussed) analysis of the Arab Spring uprising than it does with the colonial structures of citizenship that relied on education levels, language skills and wealth to recognise citizenship of the nation state. This enhances the claim I made in opening this article, that reimagining what it means to be a citizen in the face of oppression is in fact not a new phenomenon. It is instead a phenomenon also present in the work of Nyerere, and as we will see in the following section, also Senghor.

As previously mentioned, regardless of the promises, and determination in the language in which the idea was presented to the people, the practical implementation of the Ujamaa Vijijini project failed to deliver the conditions promised by the Arusha Declaration. This is not to suggest that Nyerere's belief in the need to provide certain conditions for his people was falsified, but rather, that his abilities in theory and practise differed. As the project developed it became clear that many of the rural population were uncomfortable with being uprooted from their family homes and moved into artificially created villages. In one interview Nyerere even admitted to 'decent modern houses that had been bulldozed flat because they were not sited in the ujamaa village' (Bailey 1998, v). It became clear in these cases that the realisation of the ideology was taking precedence. Commentators spoke of situations in which 'the President ... condoned, and apparently even prompted, the use of certain "mildly" coercive measures (usually in the form of restricting famine relief (only) to residents of ujamaa villages)' (Schneider 2004, 369). Furthermore, 'different degrees of persuasion and coercion (were used) by administrative and political officials ... (for example) material rewards in the form of expanded services or direct support from the government' (Boeson, Moody, and Madsen 1977, 15) were given to those villagers producing the crops required by the state. These policies led to a situation in which the policy altered completely from a 'voluntary movement to a highly coercive system' (Seftel and Smyth 1998, 131) in which the villagers were treated by the state as means to a further end: productivity. The high levels of coercion led, according to Schneider, to:

> The historical end-result of the policy of ujamaa vijijini (which) was the compulsory settlement of the majority of Tanzania's rural population into approximately seven thousand villages, which began in 1968, was greatly accelerated in 1973, and declared largely completed by late 1975. The basic modus operandi of villagisation was coercive and top-down, and it is generally agreed that it did not improve the majority of rural Tanzanians' lot, as had been hoped. (Schneider 2004, 345–346)

However, as previously suggested, the focus of this article is on the normative ideas underpinning these claims; whilst it was important to mention the failings in passing, the fundamental focus of this section was on utilising Isin's vocabulary to better understand the process Nyerere was advocating for in which the people of Tanzania could develop themselves; Nyerere's 'act' of transforming not only understanding of the village, but also the broader state community. Enabling the individuals to view themselves, and be viewed by the state, as actors rather than passive members: to focus on Nyerere as transforming understanding of citizenship in a way that had previously been ignored by the oppression of the colonial condition, as something beyond a relationship with the nation state.

To summarise, Nyerere presented his policies on the basis of improving development for the people, reimagining the role of villages as sites in which exploitation would be eradicated and opportunities would be created for individuals and communities to play an active role in government, respected as having individual agency as citizens of both the village and the wider community. The article does not make the claim that this was in fact a successful approach but rather that it was one attempt utilised to overcome the concept of victimhood imposed on the colonised by the colonisers. The article now turns to a second reimagining of space in the face of the dehumanising effects of colonialism; the pan-national community. To reiterate an earlier point, I am not suggesting that these sites of citizenship do not interlink. It is clear, for example, from discussion of ujamma vijinni that involvement in a village, it was hoped, would spark greater national involvement as development of actors occurred, as well as greater international integration. However, considering the two spaces separately in this article does provide for a more detailed analysis of the particular philosophies and policies presented by the Nyerere and Senghor in relation to each site.

Pan-nationalism

Expanding on discussions of localised conceptions of citizenship this section focuses on the concept of pan-national identities, as understood by the 'philosopher statesmen' as a space reimagined as important in evoking solidarity and 'fraternity' (Isin 2012, 45), and transforming the understanding of what it means to be an individual with citizenship. Julius K. Nyerere was heavily involved in the pan-African movement as well as the continent-wide struggle for independence; whilst Léopold Sédar Senghor's conception of Négritude heavily emphasised an understanding of identity divorced from national boundaries and borders but heavily attached to a conception of race and a desire to overcome colonial oppression.

What makes this element of their political thought particularly interesting is the reliance and emphasis on African values, both within their own political states, and as a foundation for the arguments they made for a collaborative African project. Each scholar focused in their writings on pan-national community on a conception of citizenship similar to that proposed by Isin. The argument that 'to imagine citizens without nations requires a genealogy of fraternity' (Isin 2012, 465), a sense of togetherness or brotherhood bonding people beyond associations of birth right often associated with national citizenship.

The article argues that the reliance on African values was intended by these theorists to reimagine the continent as a federalised community, bonded by values, in which African's viewed themselves as activist citizens defining the continent and establishing a system of corresponding rights and duties, transformed from the situation of colonialism. Similar to the discussion of local identities in the previous section, and highlighting a dynamic and interconnected relationship between the different sites, this final discussion focuses on the 'philosopher statesmen's' reimagining of the international space as a site of activist citizenship; suggesting that in developing the pan-African movement they were not only making claims to a new and transformative conception of citizenship of the imagined space, but also that they viewed it as a method of inspiring others to overcome the systematic subjugation of the colonial movement.

When providing examples of successful pan-national collaborations the most common example discussed, either favourably or negatively, is the European Union. Discussing membership of the EU in terms of citizenship does exist in the literature (Checkel 2001). Whilst EU integration maintains a strong focus on national borders and identity, and is established alongside the rights and duties owed to the state, the initial project set forth by Nyerere emphasised pan-African citizenship and identities as a positive force for transforming the continent. It viewed individuals from across the continent as primarily Africans. It is on this basis that the article suggests that the model presented by the two presidents can be viewed as a transformative act of citizenship: the purpose was in altering the conception of what it means to be a citizen, expanding it beyond the limiting borders of national identity and viewing membership of the broader continent in terms of citizenship. Understanding, like Balibar, that 'national identity, however effective it has been in modern history, is only one of the possible institutional forms of the community of citizens, and it neither encapsulates all of its functions nor completely neutralizes its contradictions' (Balibar 2012, 438). Beyond this, and as will be discussed in what follows, Senghor also made reference to a universal citizenship, seeing citizenship as something that goes beyond all borders and is in fact a condition of humanity (Senghor 1962). This in and of itself was a new and disruptive conception of what it means to have citizenship, one that has since been supported by scholars such as Balibar who recognise that community does not have to be associated with a state, but at the time could be classified as a disruptive conception. A conception that had previously been largely marginalized from a Western literature that focuses on the nation state.

In contrast to the negative connotations associated with national identity, prevalent in contemporary Western literature, as being something 'ideologically important and dangerous' (Berlin 1980, 341) this section suggests that the 'philosopher statesmen' in fact viewed pan-national or cultural identities as being empowering, reimagining them as spaces in which individuals could establish themselves as 'insiders' rather than 'aliens or subjects' (Isin 2009); identities that they saw themselves as having as well as hoping to enable a process of becoming for those under their rule. Standing in opposition to the colonial model, premised on the idea of exclusion, pan-national identity is presented normatively as an inclusive conception of space. George Padmore describes it as arising as a 'manifestation of fraternal solidarity among Africans and people of African descent' (Padmore 1972, 95). A restorative process premised on claims to community for those individuals silenced by oppressors.

The 'philosopher statesmen' presented pan-national identities, as well as more traditional conceptions of the nation (although this is not the focus here), as the first step in a process of becoming agents and overcoming the notion of the inactive subject. Padmore, like myself, is of the opinion that the local, the national and the pan-national in fact interact in the views of pan-Africanists; transformation of the pan-African can successfully alter the position of the national. He claims that W.E.B. DuBois saw the movement as 'an aid to the promotion of national self-determination' Padmore 1972, 106).

To further situate this discussion within the citizenship literature it is necessary to think in terms of informal grounds of citizenship. The article is arguing not only that the 'philosopher statesmen' were in a position to implement the necessary legal and institutional frameworks, and in the case of the villagisation projects it can be argued that they took on a formal institutionalised approach, but that their rhetoric highlights that 'what is important is not only that citizenship is a legal status but that it also involves practices of making citizens- social, political, cultural and symbolic' (Isin 2008, 17). Whilst in contemporary Western terms concepts such as nationalism can be viewed as an argument for exclusion, in this example it can be viewed as a model for inclusivity: a desire to establish a site for informal citizenship based on social, political, cultural and symbolic norms. As a first stage which enables individuals to reassert their own citizenship outside of institutional interpretations and to then claim their more formal rights as institutionalised citizens. As Jabri suggests: 'the challenge for the new state was hence the challenge of government, not just government of ethnic or tribal relations, as most Eurocentric renditions of the postcolonial would suggest, but primarily the government of populations' (Jabri 2013, 97); the embodiment of a shared pan-national identity could be viewed as one remedy to this, easing the task of government and providing a site for citizen engagement. It is only through the recognition that the 'resources of the political community were paramount not simply in relation to the provision of welfare, but in the reconstitution of this community as an independent entity' (Jabri 2013, 97) that it is possible to fully understand the value of continentalist ideals in the struggles of the post-colonial states. To best understand this framing of pan-nationalist ideals the section discusses each thinker individually. The first example being Leopold Sedar Senghor's model of Négritude (roughly translated into English to be Blackness), and his claims for viewing the movement as enabling previously colonised individuals to undergo a process of becoming based on the traditionally exclusionary identifier of race. This is followed by consideration of his conception of the universal citizen (1962), and his belief in the somewhat marginalised position that citizenship is not grounded in discussions of national borders.

Whilst there is a vast literature on the Négritude movement it is impossible within the remits of this article to consider it in any depth. However, a brief introduction of Senghor's views is required to provide the context for the remaining argument. As a political, artistic and cultural movement it originated amongst the diasporic communities in Paris in the late 1930s amongst the West-African and Caribbean elite. It maintained its reactionary spirit, as an ideological damnation of the political and moral domination of the Western colonial enterprise until the start of the 1960s. On becoming the first president of independent

Senegal, Senghor maintained a strong political and academic relationship with France. He argued for a system of development supported by, and in collaboration with, Europe: 'We must build our own development plan, based on European, socialist contributions and also on the best of Negro African civilisation' (Senghor 1962, 60). This is not to say that he intended to copy the West, but rather that he underwent a process of reimagining development and citizenship as a collaborative project. He suggested that having successfully re-built individual states, and a federal state of Africa, the continent should remain 'freely associated with France in a Confederation' (Senghor 1962, 15). In making these choices he was rethinking citizenship beyond the nation state, envisioning it instead as a process of confederation and collaboration in which he viewed his own citizenship as not being constrained by borders, instead seeing himself as an international citizen shaped by different cultural, social and societal experiences.

Senghor believed that the strength of the Négritude movement was in guiding Black people to recognise the value of their Blackness, and to use this to contribute to the future of not just Africa, but the world more generally. In defining this mission, he suggested that it was the role of Africans not only to shape their own future but rather to create a model suitable not only to fit 'Africa and the twentieth century, but first of all to fit man' (Senghor 1962, 17). In a recent article published in 'African Studies', Shiera el-Malik suggests that the poetry and politics of the Négritude movement, particularly Senghorian Négritude, can be viewed in terms of disruption, and in particular 'he aimed to show that heretofore subjugated knowledges are fundamental components of dominant forms of knowledge' (el-Malik 2015, 49–50). Senghor claimed that it was the role of the Black man to 'bring, like a leaven, his message to the world to help build a universal civilisation' (Senghor 1962, 85) and in doing this he would disrupt the dominant narrative that constituted an understanding of what it meant to be a citizen in/ of the world. On addressing these ideas it is possible to suggest that, for Senghor, the role of Négritude as an expressly cultural–political movement, was intrinsically linked with his international political aims, to shape the wider global community, but that to achieve these aims required individuals who had previously viewed themselves as subjects to recognise themselves, instead, as citizens. He argued that it was Africa's time to contribute to what he referred to as the Universal Civilisation (a concept which in and of itself makes interesting claims regarding citizenship). However, he believed that to be able to achieve this, colonised groups not only needed to be granted their freedom by external forces, but also to come to terms with their own worth as active participants undergoing a transformative process, enabling them to view themselves no longer under the cloud of dehumanised colonial subjects. It was this that he claimed was the role of Négritude: not only to define what it meant to be Black, but also to establish a sense of self-belief amongst Black individuals to enable them to share their knowledge and experience internationally. In this sense, he argued that achieving citizenship not only had the opportunity to improve the lives of individuals but also of the wider 'universal' community: a claim that refers to a process of becoming beyond the nation state.

As commentator Barrend van Dyk Van Niekerk observed, for Senghor,Négritude is 'the explanation and interpretation by the black man of his own position in the universe' (Van Niekerk 1970, 100). It was viewed as an act of self-discovery that enabled individuals to position themselves in the world. In discussing Senghor's approach as being one akin to an act of self-definition, parallels can be dawn between the philosophical underpinnings of the debates surrounding Senghorian Négritude, as a force for emancipation, and the question of 'activist citizenship' as defined by Isin (2008). It is clear from Senghor's imagery, 'bring like a leaven', that the movement is an act of self-definition, and self-mastery. It is a personal act to bring, rather than to be given, one's freedom, and this was at the heart of Senghor's understanding of the movement he helped to create. Similarly, as previously referenced, Isin claims that

> we define acts of citizenship as those acts that transform forms ... and modes (citizens, strangers, outsiders, aliens) of being political by bringing into being new actors as activist citizens (claimants of rights and responsibilities through creating new sites and scales of struggle). (Isin 2008, 39)

Through embarking on this process Senghor hoped to inspire his nation, and the wider African and global communities, to reimagine themselves in terms of belonging, of being, not members of the other, but as agents with rights and responsibilities to both their own communities and states, and, as Senghor envisioned it, the Universal Civilisation. Thus, it can be argued that his writings were transformative; the notion of a Universal Civilisation in and of itself suggests a wider understanding of the concept of citizenship, in fact corresponding with Cosmopolitan views of agents as citizens of the world. Whilst there is not space in this article to analyse a potential Cosmopolitan reading of Senghor, it is worth noting that in much of Senghor's work, discussing both the national and the international, there is an underlying assumption that citizenship on any scale first requires an 'act' of becoming. According to Senghor, the Négritude movement had the potential to facilitate this transformative process amongst previously subjected people, to enable them to claim their rights as agents. Having discussed Senghor's Négritude in terms of an activist model of citizenship focus now turns to the broader pan-African views of Nyerere.

The broader pan-African movement with which Nyerere is often associated originated in the late 1890s, early 1900s with the first pan-African conference taking place in London in 1900. The movement is associated with a wide range of politicians, activist and scholars, becoming particularly popular in the 1920s when it was associated with the academic writings of W.E.B. DuBois, and the activism of Marcus Garvey. It was grounded in feelings of oppression, alienation and a loss of dignity deemed to be shared by all individuals of African descent spread across the globe. Similar to Senghor's Négritude it relies on a common identity associated with individuals of African descent that tie them together. Scholars such as Esedeke (1977) and Chrisman (1973) recognise that the pan-African vision 'has as its basic premise that we the people of African descent throughout the globe constitute a common cultural and political community by virtue of our origin in Africa and our common racial and political oppression' (Chrisman 1973, 2). Thus, to 'regain dignity is the mainspring of all their actions ... the intellectual superstructure of Pan-Africanism has meaning only if one constantly reminds oneself that at its roots lie these deep feelings of dispossession, oppression, persecution and rejection' (Legum 1965, 15).

Beyond its origins in the work of DuBois the movement transformed into a political call associated with the views of the Presidents' of the newly independent African states in the 1950s and 1960s. The second strand of the pan-African movement was, like the first, rooted in three key themes: alienation, the necessity to reassert dignity and a shared sense of unity between all African people. Each of these themes, as will become clear, can be read as an intention to transform the political understanding of what it means to be a citizen. That is to say, for the political class in particular, these themes constituted more than just a philosophical goal; they also established the necessary conditions to progress towards the federalisation of the African continent. In the late 1950s, as a greater number of African states began to gain their independence, there was a political move from figures such as Léopold Sédar Senghor, Kwame Nkrumah, Ahmed SekouToure, Jomo Kenyatta and Julius Nyerere, to name a few, to federate (to a greater or lesser extent) to create a collective movement that was not pro-West, pro-communism, pro-nationalism, but was instead 'pro-African' (Legum 1965, 13). Leaders from across the political and ideological spectrum, supporting national states grounded in democracy, one-party politics, socialism and capitalism, were willing to set aside differences in the name of a pan-African federation. However, the underlying differences in leadership put a strain on this relationship. Whilst there was a shared belief in the unity of all Africans, the movement was riddled with issues of political contestation between the various leaders of the newly independent states.

Not only were there these issues arising between the states, regarding their abilities to work collectively, there was also a question of what exactly each state wanted the outcomes of a unified Africa to be. Was it a political ideal? Or was the goal of collaboration only for the purposes of economic security? Why should the leaders that had fought so hard in the anti-colonial struggles, give up the sovereignty they had just won? Who would lead a federalised continent? For these reasons the various charters detailing the plans for a unified continent (Casablanca, Sanniquellie, and Monrovia) fell through, and the pan-African dream was never realised. Nonetheless, the movement intended to set in motion an idealised political model of the African citizen as one able to interact as equals with global partners. As with discussion in the previous section, the practical realities of this were marred with issues, stemming not least from a naiveté about the capabilities of government. However, in terms of the purpose of this article, to demonstrate an attempt to transform the political understanding of citizenship as a model outside of the colonial focus on borders and oppression in the writings of Nyerere, this discussion is particularly relevant. The article turns now to that very discussion.

For Nyerere and his contemporaries the purpose of unification was the potential for improved opportunities for Africans interacting with the rest of the world. Similar to Jabri's observation regarding unequal global institutions (Jabri 2013) they recognised the inequalities of the global system. A divided continent was, for Nyerere, one of the greatest risks facing a newly independent Africa. He strongly believed that squabbling within the continent would weaken the relative position of every nation as well as the continent in its entirety. In his speech 'Africa must not fight Africa', Nyerere defended his belief that

> the weakness of Africa is a constant invitation and a constant encouragement to the exploiters of Africa to suck Africa with impunity. Only a strong Africa can stop this. But there can be no strong Africa and no salvation for Africa except in unity. (Nyerere 1966, 219)

It was his belief that this issue was rooted in Africa's constant economic race to the bottom as a method for encouraging investment, as well as the continents choice to politically imitate and court the West or East to encourage aid. Nyerere, supported a system of unification that respected the sovereignty of each individual state and the people of those states. However, the question remained, on what grounds Africa could overcome political, economic, and cultural differences, and unify. At the root of Nyerere's solution was what he referred to as a 'sentiment of "African-ness"', a feeling of mutual involvement, which pervades all the cultural and political life. There is, in other words, an emotional unity which finds expression in, among other things, concepts such as the "African personality"' (Nyerere 1967, 188). It was on the controversial grounds of a shared meaning of what it meant to be African, similar to the claims being made by the Négritude movement, that it was claimed unification could be possible and through a reimagining of such identities that rather than restricting individuals, rather it could transform them.

Nyerere's argument was not grounded in a denial of difference; he did in fact recognise that Africa was a continent made up of diverse political and cultural values. Like contemporary scholars he recognised that 'citizenship as a political principle cannot exist without a community, but this community cannot be completely unified' (Balibar 2012, 438). It was his argument that differences, rather than being seen as barriers to unification, should in fact be included in a pan-African model:

> It is no use waiting for differences of approach, or of political belief, to disappear before we think of working for unity in Africa. They will not disappear. If we are ever to unite, the differences must be accommodated within our growing unity, and our growing unity must be shaped in a manner which allows for the existing differences. (Nyerere 1973, 13)

Such conceptions of citizenship beyond the unified nation state, instead focusing on differences are a further example of a disruptive conception that has previously been ignored by traditional citizenship studies. This is not to suggest that these ideas are not being discussed now, as it is clear by the reference to Isin and Balibar that this is not the case, but rather, that a re-reading of these African scholars provides a previously marginalised contribution to these discussions. On consideration of these claims a further question is raised: If Nyerere recognised the differences that existed between the various political conditions of the African continent, on what grounds did he believe collaboration could be based? Although he did not directly make this claim, it is possible to assert that, in appealing to the possibility of a pan-African state, he was making an assumption based on a shared desire for becoming as a method of overcoming oppression, and, in that sense, we can once again view the concept of pan-Africanism as a process within the decolonisation movement that offers a perspective on the politics of identification, solidarity and becoming. It offers a way of tracing a citizenship which extends beyond the nation state to a wider, international, conception of identity and is viewed by these thinkers as a step in the process of encouraging the transformative process of an oppressed people towards being engaged citizens.

Concluding remarks

This article has focused on the previously marginalized transformative narratives of the 'philosopher statesmen' which reimagined citizenship as a process under which previously oppressed individuals could be viewed as citizens not only on a national level but also local and pan-national, subject to corresponding rights and duties. What has been investigated was the focus on different identities as enabling 'subjects (to) transform themselves into citizens' (Isin 2008, 18); understood as being actors recognising themselves as right holders, making claims for these rights and viewing themselves not as dehumanised subjects as the colonial movement would have had them believe, but rather as autonomous agents and citizens, not simply members, of a community. This article has discussed the claims of Julius Nyerere and Léopold Sédar Senghor, each of whom proposed an understanding of the local or pan-national as being sites of solidarity and fraternity in which citizens could actively rediscover themselves, undergoing the process of becoming citizens and in doing so played a role in transforming political understanding of what it means to have citizenship. As Isin clarifies, 'acts of citizenship are those acts through which citizens, strangers, outsiders and aliens emerge not as beings already defined but as beings acting and reacting with others … they actualise ways of becoming political' (Isin 2008, 39). Through a reimagining of shared local and pan-national identities, it has been suggested by this article, that these thinkers presented a process through which subjects were intended to embark on a process of becoming, and in imagining this process they, themselves, were able to transform contemporary understandings of citizenship, a narrative that has previously been marginalized and ignored. It has been suggested that these views, previously silenced by dominant Western narratives can, and should, contribute to contemporary debates surrounding post-sovereign citizenship.

In concluding, the article agrees with Jabri that the Arab Spring has involved a 'renewed notion of political community' (Jabri 2013, 1) and a reimagining of what it means to be a member of said community in the face of oppression. However, it argues that such a process is not particular to contemporary revolutions, but rather analysis of the 'philosopher statesmen' discussed in this article suggests that, although marginalized, reimaginings of what it means to be a citizen in the face of colonial oppression have occurred in the past and the study of these narratives has the power to provide lessons for the future.

Disclosure statement

No potential conflict of interest was reported by the author.

References

Agamben, G. 1993. *The Coming Community*. Minneapolis: University of Minnesota Press.
Bailey, J. 1998. "Preface." In *The Story of Julius Nyerere Africa's Elder Statesman*, edited by A. Smyth and A. Seftel. Tanzania: Mkuki na Nyota.
Balibar, E. 2004. "Citizenship without Community." In *We, the People of Europe?: Reflections on Transnational Citizenship*, edited by E. Balibar, 51–77. Princeton: Princeton University Press.
Balibar, E. 2012. "The 'Impossible' Community of the Citizens: Past and Present." *Environment and Planning: Society and Space* 30: 437–449.
Berlin, I. 1980. "Nationalism: Past Neglect and Present Power." In *Against the Current: Essays in the History of Ideas*, edited by H. Hardy, 420–448. London: Hogarth Press.
Boeson, J., B. Madsen, and T. Moody. 1977. *Ujamaa: Socialism from Above*. Uppsala: Scandinavian Institute of African Studies.
Checkel, J. 2001. "The Europeanization of Citizenship." In *Europeanization and Domestic Change: Transforming Europe*, edited by M. Cowles, J. Caporaso, and T. Risse, 180–197. London: Cornell University Press.
Chrisman, R. 1973. "Aspects of Pan-Africanism." *Black Scholar* 4 (10): 2–5.
el-Malik, S. 2015. "Interruptive Discourses: Léopold Senghor, African Emotion and the Poetry of Politics." *African Identities* 13 (1): 49–61.
Esedeke, P. 1977. "New Pan-African Trends." *The Journal of Pan African Studies* 3 (4): 85–100.
Esposito, R. 2010. *Communitas: The Origin and Destiny of Community*. Stanford: Stanford University Press.
Hoskins, B., and M. Mascherini. 2009. "Measuring Active Citizenship through the Development of a Composite Indicator." *Social Indicators Research* 90 (3): 459–488.
Isin, E. 2008. "Theorizing Acts of Citizenship." In *Acts of Citizenship*, edited by E. Isin and G. Nielsen, 15–43. London: Zed Books.
Isin, E. 2009. "Citizenship in Flux: The Figure of the Activist Citizen." *Subjectivity* 29: 367–388.
Isin, E. 2012. "Citizens without Nations." *Environment and Planning: Society and Space* 30: 450–467.
Isin, E., and B. Turner. 2002. "Citizenship Studies: An Introduction." In *Handbook of Citizenship Studies*, edited by E. Isin and B. Turner, 1–10. London: Sage.

Jabri, V. 2013. *The Postcolonial Subject: Claiming Politics/Governing Others in Late Modernity*. Oxon: Routledge.

Kearns, A. 1992. "*Active Citizenship and Urban Governance.*" *Transactions of the Institute of British Geographers* 17 (1): 20–34.

Legum, C. 1965. *Pan-Africanism: A Short Political Guide*. New York: Frederick A. Praeger.

Nancy, J. 1991. *The Inoperative Community*. Minneapolis: University of Minnesota Press.

Nyerere, J. 1966. "Africa Must not Fight Africa." In *Freedom and Development: A Selection from Writings and Speeches*, edited by J. Nyerere, 1968–1973. New York: Oxford University Press.

Nyerere, J. 1967. "The Dilemma of the Pan-Africanist." In *The Inaugural Lectures of the University of Zambia*, edited by J. Nyerere, D. Nicol, and C. Pratt. Manchester: Manchester University Press.

Nyerere, J. 1973. "All Men Are Equal." In *Freedom and Development: A Selection from Writings and Speeches*, edited by J. Nyerere, 1968–1973. New York, NY: Oxford University Press.

Otunnu, O. 2015. "Mwalimu Julius Kambarage Nyerere's Philosophy, Contribution, and Legacies." *African Identities* 13 (1): 18–33.

Padmore, G. 1972. *Pan-Africanism or Communism: The Coming Struggle for Africa*. New York, NY: Anchor.

Schnapper, D. 1994. *Community of Citizens: On the Modern Idea of Nationality*. New Brunswick: Transaction Publishers.

Schneider, L. 2004. "Freedom and Unfreedom in Rural Development: Julius Nyerere, Ujamaa Vijijini, and Villagization." *Canadian Journal of African Studies / Revue Canadienne Des Études Africaines* 38 (2): 344–392.

Senghor, L. 1962. *Nationhood and the African Road to Socialism*. Paris: Présence Africaine.

Seftel, A., and A. Smyth. 1998. *The Story of Julius Nyerere Africa's Elder Statesman*. Tanzania: Mkuki na Nyota.

Stephens, A., and V. Squire. 2012a. "Guest Editorial." *Environment and Planning: Society and Space* 30: 434–436.

Stephens, A., and V. Squire. 2012b. "Politics through a Web: Citizenship and Community Unbound." *Environment and Planning: Society and Space* 30: 551–567.

Van Niekerk, Barrend van Dyk. 1970. *The African Image in the Work of Senghor*. Cape Town: A. A. Balkema.

White, M. 2008. "Can an Act of Citizenship Be Creative?" In *Acts of Citizenship*, edited by E. Isin and G. Nielsen, 44–56. London: Zed Books.

Young, T. 2003. *Readings in African Politics*. London: The International African Institute.

Index

www.ingramcontent.com/pod-product-compliance
Ingram Content Group UK Ltd.
Pitfield, Milton Keynes, MK11 3LW, UK
UKHW010020280225
455677UK00023B/711